SKETCH MAP
Showing position of
WARWICKSHIRE.
Scale
0 10 20 30 40 50 Miles

DISTANCES BY RAIL.

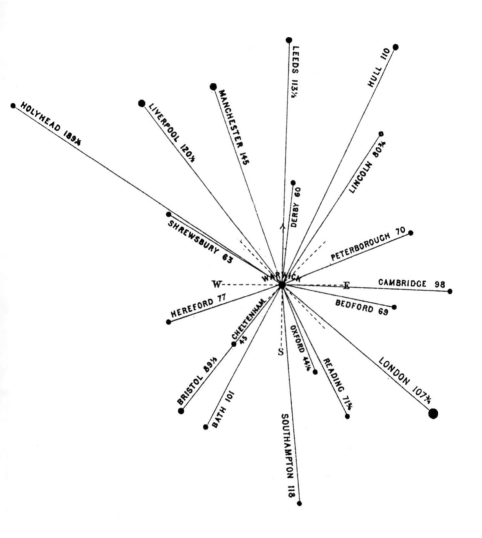

C. Stanfield. R.A.

Warwick Castle.

W. Miller.

BLACK'S

GUIDE TO

WARWICKSHIRE

SIXTH EDITION

Illustrated by Maps, Plans, & Illustrations

SHAKSPERE'S HOUSE.

EDINBURGH
ADAM AND CHARLES BLACK

1881

Published by:
Country Books
Courtyard Cottage, Little Longstone, Bakewell, Derbyshire DE45 1NN England
Tel/Fax: 01629 640670

ISBN 1 898941 23 8

From the 1850s until the end of the nineteenth century, Adam & Charles Black of Edinburgh published a series of guide books covering the country at a time when the railways and the industrial revolution were in their infancy. Who would have thought in 1881 that the country would have been covered in a road system simply to accomodate the motor car?! Only the aristocracy and the wealthier middle classes could afford to travel and so the books were produced in small numbers — original copies are now both scarce and expensive. Many of the early volumes were sponsored by advertisements for services, products and goods and as these are part of the period feel, they have been included. Whatever happened to the mourning warehouse?

The **Black's 1881 Guide to Warwickshire** contains a diagram of distances, folding maps of the county and the Great Western Railway, and plans of Birmingham and Leamington. There are numerous steel engravings of Warwick (castle, tomb of Leicester & statue of Guy); Stratford (Shakespere's house in 1807 prior to alterations, his birthplace, interior of the church, Ireland's view of New Place, plan of New Place, & Shakespere's crest); & Kenilworth (castle, restoration of the castle, bird's-eye view, gateway, ground plan, Leicester's chimney-piece, Caesar's tower, Mervyn's tower, great hall, Leicester's buildings, water tower, coat of arms, parish church, remains of abbey & seal of the priory). Note the Victorian spelling of Shakespere!

COUNTRY BOOKS are in the process of reprinting the entire series of Black's Guides. Please ask for a prospectus on other counties of interest. Numbered limited editions in cloth or leather bindings are available only by subscription from the publisher.

Printed in Englnad by:
MFP Design & Print, Longford Trading Estate, Thomas Street, Stretford, Manchester M32 0JT
Tel: 0161 864 4540

CONTENTS.

GENERAL DESCRIPTION OF THE COUNTY

ALPHABETICAL DESCRIPTION.

ILLUSTRATIONS.

---+---

MAPS.

VIEWS.

WARWICKSHIRE.

GENERAL DESCRIPTION OF THE COUNTY.

SITUATION, GEOLOGY, AND PHYSICAL FEATURES.

ARWICKSHIRE, from its central situation, has been called "the heart of England." It is bounded on the north by Staffordshire and Leicestershire; on the east by Northamptonshire; on the south by Oxfordshire and Gloucestershire; and on the west by Worcestershire. The south-eastern part of the county consists of the lower formations of the oolitic series, rising into two moderately elevated ranges of hills, separated by a narrow valley. On some of these elevations, especially near Fenny Compton, there are extensive quarries of gritstone. The valley of the Stour and the vale of the Red Horse belong to the lias formation, which towards its north-western limit rises into gentle elevations at Walton or Bath Hill, Morton Hill, and Dunsmore Heath, admitting of the red marl and new red sandstone group cropping out below it. This group occupies the rest of the county with a few exceptions, forming moderate ranges of high ground near Alcester, Henley-in-Arden, Warwick, Solihull, and Coleshill. A coal-field, sixteen miles in length by about three in breadth, extends from the neighbourhood of Coventry to the border of Staffordshire, east of Tamworth. The highest points in the county are at Corley, in Hemlingford Hundred, and in the neighbourhood of Packington. Ancient writers divide the county into parts—*the Feldon*, or plain country, and *the Arden*, or woodland, the river Avon separating them; but the growth of population and industry has long ago abolished the distinction. The principal rivers are the Avon, Leam, and Tame.

ANTIQUITIES.

The county contains interesting remains of the several nations under whose sway, in succession, the county has been. Three Roman roads pass through it —viz. Watling Street, Ikenild Street, and the Foss Way. Watling Street divides Warwickshire from Leicestershire; and very distinct and interesting remains of it are to be seen at Mancester and elsewhere. Ikenild Street, which traverses the kingdom from Southampton to Tynemouth, may be seen to advantage in the neighbourhood of Sutton Coldfield. The Foss Way may be traced, more or less distinctly, in various places, as, for instance, at Chesterton, where the remains of a camp may be seen. In various parts occur earth-works, which are attributed to the Saxons or early Normans.

EMINENT NATIVES.

Besides Shakspere, the glory of Warwickshire and of England, this county has given birth to Michael Drayton, one of the most esteemed of our early poets; William Somervile, author of "The Chase;" and Richard Jago, author of "Edge Hill." Other distinguished names in connection with literature are those of John Rouse, author of many historical and antiquarian works, mostly connected with this county;

Sir William Dugdale, author of "The Antiquities of Warwickshire;" Edward Cave, the founder of the "Gentleman's Magazine;" Nehemiah Grew, M.D., the celebrated botanist. Several of the Earls of Warwick acted very important parts in the history of the kingdom in former times. The chief of these were the renowned Guy, the subject of numberless legendary tales ; Richard de Beauchamp, "the father of courtesy;" and Richard Neville, "the setter up and plucker down of kings." Among other famous natives may be mentioned John de Stratford, Archbishop of Canterbury in the reign of Edward III. ; Laurence Sheriff, the founder of Rugby School; and Henry Compton, Bishop of London. The preceding names, as well as some others, will come to be noticed in the course of this work, in connection with the places of their birth or residence. We subjoin a list of natives who, though less noted, are sufficiently distinguished to be here recorded :— Daniel Rogers, a Latin poet of considerable ability, born 1540, died 1590 ; Fulke Greville, Lord Brooke, an elegant poet, and a liberal patron of learning, 1554-1628 ; Francis Holyock, rector of Southam, a learned and laborious lexicographer, 1567-1633; Sir Nathaniel Brent, a distinguished lawyer, 1573-1652 ; Nicholas Byfield, a Puritan divine of considerable eminence, 1579-1622 ; Humphrey Wanley, a noted antiquary, 1561-1626 ; Sir Thomas Overbury, a writer of some reputation in prose and verse, 1581-1613 ; Samuel Clark, minister of St. Bennett's Fink, whose "Marrow of Ecclesiastical History" displays much learning and industry, 1579-1682; Samuel Annesley, a celebrated Nonconformist, 1620-1696 ; Richard Claridge, a Quaker writer of some eminence, 1649-1723 ; Thomas Wagstaff, a non-juring divine, and writer of considerable ability, 1645-1712 ; Samuel Johnson,

chaplain to Lord Russell, and rector of Corring-
ton, remarkable for his learning and his steadiness
in suffering, 1649-1703 ; Peter Whalley, historian of
Northamptonshire, 1722-1791 ; Matthew Boulton, the
distinguished engineer and inventor, colleague of James
Watt, born 1728, died 1809 ; Valentine Green, an
eminent engraver, topographer, and antiquary, born
1739, died 1813. To these we may add the following
literary names associated with this county by their
works :— Dr. Thomas, the continuator of Dugdale ;
William Hutton, the historian of Birmingham ; Robert
B. Wheler, the historian of Stratford-on-Avon ; J.
Norris Brewer, author of an interesting and well-
written account of Warwickshire, etc. Not a few
illustrious names might be mentioned as connected
with this county by residence or otherwise. Addison
has made Bilton Hall classic ground. The learned
Samuel Parr, LL.D., was curate of Hatton, where he
died and was interred. The philosophic Dr. Priestley
was a Dissenting minister in Birmingham ; and there
he pursued his studies in chemistry and electricity.
James Watt's name will always be associated with the
steam-engine manufactories of Soho, near Birmingham.
The late Sir Robert Peel has invested the ancient town
of Tamworth with a fresh interest. Thomas Attwood
of Birmingham was the founder of the " Political
Union " which secured the passing of the Reform Bill.

MINERAL PRODUCTIONS.

The mineral productions of Warwickshire are coal,
ironstone, limestone, freestone, blue flagstone, marl,
blue clay, manganese, etc. In 1862 sixteen coal-mines
were in operation, yielding a return of 678,000 tons.
Of iron-ore, during the same period, the yield was
14,750 tons.

Besides the celebrated medicinal waters of Leamington, there are mineral springs at Stratford-on-Avon, Ilmington, Southam, Willoughby, King's Newnham, etc.

AGRICULTURE.

The county, from its situation, and from the absence of steep and precipitous ground, is well adapted for agriculture. The climate is mild and healthy, and vegetation early. It is calculated that about 240,000 acres are in pasture, and at least 70,000 under cultivation. The average of farms has hitherto been under 100 acres; but there has been a tendency of late years to increase their size by diminishing their number. Cattle are of the usual breeds. The large polled or ancient Warwickshire sheep is advantageously crossed, particularly with the Leicestershire. The stock of sheep is about 350,000, and the produce of wool between 8000 and 9000 packs annually.

POPULATION.

Though only twenty-fourth among the counties of England in point of extent (its area being 881 square miles, or 563,946 statute acres), Warwickshire ranks eighth in point of population. At the last census of 1871 the population was 633,902, or 307,207 males and 325,685 females ; and the inhabited houses numbered 131,775. The increase of population since the previous census amounted to 72,047.

OCCUPATION OF THE INHABITANTS.

Commencing with the ownership and cultivation of the soil, we find there are 302 males and 414 females who are land proprietors ; 3620 males and 354 females who are farmers and graziers ; 19,830 male and 635 female agricultural labourers ; 627 shepherds ; 2794 male and 660 female servants, in-door. The following are the principal figures in manufactures :—Watches, 2794 males and 84 females; guns, 5884 males and 361 females ; engines and machines, 2277 men ; needles, 1089 men and 898 women ; tools, 1239 men ; miscellaneous in tools and machines, 1491 men ; steel-pens, 1240 women; silk, 10,057 women and 2930 men ; ribbons, 4772 women and 3805 men ; buttons, 3058 women and 2158 men ; lace, 106 women ; gloves, 439 women ; French-polishing, 450 women and 88 men ; japanning, 465 women and 428 men ; coal-mines, 1888 men ; bricks, 1264 men ; glass, 1350 men, 151 women ; goldsmiths, 4171 men, 629 women ; plating, 1028 men ; miscellaneous in plating, etc., 746 men, 978 women ; brass, 6326 men, 1770 women; pins, 160 women ; lacquering, 413 women ; wire-drawing and weaving, 1261 men ; iron, 2356 men ; nails, 807 men, 296 women ; screws, 903 women ; boots and shoes, 5796 men, 1091 women ; toys, 278 women, 23 men.

Divisions, Representations, etc.

The county is divided into five hundreds, or two divisions, and contains 1 city, 1 county town, 14 market towns, and 158 parishes. It is in the province of Canterbury, partly in the diocese of Lichfield and Coventry, and partly in that of Worcester. Eleven members are returned to Parliament (exclusive of two for Tamworth, which is on the borders of the county, and partly situated in Staffordshire)— viz. two for each division, two for the borough of Warwick, three for the town of Birmingham, and two for the city of Coventry. The annual value of real property, assessed to the income and property-tax, in 1871, was £3,277,683.

WARWICK CASTLE.

Every one will be glad to learn that the damage done to Warwick Castle, by the great fire that occurred in December 1871, has been restored, and that the work has been successfully finished. The walls of the burnt portions having been found much injured, some parts had to be strengthened and repaired, and others entirely rebuilt. The grand baronial hall, the private apartments, and the library were completely restored, precisely as they were before the fire. Even the internal decorations of the various apartments were reproduced. The renewed portions of the building have been made as nearly as possible fire-proof, so as to lessen the possibility of the castle being again imperilled in the same way.

It is much to be regretted, however, that a number of valuable contents were destroyed which could not be replaced. The fire it seems was discovered at half-past one in the morning by the steward fire-boy and two footmen, who were awoke by what they at first thought were hailstones rattling outside, and then some one breaking into the castle. It appears to have commenced in Lady Warwick's apartments in the east wing. The whole of this was speedily gutted, and only the blackened walls and *debris* remained. So rapidly did the fire extend that a few books from the library and some of the more valuable pictures could alone be saved. The flames leapt across the grand staircase to the *baronial hall*, and having got possession of the apartment soon ravaged the richly-carved Gothic roof, emblazoned with heraldic devices, and sadly damaged the floor of Venetian marble. The antique oak wainscoting was hung round with armour, swords, and matchlocks, all of which, with numerous other treasures, varied and costly, were destroyed. For hours it seemed as if the entire castle was doomed to destruction. Having burnt itself out in the east wing, the fire spread through *the grand hall* in the direction of the state apartments, and for a time the efforts of the fire-brigades to arrest its progress appeared fruitless. Preparation was accordingly hurriedly made for the worst. One by one, as quickly as the work could be accomplished, the red drawing-room, the gilt drawing-room, the state bed-room, and the state dressing-room were stripped of all their rare and costly contents that were portable. The pictures by distinguished masters, each work a gem in itself—were torn from their frames, and carried out into the courtyard. There were placed the masterpieces of Rubens, Rembrandt, Murillo, Vandyke, Teniers, and Lely—of which the successive possessors of the castle have been justly proud. The rich Brussels tapestry of the state bed-room was rent from the walls; a Queen Anne's bed, presented to Earl Warwick by George III., was pulled down, and carried away piecemeal. Stripped of their costly treasures and everything portable, the rooms presented a sad scene of destruction. Happily at this juncture, when the worst appeared inevitable, the strenuous exertions of the firemen arrested the flames at the end of the baronial hall.

BIRMINGHAM.

HOTELS.—THE GREAT WESTERN, Snow Hill; QUEEN'S, New Street Station. There are numerous boarding-houses in the principal streets.

From London, 112¼ miles; Manchester, 85; Coventry, 18½; Warwick, 20 : Edinburgh, 300¼.

THIS great manufacturing town, unsurpassed in England, or in the world, for the variety, quantity, and quality of its products, is situated in the north-western extremity of Warwickshire, its suburbs extending into the neighbouring counties of Stafford, and Worcester. It is built on a series of elevations of the new red sandstone formation—a site favourable both for beauty and salubrity. The origin of the name has been the occasion of much discussion. Some writers suppose it to have been the *Bremenium* mentioned in the Itinerary of Richard of Cirencester, and consequently ascribe it to the Romans ; but it has been conclusively shown that this opinion is groundless. The name has been found in upwards of a hundred different shapes in ancient documents. During the last four centuries eight different ways of spelling it have been used : Brumwychcham, Bermyngeham, Bromwycham, Burmyngham, Bermyngham, Brymyngham, Bromichan, and Birmingham. Dugdale regards the name as of Saxon origin. He adopts the spelling Bromwycham, and supposes the first part of it to be the name of a Saxon owner, the syllable *ham* denoting a dwelling. Hutton, the historian of Birmingham, says that *brom* signifies broom, and *wych* a dwelling. Whatever the time of the origin of the name, there seems thus to be no reason to doubt that it is of Saxon etymology. Birmingham was a place of some consequence before the Conquest, as is shown by the fact that, in 1309, William de Birmingham, then lord of the manor, proved that his ancestors had held a market here, and levied tolls under the Saxons. The De Birmingham family had a castle here, erected about 1154, and on several occasions took an active part in public affairs, particularly in the wars of the barons. Edward, the last of this ancient family, was, in the reign of Henry VI., tricked out of the lordship by John Dudley, Earl of Warwick and Duke of Northumberland, upon whose execution for treason it reverted to the crown. During the war between Charles I. and his Parliament, Birmingham sided with the Parliament, supplying its troops with about 15,000 sword-blades, and seizing the royal plate and furniture, which the King had left behind him at Aston Hall on his way southward. A few months after, Prince Rupert inflicted signal vengeance on the town, by burning and plundering it to the extent of £30,000. In 1665 Birmingham was almost depopulated by the plague. The Restoration gave an impetus to its trade from the many gilded trifles that were used by the ladies and cavaliers of the time. William III., it is said, founded the gun trade. He was lamenting the necessity of depending upon Holland for this species of arms, when Sir R. Newdegate, a member of Parliament for Warwickshire, directed his attention to Birmingham as able satisfactorily to execute his orders. From that time the gun trade of Birmingham continued to grow in importance. The next point in the history of Birmingham is the riots of 1791, which resulted from the indignation of the mob at a dinner held by about eighty persons to commemorate the French revolution. For three days the populace were in possession of the town, and indulged in wanton and brutal excesses. The damage done was estimated at £60,000. Among those who suffered most severely was the celebrated Dr. Priestley, whose philosophical apparatus, library, and valuable manuscripts, were destroyed along with his house. The year 1831 witnessed the establishment of the Political Union, with Thomas Attwood as its chief. The effect of the Union in securing the passing of the Reform Bill is well known. With the exception of the Chartist riots in 1839, and several royal visits, there is nothing further in the history of Birmingham calling for mention.

Many names of note are connected with Birmingham, most of them by residence. Richard Smallbroke, bishop of Lichfield and Coventry, was born here in the beginning of last century, and distinguished himself by his works in refutation of Woolston. James Watt, the inventor of the steam-engine, having in 1775 entered into partnership with Matthew Boulton of Soho, himself a distinguished engineer (born in Birmingham in 1728; died 1809), here developed the wondrous powers of the agent which was so soon to revolutionise the world. He died in 1819. "Birmingham, when Watt went to settle at Soho," remarks M. Arago, "could reckon among the inhabitants of its neighbourhood Priestley, whose name says everything; Darwin, the author of the 'Zoonomia,' and of a well-known poem on the 'Loves of the Plants;' Withering, an eminent physician and botanist; Keir, a chemist, distinguished by his notes on his translation of Macquer, and by an interesting paper on the crystallisation of glass; Galton, to whom we owe an elementary treatise on ornithology; Edgeworth, the author of various works, justly esteemed, and the father of Miss Maria, well known to fame." John Baskerville, the eminent typefounder and printer, though not a native, lived and died here. Dibdin says of his typography : —" It is eminently beautiful ; his letters are generally of a very slender and delicate form, calculated for an octavo, or even a quarto, but not sufficiently bold to fill the space of an imperial folio, as is evident from a view of the great Bible. . . . In the italic letters, whether capital or small, he stands unrivalled, such elegance, freedom, and perfect symmetry, being in vain to be looked for among the specimens of Aldus and Colonæüs." After Baskerville's death, which occurred in 1775, his types were purchased by a literary association in Paris for £3700, and were employed in printing a magnificent edition of the works of Voltaire. Thomas Attwood, Esq., the chief originator of the Political Union, and one of the first representatives of the newly-enfranchised borough, has been already alluded to in our brief sketch of the history of the town. He died, full of years and honours, in 1856. The clergy of Birmingham, Established and Dissenting, have, both in former and recent times, occupied a worthy place in connection with the literature of the country.

POPULATION AND TRADE.

The population of Birmingham at last census amounted to 343,696. But to get the full increase of population the two districts of King's Norton and Aston must be taken into amount. These being included, raise the population of Birmingham to 444,545. There were 65,371 inhabited houses. This shows an increase of 471,620 persons since the previous census, when the numbers were 296,076 persons. The growth of the town in population and wealth may be conceived when it is stated that in 1801 the inhabitants numbered only 73,670. In 1831 the population was 142,251 ; in 1841, 182,922 ; and in 1875 (estimated) 360,000, or an increase of a hundred per cent in 34 years.

It may be interesting to note here the chief occupations of the inhabitants, as supplied by the census returns of 1861. As the parish of Ashton is virtually a part of Birmingham, the figures relating to it are here included. Commencing with the occupations of males, we find the gun manufacture employing 4328 persons; brass foundries, 3892 ; engines and machines, 1661 ; the iron manufacture, 1561 ; buttons, 1578 : glass, 1002 ; copper, 133 ; tin, 355 ; zinc, 56 ; lead, 91. There were 2497 goldsmiths, 787 manufacturers of plated ware, 959 toolmakers, 203 filemakers, and 1763 persons employed about engines and tools, without their special work being stated. Buttonmakers numbered 1578 ; wire-drawers, 647 ; wire-weavers, 247 ; nailmakers, 509 ; japanners, 368. Coach-building found employment for 1148 persons ; harness for 526 ; and whips, 156. Women take a share in many of the manufactures. At the last census 232 were employed in the manufacture of arms, 698 upon steel pens, 132 on toys, 576 on screw-cutting, 190 on nails, 73 on pins, 230 on lacquering, 1016 otherwise in brass, 72 in copper, 93 in glass, and 86 in earthenware. French-polishers numbered 291, and japanners 322. The silk manufacture employed 61 ; ribbons, 27 ; lace, 46 ; and cotton, 29. Goldsmiths and jewellers number 320 ; besides 449 not specified, coming under the same class.

With the increase of its population, which is at the present time probably from 8000 to 9000 annually, the growth of the town keeps pace. It is pleasing also to find that, as Birmingham increases in extent, it exhibits a growing regard for architectural beauty, both in public and private buildings. Scarcely a year passes without something being done to improve the town in this respect.

Birmingham forms a centre of railway communication with every part of the kingdom. It has been named by Burke "the toy-shop of Europe." Many of its "toys" are used in the most serious of all games. The annual value of the borough rateable property in 1874 was £1,254,911. The borough is represented in Parliament by three members.

CHURCHES AND CHAPELS.

From ancient records we discover that several religious houses existed here at an early period. The Hospital of St. Thomas the Apostle was founded in 1285, and appears to have been richly endowed, though its annual revenues at the Dissolution amounted to only £8 : 8 : 9. The Priory buildings stood on the spot now called the Old Square. They were probably destroyed soon after the Reformation. Another religious house was founded a century later, under the name of the Guild of the Holy Cross. This fraternity, which included both monks and nuns, had an annual income of £31 : 2 : 10 when it was suppressed by Henry VIII. The buildings of the Guild and their revenues were subsequently bestowed by Edward VI. on the citizens of Birmingham for the foundation of the Free Grammar School, which now occupies their site.

St. Martin's Church is the oldest ecclesiastical edifice in Birmingham, but the date of its original foundation and the name of its founder cannot be ascertained. The present structure is supposed to belong to the early part of the thirteenth century. It has undergone various alterations, the principal one being in 1690, when the church and tower were cased with brick. In 1781 part of the spire was rebuilt, forty feet of it having been injured by lightning. Five years later, upwards of £4000 were expended on alterations and repairs on the church, especially in the interior, when little respect was shown to the ancient monuments which it contained. In 1853 the tower was found to be in a dangerous condition, and, together with the spire, was rebuilt. During the operations various interesting discoveries were made. The mouldings and other architectural ornaments, though much deteriorated by the effects of time and weather upon a soft friable stone, were found to have been extremely beautiful. Mr. Hardwick of London, the architect to whom the work was entrusted, referred the oldest part of the tower to about the year 1180, while the upper part and the spire he ascribed to a period more recent by a hundred years. In 1873 a further reparation took place, but without disturbing the monuments; and the old edifice has been enlarged at a cost of £30,000.

The church contains some curious ancient monuments of the De Birmingham family, more or less defaced. Hutton, the historian of Birmingham, has remarked that even Westminster Abbey, famous for departed glory, cannot produce a monument of equal antiquity. The oldest of them—that in the fifth window-opening of the south aisle—is supposed to represent Sir William de Birmingham, who distinguished himself in foreign service in the reign of Edward I. Next in antiquity to this is an effigy, supposed to represent another member of the family of the same name, who lived in the reigns of Edward II. and III. A third tomb bears the image of a knight in plate armour, said to represent John de Birmingham, sheriff of Warwick and Leicester shires in 1379, as well as knight of the shire in the parliament held at Westminster in 1382. He built the two western towers of York Cathedral about 1402. Another very interesting monument is the effigy of an ecclesiastic, on a high altar-tomb of alabaster. It is supposed to represent one of the members of the family of Marrow, upon whom the lordship was conferred by the crown after the execution of the Earl of Warwick. This has been pronounced by an authority in such matters to be one of the most curious monumental effigies extant. The church is adorned with some fine stained glass, and can accommodate upwards of 2000 persons.

St. Philip's—the other parish church—a handsome structure in the mixed Italian style, was commenced in 1711, and finished in 1719. It will be observed from the steeple and cupola that the architect has been to some extent indebted for his design to St. Paul's, London. This edifice occupies the most elevated spot in the town, and a fine view of Birmingham may be obtained from the top of its steeple. It contains no monuments of any interest.

St. George's, Tower Street, was built in 1820 from the designs of Mr. Rickman. It is in the Decorated style, and consists of nave, aisles, and chancel, with a tower at the west end surmounted with battlements and pinnacles.

Holy Trinity Church, Bradford Street, erected in 1823 at a cost of about £14,000, is in the Perpendi-cular style, and consists of nave, aisles, and chancel. It has for an altar-piece a painting by Foggo represent-ing our Saviour healing the paralytic man at the pool of Bethesda.

Christ Church, New Street, erected in 1815, is Grecian in style, and has a lofty portico of Doric

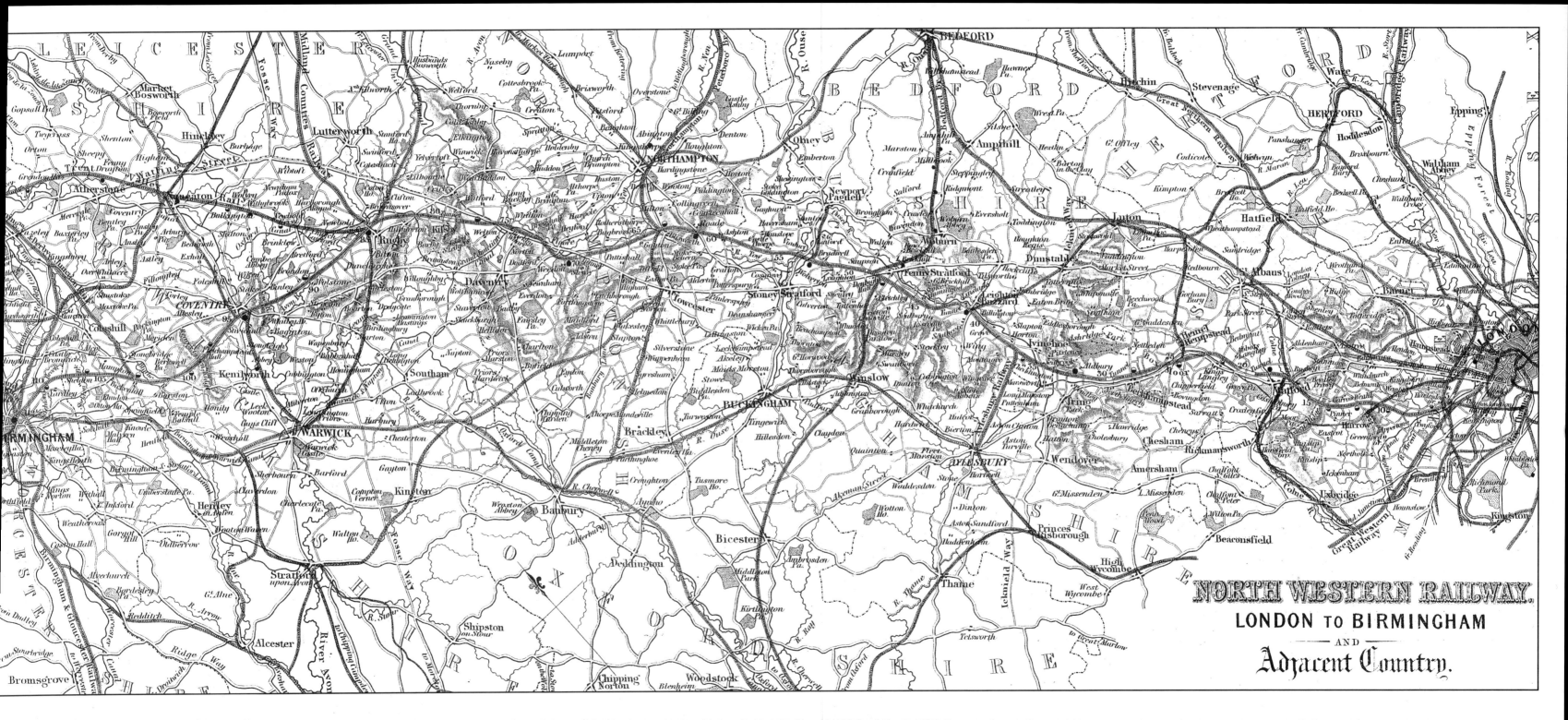

NORTH WESTERN RAILWAY.

LONDON to BIRMINGHAM

AND

Adjacent Country.

columns, surmounted by a pediment, above which rises a tower ending in a spire.

ST. PETER'S, in Dale End, and ST. THOMAS'S, at Holloway Head, are both Grecian in style. The former was erected in 1827, the latter in 1829.

There are many other churches ; but they are not of sufficient architectural importance to justify a detailed account. Exclusive of places temporarily licensed for religious worship, there are nearly forty churches in Birmingham.

Dissent is strong in Birmingham, all the principal denominations being represented.

The INDEPENDENTS have numerous places of worship. The first congregation took their origin in a secession from the Unitarians in 1748. Their chapel in *Carr's Lane* has become interesting to the Christian world by the labours of the Rev. John Angell James, who occupied this charge for more than fifty years. Mr. James died in 1859, aged 74. The present building was erected in 1820, and possesses no features of interest. *Edgbaston Chapel*, in Francis Road, is a very elegant edifice in the Decorated style, with a tower surmounted by a spire, rising to a total elevation of 170 feet. It was erected in 1855 in commemoration of Mr. Angell James's jubilee. Also deserving of notice on account of the elegance of its interior is the *Lozell's Chapel*.

The BAPTISTS have two chapels worthy of mention— *Christ Church*, in Aston Park ; and *Wycliffe Chapel*, Bristol Road, a very beautiful building in the Decorated style, and certainly one of the handsomest Dissenting chapels in Birmingham.

The METHODISTS, though possessing numerous meeting-houses, have only within the last few years shown any disposition to make architectural elegance a characteristic of their places of worship. The *Martin Street*

Chapel, Islington, is a good building in the Decorated style; and the *Bristol Road* and *Aston Viila Chapels* are also tasteful structures.

The ROMAN CATHOLICS have several places of worship. One of considerable pretensions, called the *Cathedral*, and dedicated to St. Chad, stands in Bath Street. The building is of brick, with stone dressings, and is a good rendering of the Decorated style with such materials. The west front, which contains the principal entrance, through a deeply-recessed arch, has on either side a lofty tower ending in a slated spire. Above the entrance is a fine window of six lights. The church consists of nave, aisles, transepts, and chancel. The aisles are divided from the nave by six clustered columns on either side, supporting pointed arches 75 feet high. Many of the windows are filled with good painted glass. The internal decorations of the edifice are in general very rich and tasteful. The Cathedral, which was built from the designs of the late Mr. Pugin, was consecrated in 1838, and cost about £29,000. The Roman Catholics have a convent of " Sisters of Mercy," an orphanage, " Little Sisters of the Poor," etc.

The UNITARIANS possess one very elegant place of worship in the *Church of the Messiah*, Islington. It is in the Decorated style; and besides a beautiful arcaded entrance, richly adorned, possesses a graceful spire about 150 feet high. The interior is handsomely fitted up, and contains a monument of Priestly, with a medallion portrait in profile, and an inscription by Dr. Parr.

PUBLIC BUILDINGS.

THE TOWN HALL, the principal architectural ornament of Birmingham, is a magnificent specimen of

Grecian architecture, and is universally admired for its thoroughly classic style. It occupies a fine site at the top of New Street. This noble building was commenced in 1832, but was not perfectly completed till 1850. It is constructed of Anglesea marble, and is the work of Messrs. Hansom and Welch. We quote its principal dimensions:—

Height of the basement	. . .	23 feet.
Height of the columns	. . .	36 feet.
Diameter of the columns	. . .	3 feet 6 inches.
Height of the capitals	. . .	4 feet.
Weight of each column	. . .	26 tons.

The principal room in this splendid building is open for inspection (without charge) every day except Sunday, and the tourist will do well to pay it a visit. Its dimensions are—length, 145 feet; breadth, 65 feet; height, 65 feet. It can afford comfortable sitting-room for upwards of 4000 persons; and double that number have often stood beneath its roof, entranced by the eloquence of Mr. Bright and other great popular orators. The decorations are of the most elegant and tasteful description. The lower part of the walls is painted grey, toned with red and yellow; the upper part being enamelled in imitation of Sienna marble. The pilasters are richly gilt, strict attention being paid to classical models in their various details. The gallery fronts are in bronze and gold, and are lined with crimson cloth. The covered sides of the roof are divided into recessed panels, and are adorned with the egg and tooth moulding, and richly gilt and painted. The ceiling, the gilding and painting of which are very gorgeous, is divided into three compartments, each inclosing a large circle, and divided into deeply-recessed radiating panels, diminishing in size towards the centre, where there is a magnificent sunlight gas-burner. At the back of the

orchestra is a splendid organ, said to be unsurpassed
by any in Europe. This organ, which is the property
of the Governors of the General Hospital, was erected
for the triennial musical festivals which are held here
for the benefit of that institution. Its weight is about
45 tons ; and its trackers, if laid out in a straight line,
would extend above five miles. The orchestra is further adorned with a colossal bust of Mendelssohn.

THE CORPORATE BUILDINGS are situate in Ann
Street, in close proximity to the Town Hall. It is an
imposing structure, built in the Italian style at a cost
of £200,000. It gives accommodation to the town-
council, law courts, public offices, and the mayor of
the borough.

The EXCHANGE, in New Street, adjoining the Central Railway Station, is one of the most recent additions
to the architectural beauties of Birmingham. This is
an imposing edifice in the domestic Gothic style, having a frontage of 180 feet to Stephenson Place, and
of 63 to New Street. The ground-floor is devoted
to shops, the front of each of which presents an arcade
of three arches, one serving for the doorway. The
entrance to the Exchange Rooms is in the centre of
the main elevation in Stephenson Place, and consists
of an elegant pointed arch under a tower, which, with
its slated spire, rises to a height of about 100 feet.
The several storeys above the ground-floor (three in
number) present continuous arcades of pointed windows.
Altogether, the effect of the building is light and graceful as well as imposing, and it is generally allowed to
be a very successful example of the application of the
Gothic style in the construction of a building for commercial and other purposes. It was built after the designs of Mr. Edward Holmes of Birmingham.

Besides the Exchange, which is a handsome room,

70 feet by 40, and 23 feet high, the building has a room for the meetings of the Chamber of Commerce, an assembly-room, dining-rooms, a hall for masonic meetings, committee-rooms, etc.

The statue of Thomas Attwood stands at the junction of Stephenson Place and New Street, opposite the Exchange (p. 23).

The CENTRAL RAILWAY STATION, at the foot of Stephenson Place, off New Street, and in the immediate vicinity of the Exchange, may be conveniently noticed here. It is a large and very elegant building in the Italian style, consisting of a centre and wings. The centre, which is 120 feet long, projects 20 feet from the wings, and is four storeys high. The lower storey is constructed of Derbyshire stone; the rest of the building of white brick. The lower storey is an arcade, and along with the other parts of the building exhibits much correctness and taste in its various details. The building includes a hotel and refreshment-room, as well as the usual offices. The roof is a triumph of art. It is composed of iron and glass, and measures 1100 feet in length, and 212 in width, and is 80 feet high ; yet it has no support except that afforded by the pillars on either side. The arches of iron that span the space from pillar to pillar weigh about 25 tons each. The glass of the roof is said to weigh 115 tons, and the iron at least 1400 tons. The roof was constructed by the well-known firm of Fox, Henderson, and Co. The traffic of the London and North-Western and Midland Railways, and their many branches, is carried on in this station. The station of the Great Western Railway is at Snow Hill, about ten minutes' walk from New Street. The Great Western Hotel is connected with the Station.

The PUBLIC OFFICE, Moor Street, erected in 1806,

and considerably enlarged in 1861, is mainly Grecian
in style, and is used for the Borough Court of Quarter
Sessions, the general Police Court, and other purposes.
It may be mentioned here that the BOROUGH GAOL is
at Birmingham Heath, on the outskirts of the town.
It is a large and handsome building of brick, in the
Romanesque style, and contains about 600 separate
cells.

The MARKET HALL, which extends from High Street
to Worcester Street, is a vast building in the Grecian
style.   An Act of Parliament was procured for its
erection in 1828, but it was not begun till 1833.   It
cost about £67,261.   There are twelve entrances, the
principal one being that towards High Street.   The
entire length of this building is 365 feet ; the width,
108 ; the height, 60.   Its area (4380 square yards)
affords accommodation for 600 stalls.   The Market
Hall is open every day, but the principal market-day
is Thursday.

The CORN EXCHANGE, also situated in High Street,
was completed in 1847, at a cost of £6000.   In its
external appearance there is nothing to attract admiration ; but its interior, which is of the Italian-Doric
style, is very elegant.

The THEATRE ROYAL, in New Street, presents to
the street a piazza surrounded by a colonnade, with a
wing on either side, ornamented respectively by medal-
lions of Shakspere and Garrick.   The interior is tastefully fitted up, and affords accommodation for two
thousand persons.   Mr. Macready was trained on this
stage, and many other actors of eminence made their
first appearance here.

The Prince of Wales Theatre, in Broad Street, also
affords entertainments of a dramatic kind.

MONUMENTS.—It may be convenient to the tourist

to have the various monuments noticed under one heading.

Nelson's Monument, in the Bull Ring, opposite St. Martin's Church, consists of a bronze statue of the admiral standing on a circular marble pedestal, his left arm resting on an anchor, and the model of a ship of war behind him. The pedestal is ornamented with appropriate sculptures. The monument is the work of Westmacott, and is worthy of that eminent sculptor. It was inaugurated in 1809.

The *Statue of Sir Robert Peel* stands in the open space near the Town Hall. The figure, which is in bronze, and is considered a good likeness as well as an excellent work of art, was executed by Mr. Peter Hollins of Birmingham, and cast by Messrs. Elkington, Mason, and Co., of Newhall Street. It was erected in 1855.

The *Attwood Statue,* New Street, was erected in 1859, in memory of the veteran father of political unions. Thomas Attwood died in 1856. The statue, which is of marble and the work of Mr. Thomas of London, is a very effective likeness. It cost about £1000.

The *Sturge Statue,* Five Ways, was inaugurated in 1862. It represents the eminent philanthropist, Joseph Sturge, on a pedestal, between fine allegorical figures of Charity and Peace. The sculptor of this monument was Mr. Thomas of London.

A Statue of James Watt is set between the Town Hall and the Midland Institute, and statues of the late Prince Consort and Sir Rowland Hill are in progress.

EDUCATIONAL INSTITUTIONS.

The FREE GRAMMAR SCHOOL, New Street, justly regarded as one of the chief architectural ornaments of

Birmingham, was founded in 1552 by Edward VI., who endowed it with the possessions of the ancient Guild of the Holy Cross, which had come to the crown at the Dissolution. The original building, composed of wood and plaster, was taken down in 1707 ; but that by which it was displaced falling into decay, an Act of Parliament was obtainĕd by the governors to rebuild it, and extend the usefulness of the foundation by the establishment of branch schools in various parts of the town. Accordingly the edifice was erected in 1834, from the plans of Sir Charles Barry, in the decorated Elizabethan style, since employed in the new palace at Westminster. The cost of the buildings, furnishings, etc., amounted to £67,000. The edifice is quadrangular in form, extending 174 feet in front, and 125 in the flanks, and having an elevation of 60 feet. The head-master's salary is £400 a-year ; but there are additional emoluments derived from fees which may make his salary amount to £1000. Ten exhibitions of £50 a-year each, for four years, at either of the universities, are attached to the school. About 470 boys are educated here.

THE SCIENTIFIC COLLEGE in Edmund Street, at the back of the Town Hall, is a handsome building designed in the Gothic style of architecture. It has been erected with the view of providing scientific instruction to the inhabitants, and was endowed and erected by Sir Josiah Mason at an expense of £100,000.

The QUEEN'S COLLEGE, in Paradise Street, near the Town Hall, somewhat resembles the Grammar School in style, but is less extensive and magnificent. It was incorporated by royal charter in 1843 ; and chiefly owes its origin to the munificence of two individuals, W. Sands Cox, Esq., F.R.S., and the Rev. S. Wilson Warneford, LL.D. The object of this institution is to provide instruction for students in medicine and surgery, civil architecture and engineering, and theology. Medical students are qualified by its lectures for becoming candidates for the medical degrees of the University of London, the diplomas of the Royal Colleges of Surgeons, London and Edinburgh, and the licence of the Society of Apothecaries. Students of this college have also the privilege of presenting themselves for examination for the B.A. degree of the University of London. The theological department is under the patronage of the bishop of the diocese, and prepares students for ordination.

SPRING HILL COLLEGE, for the education of young men for the ministry in connection with the Independent denomination, owes its origin to the benevolence of George Storer Mansfield, Esq., and his sisters. These excellent persons having resolved to carry out their pious design in their lifetime, Mr. Mansfield handed over to trustees certain landed estates for the maintenance of the institution, and his sisters gave their house for a college, in 1838. In 1856 the college was removed to its present more convenient site, which was acquired for £18,000, raised by subscription. The college has residences for the professors (three in number), class-rooms, studies and dormitories for thirty-six students, an extensive library, etc.

SYDENHAM COLLEGE, in Summer Lane, established in 1851, is a medical school. Attendance at its lectures qualifies for admission to examination at the various medical boards of the United Kingdom.

The BIRMINGHAM AND MIDLAND INSTITUTE, adjoining the Town Hall, at the top of New Street, was opened in 1857. This handsome pile of buildings is devoted to the various uses commonly aimed at by general scientific and literary institutions. It includes a reading-room, museums, lectures, classes for instruction in industrial science, a gallery of fine arts, etc. In close proximity to the institute is the FREE LIBRARIES, a building designed after the Italian style, and the ART GALLERY which fronts Edmund Street. Both of these institutions are well worthy of a visit.

The GOVERNMENT SCHOOL OF DESIGN also occupies a part of the Midland Institute range of buildings. This is a very important institution, having for its object the fostering of that taste in workmen and designers which is necessary for the blending of the beautiful with the useful in manufactures. It was opened in 1843, under the auspices of Government, and at first received a public grant of £600 annually. This grant was subsequently withdrawn ; but it is satisfactory to know that, notwithstanding, the institution continues to prosper. It is now regarded as the largest and most important of the kind in the kingdom. The number of pupils is upwards of 500.

CHARITIES.

The GENERAL HOSPITAL, Summer Lane, erected in 1779, and enlarged in 1791 and 1857, is a noble institution, established for the relief of the suffering poor of the town and neighbourhood. The number of patients admitted annually is nearly 3000 ; while the number visited in their own dwellings is about 14,000. The triennial musical festivals in aid of this admirable institution are well known. They are held in the Town Hall, last four days, and usually bring a profit of from four to five thousand pounds.

The QUEEN'S HOSPITAL, a large and elegant building in Bath Row, is another institution of the same kind, receiving 2000 in-patients annually, nearly 7000 out-patients being visited in the same time.

Among other institutions for the relief of the suffering poor, are the *Children's Hospital*, in Steelhouse Lane, established in 1862; the *Homœopathic Hospital*, in the Old Square; the *Dispensary*, in Union Street; the *Eye Hospital*, Temple Row; the *General Institution for the Blind*, Edgbaston; the *Institution for the Deaf and Dumb*, also at Edgbaston; the *Magdalen Asylum*, etc.

The REFORMATORY INSTITUTION, a very important and deserving charity, is at Saltley, on a site freely given for the purpose by Mr. Adderley, M.P. The object of this charity is sufficiently indicated by its name. There is accommodation for 75 boys, who are trained to industrial occupations. There are agencies in Canada, Natal, and Tasmania, for assisting boys who wish to emigrate when their period of detention is over. A similar institution for the reformation of girls exists at Smethwick. The *Discharged Prisoners' Aid Society* is an admirable charity. Its object is to enable discharged prisoners to return to the paths of honesty and virtue, by procuring lodgings and employment for them, and otherwise rendering them such assistance as they may need. The *Industrial School*, Penn Street, takes charge of vagrant and neglected children.

PARKS, ETC.

Few towns had more need of spaces of free open ground to serve as the lungs of labour, and few are better supplied than Birmingham. On its northern border is ASTON PARK, which was acquired a few years ago. Portions of it have been disposed of for building purposes, but there is enough of these fine grounds left to make free access to them a boon to the people of Birmingham. The ADDERLEY PARK, at

Saltley, was the gift of the Right Hon. C. B. Adderley, M.P., in 1856. CALTHORPE PARK, in the Pershore Road, the gift of Lord Calthorpe, was opened in 1857. The CEMETERIES may be conveniently noticed here. They are well kept, and are favourite resorts of the inhabitants. The *Witton Cemetery*, about 3½ miles from the centre of the town, is of great extent. It is the property of the Corporation, who have expended on it about £75,000. The *Church of England Cemetery*, on the north-western border of the town, between Vyse Street and Ikenild Street, was consecrated in 1848. It is laid out with much taste, and has a handsome church in the Perpendicular style, dedicated to St. Michael, and used for worship. The *General Cemetery* is in the immediate vicinity of ·that just noticed, and is, like it, planned very tastefully. It contains a chapel for the conducting of the burial service. Some of the monuments are worthy of notice.

MANUFACTORIES.

The manufactories of Birmingham are so numerous and extensive that it would require an entire handbook to do them justice. They date from a very early period ; for we find Leland, who wrote in the reign of Henry VIII., saying : " There be many smithes in the towne, that use to make knives and all manner of cutting tooles, and many lorimers that make bittes, and a great many naylours ; so that a great part of the town is maintained by smithes, who have their iron and sea coal out of Staffordshire." Hutton is even of opinion that " the Britons were supplied with their implements of war and husbandry from the black artists of the Birmingham forge long before the landing of Cæsar ;" but this, though not improbable, is necessarily only a matter of conjecture. Swords were manufactured in great numbers in the reign of Charles I. We have already stated that the manufacture of gilded ornaments originated at the Restoration, and that of guns in the reign of William III. From that period the productions of Birmingham increased in number and extent; and at the present moment its manufactures, whether for variety, or value, or quantity, are unequalled in the world. The excellence of the manufactures of Birmingham was sufficiently shown at the local Exposition of 1849, and again at the Great Exhibitions of 1851 and 1862. It was the Birmingham Exposition of 1849 which suggested to Prince Albert the idea of an exhibition of the products of the industry of all nations. The Crystal Palace, in which the latter exhibition was held, and many of its most prominent ornaments and articles of usefulness and elegance, were the production of Birmingham.

BUTTON-MAKING is one of the earliest manufactures; at least it is that which in earlier times contributed most to the prosperity of the town. Immense fortunes have been made in the button trade—one eminent manufacturer having acknowledged that by a single improvement he realised £40,000. Buttons are made of brass, copper, steel, pewter, cloth, glass, pearl, horn, shell, bone, wood, and porcelain. The gilt button has gone out of use for gentlemen's dress, but is still extensively used for military and other uniforms. Formerly it employed thousands of persons; and it is stated that John Taylor, who was the first to embark largely in its manufacture, acquired a fortune of £200,000. This trade is still carried on at the manufactories of Hammond, Turner, and Co., Snow Hill, and Smith and Wright, both of which houses produce other varieties of buttons of great beauty. Allen and Moore, Great

Hampton Row, manufacture metal buttons of beautiful designs in great quantities. Their medals, too, are finely executed. The extensive manufactory of Elliot and Sons, Regent Street, sends forth millions of the Florentine or cloth button annually. There also are produced linen buttons, military and sporting buttons, etc. Among other establishments, the following deserve to be noticed :—William Kirby, Whitby Plàce, Summer Lane (hooks, eyes, and buttons) ; Banks and Hammond, Summer Row (pearl and bone buttons); and Mr. Brisband, Howard Street (pearl and bone buttons).

SWORD* AND GUN MAKING is an important branch of the trade of Birmingham. Swords were made here from a very early period—as early as the time of the Britons, Hutton thinks. It has been already mentioned that Birmingham supplied Cromwell's soldiers with 15,000 swords. This manufacture is, we believe, carried on in its greatest excellence and extent in the manufactory of Charles Reeves and Co., Toledo Works, Charlotte Street. Other important manufactories of this kind are those of Harvey, Albert Works, Glover Street ; Male, Broad Street ; and Sargent, Edmund Street.

Guns and pistols are made in great quantities ; and there are numerous establishments engaged in their manufacture. Every description of guns and pistols seems to be made at the establishment of J. Townsend, Sand Street. Other extensive producers of firearms are Cooper and Co., Woodcock Street ; Bentley and Playfair, Summer Lane ; Swinburn and Son, Russell Street ; and Hollis and Sheath, St. Mary's Square. The sporting guns of Westley, Richards, and Co., High Street, are universally known and appreciated. It is stated that Birmingham produces some 3000 rifles weekly.

In connection with the gun trade, the *Gun-Barrel Proof-Houses*, in Banbury Street, Digbeth, and in Baggott Street, deserve to be noticed. All fire-arms fabricated in Birmingham are required to be proved here. They are fired with a double charge of powder and ball, and are not examined for twenty-four hours after firing. The good barrels are stamped, and the bad ones broken to pieces in a vice.

The GOLD, SILVER-PLATE, AND JEWELLERY trade does not appear to have been carried on to any great extent till a recent period. At present a considerable portion of the jewellery disposed of in this country is produced in Birmingham. It is said that, for chains alone, at least 1000 ounces of fine gold are consumed weekly. Nearly 30,000 wedding-rings annually pass through the assay office here. At least 70 ounces of gold leaf are used every week. It is estimated that more of the precious metals are used in the manufactures of Birmingham than even in the metropolis itself. Of silver* more than 40,000 ounces are assayed annually. The principal houses in the jewellery trade are the following :—Goode, St. Paul's Square, of great extent, employing 500 persons, principally females, where the manufacture of gold chains, and the fitting up of gems, etc., may be seen to advantage ; Balleny, St. Paul's Square ; Aston and Son, Regent Place ; Betts, Fairfax, and Co., Richard Street ; Williams, Vyse Street ; C. J. Shaw, Vyse Street ; Manton and Mole, Great Charles Street ; T. and J. Bragg, Vittoria Street ; Harris, Great Hampton Street ; and Pritchard and Martin, Regent Place.

ELECTRO-PLATING is an art of much importance ;

---

* The total quantity of silver used in Birmingham for different manufactures exceeds 150,000 ounces annually. A single manufacturer has used 34,000 ounces in a year for his own consumption.

and one which holds a very prominent place among the manufactures of Birmingham. In the extensive establishment of Elkington, Mason, and Co., the different processes are carried to great perfection. Their show-room is one of the largest and most elegant in the world ; and the tourist cannot fail to be delighted by a visit to it. We have no space to describe the process by which a coating of gold, silver, or other metal is deposited on the plated articles. The effect is extremely beautiful. Specimens of the different processes are exhibited in the show-room. This firm also produces admirable groups and figures in bronze. The statue of Sir Robert Peel, in New Street, was cast by them from a model by Peter Hollins, Esq. The works of Prime and Son, Northwood Street , J. and C. Ratcliffe and Co., Suffolk Street ; G. R. Collis and Co., Church Street, also exhibit the perfection of the process in its numerous applications. The last-mentioned works were formerly the establishment of Sir Edward Thomason and Co. The show-room, besides a splendid assortment of silver and plated goods, contains a copy in bronze of the famous Warwick Vase, the construction of which occupied seven years, and a statue, also in bronze, of George IV. in his coronation robes.

In the manufacture of BRASS and BRONZE a large trade is done in Birmingham. In one establishment, R. W. Winfield and Co., Cambridge Street Works, 700 workmen are constantly employed. Messrs. Winfield received a council medal at the Great Exhibition for the superiority of the articles they displayed. Ironmongery of all kinds, plain and ornamental, is manufactured in these works. A manufactory of a similar kind is that of Peyton and Peyton, High Street, Bordesley. The manufactures of Hardman and Co

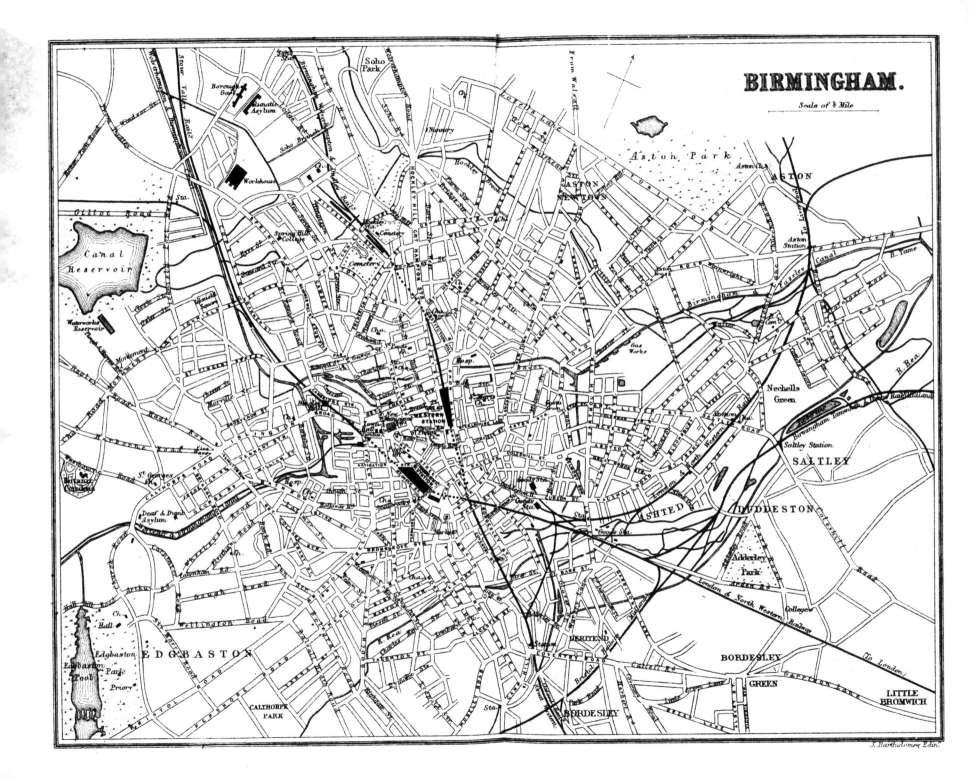

are extremely interesting, presenting faithful and tasteful imitations of the mediæval style. Messenger and Sons, Broad Street, also successfully imitate the antique in their metal work. We may mention that, among other equally well-known productions, the magnificent chandeliers of St. George's Hall, Liverpool, the staircase of Northumberland House, London, the gates of the Fitzwilliam Museum at Cambridge, and the fine fountain in the Birmingham Market Hall, were produced here.

Among the workers in IRON, we may mention Messrs. Watkins and Keen (Patent Nut and Bolt Co., Limited), who are manufacturers of all descriptions of nuts, bolts, etc., smith's work, and every kind of railway fastenings, by patent machinery, at the London Works, Smethwick, being the premises formerly occupied by Messrs. Fox, Henderson, and Co. In the same neighbourhood are the important works of Mr. Thos. Gibson, coach-spring and axletree manufacturer; Messrs. J. Astbury and Son, general iron-founders; the London Works Iron Co., etc. The steam-engine manufactory of Toy and Sons, Soho (within the boundary of Staffordshire), will be viewed with special interest, as it was here that James Watt brought the steam-engine to perfection. In company with Mr. Boulton he established here the first manufactory of steam-engines.

GLASS MANUFACTURES.—The establishment of F. and C. Osler, Broad Street, enjoys a reputation perhaps second to that of no other in the kingdom. In this establishment were manufactured the beautiful and magnificent crystal glass candelabra for the tomb of the Prophet, and for the palace of Ibraham Pasha at Cairo. The much-admired crystal fountain of the Great Exhibition was constructed in this manufactory. Other very important works, where the various

branches of the manufacture are carried on, are those
of Chance and Co., Spon Lane ; Gammon and Co.,
Great Brooke Street ; Stone, Fawdry, and Stone, Dart-
mouth Street ; Lloyd and Summerfield, Spring Hill ;
Walsh, Birmingham Heath, etc.

PAPIER-MACHE is an interesting and beautiful manufacture. The tourist may see it in its various parts in
the manufactory of J. Bettridge and Co., Barr Street,
St. George's. This establishment, which has been
repeatedly visited by royal personages, is obligingly
opened for the inspection of visitors. The firm of
M'Callum and Hodson, Summer Row, is also largely
engaged in this manufacture.

STEEL PENS.—It would be scarcely an exaggeration
to say that Birmingham supplies the whole world with
steel pens. The most noted manufactory is that of
Gillot and Company, Graham Street. The names of
Mitchell, Mason, Hinks, Wells, Brandauer, etc., are well
known in connection with this manufacture. Gold
pens are produced by Willey and other manufacturers.

It is impossible to notice in detail even the chief of
the miscellaneous manufactures carried on in Birmingham. *Wire-Drawing* is an important trade—one
establishment, that of Webster and Horsfall, Hay
Mills and Oxford Street, being said to produce weekly
eight tons of musical wire alone. The manufacture of
Oil and Gas Lamps, specially designed for the Indian
markets, has been brought to a point of high excellence
by W. Cooper and Son, Aston Road, and other houses.
The manufacture of *Railway Carriages and Waggons*
has become an important branch of trade, employing
a very large number of hands. The principal manufactories are those of the Midland Waggon Company,
the Metropolitan Company, and the Britannia Works.

THE ROYAL MINT, Heaton and Sons, Icknield Street

East, cannot fail to interest those who obtain the privilege of inspecting it. Copper coin is made here in immense quantities—82,000 pieces being struck every day.*

Vicinity of Birmingham.

THE suburbs of Birmingham afford sufficient evidence of the prosperity of the town. Not confining itself to Warwickshire, Birmingham is rapidly extending into the adjoining counties of Stafford and Worcester. Numerous handsome villas, with pleasant gardens, evince the taste and wealth of the merchants and manufacturers who here seek a partial retirement from the bustle and noise of this great seat of industry. Edgbaston appears to be the aristocratic quarter, though Aston and Handsworth are also favourite localities. It may be remarked here that the last-named place, which is geographically situated in Staffordshire, has an old church, beautifully situated, containing a fine statue of James Watt (who is buried here), executed by Chantrey, and a bust of his partner, Boulton, by Flaxman.

The extensive parish of ASTON lies on the north side of Birmingham, of which it is virtually a suburb.

Aston Hall is 2½ miles by rail from the New Street Station. It is in the Elizabethan style, and occupies a gentle eminence, at the end of a fine avenue of elms and Spanish chestnuts. The building was commenced in 1618 by Sir Thomas Holte, but not finished till 1635. In 1642 Charles I. was entertained here for two days; and the room in which he slept is still called "King Charles' Bed-room." For his attach-

---

* Should the tourist wish fuller information regarding Birmingham, he will find "Cornish's Guide" a correct and useful manual. The author of this work is indebted to it for some of the facts in the above account.

ment to the royal cause, Sir Thomas was attacked by a party of the townspeople of Birmingham, assisted by some regular troops. After a brief defence the Hall was surrendered. In this affair a cannon-ball shattered part of the staircase. The effect of the stroke may be seen to this day. Sir Thomas was heavily fined for his loyalty. The Holte family becoming extinct, Aston Hall and Park passed through several hands. It was for some years the residence of James Watt, Esq., son, of the inventor of the steam-engine. A large portion of the park had previously to 1857 been disposed of for building purposes. In that year a company was formed for the purpose of acquiring for the people the hall and what remained unfeued of the park. Great *eclat* was given to the project by her Majesty visiting Birmingham, and inaugurating the park with much ceremony, in 1858. The company having, however, failed in its object, the corporation made good the deficiency (£20,000), thereby securing the park, extending now to about 43 acres, for the people. Some of the apartments of Aston Hall are well worthy of inspection. The Great Hall, at the entrance, has a richly-decorated plaster ceiling, with a broad cornice containing the figures of various animals. The lower portions of the walls are wainscotted, and are painted with landscapes and figures of Roman emperors. The back of the grate bears the royal arms, with the initials C. R. Over the chimney-piece are inscribed the following lines :—

> " If service be thy meane to thrive,
> Thov mvst therein remaine,
> Both silent, faithful, jvst, and trve,
> Content to take some paine.
>
> If love of vertve may allvre,
> Or hope of worldly gaine,
> If feare of God may the procvre,
> To serve doe not disdaine."

The Great Staircase is enriched with grotesque carvings. Here may be seen the shattered standard and panelling in the condition to which it was reduced by the cannonading previously referred to. The Great Drawing-Room is a fine and interesting apartment. Its ornamental stone frieze, with military figures of various ages and nations, its decorated ceiling, and its splendid chimney-piece, are all well worthy of attention. The Long Gallery, said to be one of the finest in England, is 136 feet long, 18 wide, and 16 high. The walls are panelled with oak, and the ceiling is richly ornamented. The marble chimney-piece, the finest in the house, exhibits curious but graceful sculpture. This gallery formerly contained a series of family portraits; but these are now all dispersed. King Charles' Bedroom possesses some interest from its association with the haughty and unfortunate monarch. Aston Hall contains 103 apartments.

Aston Church is near the Hall. It is a graceful structure, of different periods. The tower and spire are of the reign of Henry VI. In the interior are some interesting monuments of the Holte family, and of other distinguished personages.

COLESHILL, 14 miles distant by rail, is separately described, p. 42.

EDGBASTON is noticed here more on account of its general picturesqueness than from its possessing any objects of much interest to the tourist. The *Church*, dedicated to St. Bartholomew, has undergone many alterations and additions since the Restoration, when it was rebuilt by Sir Richard Gough. Though architecturally of no importance, it is by no means destitute of picturesqueness. The *Hall*, a plain brick building, on the site of an ancient edifice destroyed at the Revolution, is situated near the church, in a finely-wooded park.

KNOWLE, 10¼ miles distant, is described in connec tion with SOLIHULL.

SUTTON COLDFIELD, 7½ miles distant by rail, is a market-town of considerable antiquity. It had fallen into great decay in the time of Henry VII., when John Vesey or Harman, Bishop of Exeter, a native of this place, by his numerous benefactions restored it to its original importance, and laid the foundation of its subsequent prosperity. He enlarged and ornamented the church, erected a town-hall and market-house, and founded and endowed a free school. The *Church* is a handsome building, consisting of nave, chancel, and two side aisles. There are no monuments of any importance. Sutton Park, containing about 3500 acres, was bestowed on the town by Bishop Vesey for the benefit of the poorer inhabitants.*

Sutton Coldfield has in its immediate neighbourhood the Roman road termed *Ikenild Street*, in many places very distinctly marked. There are also the remains of an extensive encampment, ascribed by some to the Romans, and by others to the early Britons. The works have occupied a square of 4 acres.

CHARLECOTE.

In the VICINITY OF STRATFORD-ON-AVON.

* Fuller gives Vesey small credit for his benefactions to Sutton Colefield. "He robbed his own cathedral to pay a parish church." His bishopric "he destroyed, not only shaving the hairs (with long leases), but cutting away the limbs with sales outright, insomuch that Bishop Hall, his successor in that see, complaineth in print that the following bishops were *barons*, but *bare-ones* indeed." Vesey died at the age of 103, and was buried in Sutton Church.

CHESTERTON.

˙From Southam Road Station, 3 miles.

THIS small hamlet may be reached by a pleasant walk or drive from either Warwick or Leamington, or by rail to Southam Road, whence it is distant about 3 miles. A conveyance from Southam attends several of the trains, enabling the tourist to visit that town, should he wish it, before proceeding to Chesterton. The road to Chesterton from Southam Road station lies through Harbury (p. 41), and may be shortened by a footpath, which will be pointed out by any of the country people.

Chesterton was the seat of the powerful family of Peyto in the time of Edward III., and through several successive generations. The last and most famous personage of this family was Peter de Peyto, created a cardinal in the reign of Henry VIII., to whose daughter Mary, afterwards Queen of England, he was confessor. In the reign of Mary, being appointed the Pope's legate, in place of the famous Cardinal Pole, who had come under the displeasure of the Pontiff, he was refused permission to enter the country in that capacity, when he retired to France, where he died, April 1558. The manor-house, which was built in the reign of Edward IV., and had important additions made to it about the year 1630, under the direction of the celebrated Inigo Jones, was taken down—it does not appear for what reason—by Lord Willoughby de Broke in 1802.

The CHURCH, dedicated to St. Giles, is pleasantly situated, and is worthy of a visit on account of the ancient monuments it contains. The principal one is on the south side of the chancel, and consists of an altar-tomb, bearing date of 1589, with the recumbent effigies of

Sir Humphrey Peyto, and Anna his wife—the knight
being habited in armour, and the lady in the fashion
of the time. There are two other monuments, both
bearing a couple of busts—one to the memory of Sir
Edward Peyto, who died in 1643, and Elizabeth his
wife ; the other commemorating Sir William Peyto
(son of Sir Humphrey and father of Sir Edward), who
died in 1609, and his wife Eleanora. All these monuments are in good preservation. The east window is
filled with a fine representation of the Last Supper,
erected in 1862 by Lord Willoughby de Brooke.

In the reign of Henry V., John Lucy, vicar of this
parish, afforded an asylum to Lord Cobham, one of the
most noted followers of Wickliffe. For this offence,
and for heresy, he was tried and condemned ; but
through the exertions of his friends he obtained the
royal pardon.

On a hill near the village stands a large stone windmill, erected in 1632 by Sir Edward Peyto, after a
design by Inigo Jones. It is circular in form, and
supported by six arches with pilaster capitals. This
windmill forms a convenient landmark to guide the
tourist to the Roman Camp, which is in a field a few
hundred yards west of the hill on which it stands.

The ROMAN CAMP is square in form, and of considerable extent. Gibson remarks that the Roman origin
of this fortification is evident from three circum-
stances :—" First, the name of the place, which plainly
comes from the Roman *castrum;* secondly, its nearness
to the Roman Foss, upon which it is certain that, at
convenient distances, places of entertainment were
built for the reception of the armies on their march;
the third token is, that in the compass within which
the Roman building is supposed to have stood several
old Roman coins have been dug up."

The Foss Way, which is turned to the purposes of a country road, is here well marked. A walk of about 2 miles will bring the tourist to Bishop's Tachbrook, 2 miles from Leamington, and 3 from Warwick.

HARBURY, about 2 miles from Chesterton, has a church in different styles, the oldest parts Early English. Adjoining the church is an endowed school in a dilapidated condition.

SOUTHAM (*Inns:* Craven Arms, Bull).—This small market-town, between 5 and 6 miles from Chesterton, and about 3 from the station of the same name, is pleasantly situated and picturesquely wooded.

The Church, which occupies a commanding position on the border of the town, consists of nave, aisles, chancel, with a north aisle and vestry, and a tower surmounted by a lofty spire at the west end. The edifice is in various styles, the oldest parts being the tower, which is Early English, and the nave, which is Perpendicular. The chancel and aisles have been rebuilt in the Decorated style. It contains no monuments of importance. The windows are filled with stained glass.

Just outside of the town is an *Infirmary* for diseases of the eye and ear, established and long presided over by Mr. Smith, a benevolent surgeon, whose philanthropic services are recorded on a tablet on the front of the institution. The town also possesses a National School, a Dispensary, and a Workhouse.

A mineral spring here, similar to those of Leamington, was formerly in considerable request.

UFTON, a hamlet 2 miles from Southam and 3 from Chesterton, possesses an Early English *Church*, mostly restored. In the churchyard stands a stone cross, with the inscription—" To the glory of God, this parish cross, erected about A.D. 1316, was restored A.D. 1862.'

The upper part of the cross, which is all that remains of the original structure, is in tolerable preservation. It has emblematical sculptures on each of its four sides, the front one being the Crucifixion, and the others— a bearded figure, perhaps representing Moses; the Virgin and Child; and the Virgin holding in her hand the crown of thorns.

COLESHILL AND ITS VICINITY.

From Birmingham, 14 miles; Coventry, 14; Tamworth, 10.

THIS quiet market-town consists mainly of one long picturesque street on the slope of a hill, at the foot of which flows the Cole, the small stream whence it derives its name.

The CHURCH, which occupies a very commanding position, is in the Decorated style, and consists of nave, aisles, chancel, and tower, surmounted by a noble crocketed spire. It contains some fine monuments of the Digby family. There are three altar-tombs, each bearing two figures, male and female, recumbent, with their hands clasped in prayer. One pair of these figures is coloured after life. The lady's figure and dress are particularly handsome. A monumental brass, bearing the date of 1652, and having a male and female figure cut in outline, will be found worthy of notice. The font is ancient and curious.

Other noticeable buildings are the FREE GRAMMAR SCHOOL, adjoining the churchyard, and the MARKET-HOUSE, also near the church, and bearing the inscription—". Henricus Dnx Digby hanc Porticum in usum hujus Emporii struxit, Anno 1766." Beside this building are the stocks and pillory, in tolerable condition.

In the vicinity of Coleshill are Maxstoke Castle and the ruins of Maxstoke Priory.

MAXSTOKE CASTLE, a mile and a half from Coleshill, may be reached by a pleasant footpath through the fields. This is a highly picturesque building, and is one of the few structures of the kind in England which are kept in their original fortified aspect—a considerable part of it remaining in the same state as when first erected by William de Clinton, Earl of Huntingdon, in the reign of Edward III. In the reign of Henry VI. the estate passed in exchange to Humphrey, Earl of Stafford, afterwards Duke of Buckingham, for certain manors in Northamptonshire. After various transmissions the castle and estates, about the reign of Queen Elizabeth, became the property of the Dilke family, the present owners. The castle is in the form of a parallelogram, with a hexagonal tower at each corner, and is still surrounded by a moat. The entrance is by a lofty gateway. The gates, which were erected by Humphrey, Duke of Buckingham, in the reign of Henry VI., are covered with plates of iron, embossed with his arms. Between twenty and thirty years ago an accidental fire destroyed a portion of the interior, but the principal parts are untouched. The hall and the drawing-room are especially interesting. The latter has a door and chimney-piece, curiously carved. In the walls of the Great Court are to be seen the ancient lodgments of the soldiers.

The PRIORY is about a mile to the south of the castle. This religious house was founded in 1337 by William de Clinton, and liberally endowed for canons regular of the order of St. Augustine. The remains consist of the gateway, fragments of the tower and detached parts of the building, and the boundary-wall. A small church adjoins the gateway, evidently constructed out of the ruins of the priory.

SHUSTOKE, a small village between 2 and 3 miles

distant, is the birthplace of Sir William Dugdale, the Warwickshire historian.* The *Church*, erected in the reign of Edward II., and a good example of the style of that period, contains monuments to the memory of Sir William and other members of his family.

Blythe Hall, midway between Shustoke and Coleshill, was the seat of Sir William Dugdale, and is still the property of his descendants. It occupies a somewhat low position on the small river Blythe, but is a handsome and spacious edifice. In the interior is a portrait of Sir William.

* Sir William Dugdale was born in Shustoke rectory-house in 1605. His "Antiquities of Warwickshire" appeared in 1656, being printed at his own cost. This is a work of great value, copies of it readily selling at a very high price. The eulogium of Fuller is well deserved :—" I cannot but congratulate the happiness of this county in having Master William Dugdale, my worthy friend, a native thereof ; whose illustrations are so great a work no young man could be so bold to begin, or old man hope to finish it, whilst one of middle age fitted the performance—a well-chosen county for such a subject, because lying in the centre of the land whose lustre diffuseth the light, and darteth beams to the circumference of the kingdom. It were a wild wish that all the shires in England were described to an equal degree of perfection, as which will be accomplished when each star is as big and bright as the sun. However, one may desire them done *quoad speciem*, though not *quoad gradum*, in imitation of Warwickshire." Dugdale was an indefatigable collector, and while preparing his work on Warwickshire did not neglect any antiquarian documents or monuments that fell in his way. His greatest work is the " Monasticon Anglicanum," in three volumes folio. This work gives an account of all the religious houses in England, and is the standard authority in all matters connected with them.. Dugdale also published " The Baronage of England," in two volumes ; " The History of St. Paul's Cathedral ;" and various other less important works of a heraldic and historical nature. He left between thirty and forty volumes of manuscript collections of charters, records, inscriptions, etc., which are now in the possession of the University of Oxford. In 1660 he was appointed to the congenial office of Norroy King of Arms, and sixteen years later he was advanced to the higher dignity of Garter King of Arms. He died in 1685, at Blythe Hall, and was buried in Shustoke church.

COMBE ABBEY.

From Coventry, 5 miles; Brandon Station, 3; Rugby, 7½;
Stretton Station, 3.

THE walk or drive from Coventry to Combe Abbey does not include any object of special interest. Between 3 and 4 miles from the city the road passes through the village of BINLEY, which has a tasteful little modern church, possessing a good east window with a Holy Family in stained glass. The approach to Combe Abbey from the Brandon* station is by a long avenue through a thick plantation. The vista afforded by this woodland road is magnificent, the mansion being distinguishable in the far distance. After traversing this avenue, the tourist crosses the Coventry road and enters Combe Park. The approach to the house is by a fine drive through the park, which is beautifully wooded, and contains a large sheet of water. Combe, as Dugdale informs us, is derived from the old British word *cwwm*, signifying a valley or low position, the site of the abbey being, indeed, by no means a prominent one. An abbey of Cistercian monks was founded here, in the reign of King Stephen, by Richard de Camvill. After the Dissolution, the site and estates were conferred on John, Earl of Warwick, after whose execution they passed to Robert Kelway, with whose daughter they came to Lord Harrington. The daughter and

* The hamlet of BRANDON was a place of some importance in former times, as is evidenced by the remains of a castle still to be seen near the river Avon. The manor belonged at the Conquest to Turchil of Warwick, and descended through a female Clinton to the Verdon family, by one of whom the castle is supposed to have been built. The remains consist of some massive fragments of masonry.

WOOLSTON, a pleasant village about a mile distant, was the site of an alien priory, subordinate to the abbey of St. Peter-super-Dinam in France. The church has some interesting features of Norman architecture.

heiress of the latter nobleman sold the estate to Sir William, an ancestor of the Earl of Craven, in whose family it has ever since remained. The first Earl of Craven (created baron 1626, and earl 1664) is noted for his romantic devotion to the cause of Elizabeth, daughter of James I., the unfortunate Queen of Bohemia, who had resided here under the care of Lord Harrington while receiving her education. She was married to Frederick, elector palatine, who, having accepted the proferred crown of Bohemia from the Protestants in the Thirty Years' War, was punished for his rashness by the loss of his own dominions.* Lord Craven was one of the most zealous supporters of the elector, and subsequently, when the ex-queen returned to England, widowed in love and wrecked in all her hopes, he gave her one of his own mansions for her residence. There is a tradition that she rewarded his attachment by giving him

* The history of Elizabeth of Bohemia is interesting. She was married at the early age of sixteen. The attractions of both her person and mind made her an object of idolatry to the cavaliers, who styled her the " Queen of Hearts." Sir Henry Wotton addressed to her the elegant lines, beginning—

> " You meaner beauties of the night,
>   That weakly satisfy our eyes,
> More by your number than your light,
>   Like common people of the skies,
> What are you when the moon doth rise ?"

" On her," says Mrs. Jamieson, " fell a double portion of the miseries of her fated family. She had the beauty and the wit, the gay spirits, the elegant tastes of her grandmother, Mary of Scotland ; her very virtues as a wife and woman, not less than her pride and feminine prejudices, ruined herself, her husband, and her people. When her husband hesitated to accept the crown of Bohemia this high-hearted wife exclaimed, ' Let me rather eat dry bread at a king's table than feast at the board of an elector :' and it seemed as if some avenging demon hovered in the air to take her literally at her word; for she and her family lived to eat dry bread—aye, and to beg it before they ate it ; but she *would* be a queen." She is buried in Westminster Abbey.

her hand. At all events, she bequeathed to him her pictures, which form a large part of the noble collection here.

The mansion was originally built by Lord Harrington on the ruins of the abbey, retaining three sides of the cloisters, which have been of Norman architecture. Lord Harrington followed the Elizabethan style ; but the additions made by subsequent owners, while avoiding marked incongruity, are not entirely consistent. The front towards the lake is said to be after a design of Inigo Jones.

On entering Combe Abbey, the tourist passes through a hall or corridor which contains many interesting specimens of arms, more or less ancient. The great attraction of this fine mansion, however, consists in its extensive and splendid collection of paintings, the examination of which will fully occupy all the time the visitor has to spare.

The *Great Gallery* is wholly hung with portraits, many of them of great historical interest. Among them may be mentioned the King and Queen of Bohemia, and Princes Rupert and Maurice, by Honthorst ; Charles II. at the age of 14, Gustavus Adolphus, William Earl Craven, and Sir Kenelm Digby, by Vandyke.

The *Breakfast* or *Elizabethan Room* is magnificent in size and decorations, having been fitted up for the reception of Elizabeth, Queen of Bohemia. Its chief pictures are five large and splendid landscapes of Norwegian scenery by Luytens.

The *North Parlour*, also a noble room, contains whole-length portraits of the King and Queen of Bohemia by Honthorst ; and of Charles I., Prince Rupert, Prince Maurice, and James Duke of Richmond, by Vandyke. The tourist will hardly fail to note with interest the resemblance between the Queen of Bohemia and her still more unhappy brother Charles I.

The *Vandyke Room*, so called from the artist whose productions adorn its walls, contains a fine painting of Charles I. and his queen, Henrietta Maria, executed at the desire of the Queen of Bohemia. There is also a good portrait of Vandyke by himself, as well as paintings by Rubens, Teniers, Brughel, and Frank Hals.

In the *Yellow Drawing-Room* there is a landscape by Rubens, with Christ and St. John. Among other paintings will be observed a portrait of the Duchess of Cleveland by Lely, an excellent and characteristic likeness of this shameless woman.

The *Gilt Parlour* has a whole-length portrait of William, Earl Craven, by Honthorst. He is in armour, with a baton in his hand. In this apartment there are also some choice works by Rembrandt, Vandyke, Zoust, and Mierveld.

The *Beauty Parlour* is so named from its containing the portraits of twenty-two of the ladies of the court of Charles II.

The *Cedar Room*, among other fine paintings, has a magnificent landscape by Rubens, with Moses and the Brazen Serpent for its subject ; and a sea-piece by Willarts, representing the Queen of Bohemia's passage to Holland.

The apartments thus briefly noticed are those generally shown to tourists. Besides paintings, several of them contain busts and other objects of interest. The windows of several of the rooms command fine views of the park. From the Vandyke Room, in particular, it may be seen to great advantage.

COVENTRY

Hotels.—*The Castle; the Craven Arms; Kina's Head; Red Lion; Godiva; White Lion; Commercial; Three Tuns.*

Distances :—
From London, 94 miles ; Birmingham, 18½ ; Leamington, 9 ; Stratford-on-avon, 18 ; Kenilworth, 5.

The ancient city of Coventry occupies a good position on a rising ground, whence its "three tall spires" are conspicuous to a great extent of the surrounding country. Alike from its architecture and its associations, this is a place of no common interest to the antiquarian and the general tourist.

John Rouse, the Warwick antiquary, who died in 1491, says that a nunnery existed here as early as the ninth century, and was destroyed in 1016 by Canute the Dane, when, in conjunction with the traitor Edric, he invaded Mercia. In 1043, Leofric, fifth Earl of Mercia, and his countess, Godiva, founded and very richly endowed a Benedictine monastery on the ruins of the nunnery. An idea of the opulence of this house, and of the magnificence of its embellishments, may be formed from a statement of William of Malmesbury, that "it was enriched and beautified with so much gold and silver that the walls seemed too narrow to contain it ; insomuch that Robert de Limesie, bishop of this diocese in the time of King William Rufus, scraped from one beam that supported the shrines 500 marks of silver." Leofric died in 1057, and was buried in a porch of the monastery. His lady is also interred in the same place, but the exact date of her death is unknown.

The name of Lady Godiva is so intimately associated with Coventry, that it would be unpardonable to omit

E

an account of her story. We cannot do better than
give it in the words of Sir William Dugdale, a devout
believer of the romantic tale, and an enthusiastic admirer of the noble lady :—"The Countess Godiva,
bearing an extraordinary affection to this place, often
and earnestly besought her husband that, for the love
of God and the Blessed Virgin, he would free it from
that grievous servitude whereunto it was subject ; but
he, rebuking her for importuning him in a manner so
inconsistent with his profit, commanded that she should
thenceforward forbear to move therein ; yet she, out of
her womanish pertinacity, continued to solicit him, insomuch that he told her if she would ride on horseback
naked from one end of the town to the other, in sight
of all the people, he would grant her request.   Whereunto she returned, 'But will you give me leave to do
so ?'   And he replying 'Yes,' the noble lady, upon an
appointed day, got on horseback naked, with her hair
loose, so that it covered all her body but the legs ; and,
thus performing her journey, she returned with joy to
her husband, who thereupon granted to the inhabitants
a charter of freedom.   .   .   .   In memory whereof,
the picture of him and his said lady was set up in a
south window of Trinity Church in this city, about
Richard II.'s time, his right hand holding a charter,
with these words written thereon :—

> 𝔍, 𝔏𝔲𝔯𝔦𝔠𝔥𝔢, 𝔣𝔬𝔯 𝔏𝔬𝔟𝔢 𝔬𝔣 𝔱𝔥𝔢𝔢
> 𝔇𝔬𝔢 𝔪𝔞𝔨𝔢 ℭ𝔬𝔟𝔢𝔫𝔱𝔯𝔢 ℭ𝔬𝔩-𝔣𝔯𝔢𝔢."

It is said that the inhabitants all withdrew from the
streets and from their windows, to allow the lady to
perform her delicate task with as little pain to her
modesty as possible.   One man, a tailor, could not resist the temptation to look forth, but was struck blind

for his presumption ; and to this day the effigy of Peeping Tom, to be seen in the upper part of a house at the corner of Hertford Street, stands as a monument of his disgrace.

The procession of Lady Godiva is said to have been instituted to commemorate the service thus rendered to Coventry,* but it has been satisfactorily shown that it originated in the licentious reign of Charles II. Yet, notwithstanding the sufficiently matter-of-fact way in which the show has been accounted for by antiquarians, the legend of Lady Godiva is not likely either to be forgotten or repudiated, for our Poet Laureate has "wedded it to immortal verse." A few of Mr. Tenny-

---

* The procession of Lady Godiva took place annually till within the last twenty or thirty years, and was graced by the presence of the civic authorities. More recently it has not taken place oftener than once in three or four years ; and if it is not already numbered among the things of the past, the time is not distant when it will be. The procession in its palmy days was of great length and pomp. At the front of it came the city guards in old armour, followed by St. George on horseback, and in a full suit of armour. Then came a band of music, with two city streamers, followed by the high constable of the city, preceding the principal feature of the show, Lady Godiva. Her ladyship was represented by a handsome female, not nude, in accordance with the tradition, but dressed in linen closely fitted to her limbs, and of a colour emulating their complexion. After Lady Godiva came the mayor, aldermen, and sheriffs, preceded and followed by various subordinate officials and attendants. A band of musicians brought up the rear of the civic authorities. Then followed a long array of the ancient companies of the city, with their various streamers, and attended by bands of music. Next in order came the benefit societies, greatly contributing to the gorgeousness of the spectacle with their respective insignia and decorations. These were followed by the woolcombers' company, who, besides their streamer, master, and followers, wool-sorters and combers, introduced a little boy and girl, as shepherd and shepherdess, in a rural car, Jason with a golden fleece and drawn sword, and Bishop Blaize, the great friend of the woolcombers, with combs in one hand and a Bible in the other. Another band of musicians closed the procession.

son's beautiful lines cannot fail to be acceptable
here :—

> "She sought her lord, and found him where he strode
> About the hall, among his dogs alone ;
> His beard a foot before him, and his hair
> A yard behind. She told him of their tears,
> And pray'd him, 'If they pay this tax, they starve.'
> Whereat he stared, replying, half-amazed,
> 'You would not let your little finger ache
> For such as these ?' ' But I would die,' said she.
> He laughed, and swore by Peter and by Paul :
> Then fillip'd at the diamond in her ear :
> 'O ay, ay, ay, you talk !' 'Alas !' she said ;
> 'But prove me what it is I would not do.'
> And, from a heart as rough as Esau's hand,
> He answered, 'Ride you naked thro' the town,
> And I repeal it ;' and nodding, as in scorn,
> He parted, with great strides, among his dogs.
>
> .　　.　　.　　.　　.　　.
>
> "Then she rode forth, clothed on with chastity ;
> The deep air listened round her as she rode,
> And all the low wind hardly breathed for fear.
> The little wide-mouthed heads upon the spout
> Had cunning eyes to see : the barking cur
> Made her cheek flame : her palfrey's footfall shot
> Light horrors, through her pulses : the blind walls
> Were full of chinks and holes ; and overhead
> Fantastic gables, crowding, stared : but she
> Not less thro' all bore up, till last she saw
> The white-flower'd elder-thicket from the field
> Gleam through the Gothic archways in the wall.
> "Then she rode back, clothed on with chastity :
> And one low churl, compact of thankless earth,
> The fatal byword of all years to come,
> Boring a little augur-hole in fear,
> Peep'd—but his eyes, before they had their will,
> Were shrivell'd into darkness in his head,
> And dropt before him. So the Powers, who wait
> On noble deeds, cancell'd a sense misused ;
> And she, that knew not, passed : and all at once,
> With twelve great shocks of sound, the shameless **noon,**
> Was clashed and hammer'd from a hundred towers,
> One after one : but even then she gain'd
> Her bower ; whence reissuing robed and crown'd
> To meet her lord, she took the tax away,
> And built herself an everlasting name."

Soon after the Conquest, the lordship of Coventry
devolved by marriage to the Earls of Chester, under
whose patronage the city seems to have prospered.
The Earls of Chester were succeeded by the Montalts
and Arundels. On the failing of issue it became the
property of the crown. Edward III., when he advanced his son, Edward the Black Prince, to the dukedom of Cornwall, annexed this lordship, under the
name of the manor of Cheylesmore, to the dukedom for
ever. In 1344 the town received a charter of incorporation from Edward III. The great yearly fair is,
however, of a much earlier date, having been granted
by Henry III. in 1218. In 1397 Coventry was the
scene of the famous hostile meeting between Henry
Bolingbroke, Duke of Hereford (afterwards Henry IV.),
and Thomas Mowbray, Duke of Norfolk, which has
been immortalised by Shakspere ("King Richard II."
act i. scene 3). Richard II. and a great array of his
nobles were present on the occasion. When the
champions were about to engage, the king suddenly
interfered, and banished them both from England ;
Norfolk for life, and Hereford for a term of years.
The meeting was at Gosford Green, near Coventry. In
1404 Henry IV. held a parliament in the great chamber of the priory. From the circumstance of the writs
forbidding the return of lawyers, or persons skilled in
the law, this parliament acquired the name of *Parliamentum indoctorum.* Coventry received many marks
of the favour of Henry VI. and his queen, who both
frequently visited it. It was by this monarch that
the city and certain hamlets and villages round it were,
in 1451, formed into an entire and separate county.
The charter enacted that "the bailiffs of the city shall
be sheriffs of the county, and the same coroner preside
over both." This charter was confirmed by Edward

IV. A second parliament was held at the priory in 1459. From the multitude of attainders passed by it against Richard, Duke of York, and others, this parliament has been styled *Parliamentum diabolicum.* Its acts were afterwards reversed. For the support which it had rendered to Henry VI., in the struggle which ended in the dethronement and death of that unhappy monarch, Coventry had to pay a fine of 500 marks to Edward IV. On the overthrow of Richard III. at Bosworth Field in 1485, Henry VII. was received with every demonstration of joy by the inhabitants of Coventry, who presented him with a cup and £100, in return for which compliment he knighted the mayor. Queen Elizabeth visited this city in 1565, when she was splendidly entertained by the mayor and citizens. In the year following, and again in 1569, the unfortunate Mary Queen of Scots was kept a prisoner here for some time. In 1616 her son, James I., visited Coventry, and was entertained with great pomp. On this occasion he was presented with a gold cup of the value of £160. In the war between Charles I. and the parliamentary party Coventry sided with the latter ; for which, on the restoration of Charles II., its walls and gates were dismantled. On this work 500 men were employed for 24 days.* Coventry was on several occasions subsequently honoured by the visits of royal and other remarkable personages ; but these, and the facts in its more recent history, do not call for special mention. The " New Boundary Act" put an end to

* The walls were 3 miles in circumference, 9 feet thick, and had 32 towers and gates. They were begun about 1356, and took many years to be completed. They were kept in good repair during a period of nearly 300 years, and were strong enough to admit of the citizens more than once safely bidding defiance to the royal authority. Some interesting remnants of the walls and the gates are still to be seen.

the ancient jurisdiction of the city, with respect to the "County of the City of Coventry," in 1842.

Coventry has been the birthplace of a number of eminent men. Vincent of Coventry, a distinguished Franciscan, and author of various theological works, flourished in the early part of the 13th century. He was educated at Cambridge, of which university he afterwards became a professor. William Maklesfield was general of the order of the Dominicans, and a celebrated scholar. John Bird, the head and last provincial of the Carmelites, gained the favour of Henry VIII. by his opposition to the Pope, and was appointed to the bishoprics of Bangor and Chester. Humphrey Wanley, an eminent scholar and antiquary, was born in 1671. He rendered great service to the cause of letters by his investigations regarding Anglo-Saxon and other manuscripts. The work by which he is best known is entitled "The Wonders of the Little World." He died in 1726. Samuel Carte, divine and antiquary, was born in 1652, and died in 1740. His son Thomas was a man of kindred and greater genius; and besides his eminence as a divine and historian, made some figure in the political troubles of his time. He was born in 1686, and died in 1754.

The population of the municipal borough of Coventry at the census of 1871 was 37,670, and that of the parliamentary borough, which has a larger area, 41,350, and the inhabited houses 9332. The city is represented in Parliament by two members. Numerous fairs are held, and are mostly well attended.

The chief manufactures of Coventry are ribbons, silk, and watches. The textile art can be traced to a very remote period, a weaver having filled the office of mayor in 1525; but the ribbon trade was not introduced till a century and a half ago, mainly through the immigration of French refugees, who had been compelled to leave their country in great numbers in consequence of the revocation of the Edict of Nantes. The introduction of steam-looms gave great impetus to the manufacture. A considerable depression in this manufacture took place previously to 1861, and still to a great extent continues. In 1861 it gave employment to 1407 men and 1274 women, whereas it previously occupied about 6000 persons. Silk in 1861 employed 1364 men, and 4171 women. Silk dyeing and printing employed 278 men, and other occupations connected with the manufacture 188.* Watches gave occupation to 1943 men and 43 women. The watch manufacture has recently somewhat recovered from its depressed state of a few years ago.

Coventry has a considerable amount of traffic both by canal and railway. Besides the great fair, which commences on the Friday of Trinity week, and continues eight days, there are two annual cattle fairs and two cheese fairs, as well as a monthly cattle fair. There are races in March, which are well attended.

There are numerous charities, amounting annually to about £4000, instituted for the benefit of the poor. There are about 2300 acres of land, called "Lammas" and "Michaelmas" lands, upon which freemen of Coventry have the right to feed three head of cattle each. The freemen number about 3400.

---

* The silk and ribbon manufactures are carried on extensively in the neighbouring parish of FOLESHILL, which has a population of 8140. Within the registration district, silk employs 1213 women and 253 men ; and ribbons, 2025 women and 1277 men. Watches give employment to 35 men. There are 686 coal-miners and 100 iron-miners. In the *Church*, which has some remains of old architecture, there is a font of great antiquity. Near the Church is a *Free School*, founded in 1766.

CHURCHES AND CHAPELS.

The ancient monastic establishments may be briefly noticed first. Whether or not Earl Leofric was as rough a personage as Mr. Tennyson and the legend of Lady Godiva make him, it is evident that he was a very dutiful son of the church, as we have the record of many princely endowments with which he enriched it.

The BENEDICTINE PRIORY, founded in 1043 by Earl Leofric, and honoured by the residence of kings and the meetings of parliament, with its cathedral church, met the fate of all similar institutions at the Dissolution in the reign of Henry VIII. Some few fragments of it remain, and may be seen near "New Buildings."

The WHITE FRIARS' MONASTERY stands in the southeast part of the city. It was founded about 1342. Fourteen years after the Dissolution it became the property of John Hales. After several transmissions, it was, in 1801, sold to the directors of the poor in this city, who turned it into a house of industry, for which purpose it is still used. Though it has necessarily undergone considerable alterations, there are still many portions of the original edifice in good preservation—the chief of these being the cloisters (used now as an eating-room for the paupers), the dormitory, the remains of the chapter-house, the old gateway, etc.

GREY FRIARS' MONASTERY AND CHURCH were upon the site now occupied by Christ Church. The Grey Friars settled here about 1358. The handsome spire of their church escaped destruction at the Dissolution, and still remains to do credit to the taste of the mendicant order who erected it. It forms the steeple of Christ Church, which was opened in 1832.

Of the CARTHUSIAN MONASTERY, or Charter-House, founded in 1381, few traces remain.

ST. MICHAEL'S CHURCH is said to be the largest, and is certainly one of the noblest parish churches in England, originally built as such. Sir Christopher Wren pronounced it a masterpiece of art. Its history is interesting. The erection of the steeple, which is the most ancient part, occupied twenty-two years, being begun in 1373 and finished in 1395. It is said that the tower was erected by Adam and William Botoner, who were both several times mayors of Coventry, and that the spire was added to it by their sisters, Ann and Mary, who also built the middle aisle of the church. The following rhyme is said to have been inscribed on a brass plate found in the chancel :—

> "William and Adam built the Tower,
> Ann and Mary built the Spire ;
> William and Adam built the Church,
> Ann and Mary built the Quire."

On the erection of the spire Adam and William Botoner expended £100 annually for twenty-two years. New Street, adjoining the church, was built for the accommodation of the workmen employed upon its construction. It is certain that St. Michael's was completed and used for public worship in the reign of Henry VI., for in 1450 that monarch heard mass here, and presented a golden cloth. The memory of the Botoners is still held in veneration by the inhabitants of Coventry.

The church consists of nave with aisles, chancel with aisles, transepts, and tower, surmounted by a magnificent spire, rising to a height of 303 feet. The tower is 136 feet 3 inches from the base to the battlements. Its windows are, in size and style, admirably in keeping with its proportions. The buttresses are finely orna-

mented with carvings, and the niches of the upper
part are adorned with thirty well-executed statues of
Roman saints. Above this tower rises an octagonal
prism to a height of 32 feet 6 inches. From this octagonal prism tapers the spire, which is 130 feet 9
inches high. The walls of the spire are said to be 17
inches thick at the bottom, and so finely tapered as to
recline but 4½ degrees from the perpendicular. It is
exceedingly to be lamented that the stone of which
this noble spire and church, and the neighbouring
church of the Holy Trinity, are constructed, is of a
soft, friable description, very liable to crumble under
the action of the weather. Owing to this circumstance,
much of the exquisite and delicate carving with which
these buildings are adorned appears doomed to certain
decay; indeed, many of the ornamental details are
already partially or wholly lost. The architecture of
the body of the church, though somewhat less ancient
than the steeple, is admirably in keeping with it.
"The whole," as Mr. Brewer very justly observes, "is
of the best character of Gothic; light, though august,
and impressive from a felicitous arrangement of parts."

The effect of the interior is very imposing. The
aisles and transepts are divided from the body of the
church by lofty arches rising from clustered columns.
The ceiling is of oak, finely ribbed and carved. The
east windows of the chancel and its aisles are filled
with representations of incidents in the life of our
Saviour. The window next the east one of either
aisle of the chancel is filled with fragments of old
stained glass, which, being rich and varied, produce a
fine effect. The second window from the east in the
north chancel aisle is " In memory of the great and
good Albert Emanuel, Prince Consort, who entered
into immortality Dec. 1861." Among other recent

memorial windows may be mentioned those to William Wilmot, mayor of Coventry, a benefactor of the freemen, who died in 1860 ; and Charles Dresser, churchwarden, who was the means of establishing a third service in the church, and who died in 1861.

The church contains a number of monuments, none of which, however, are of particular importance. For the benefit of the tourist who is interested in such matters, we copy a curious inscription from a brass plate, originally in a slab in the floor at the western end of the church, but now affixed to the south wall of the south transept :—

Here lyes the body of Captn. GERVASE SCROPE, of the Family
of Scropes of Bolton, in the County of York, Who
departed this life the 26th day of Augt. Anno Dni. 1705,
Aged 60.
AN EPITAPH, written by Himself in the Agony and
Dolorous Paines of the Gout, and died soon after.

Here lyes an Old Toss'd TENNIS BALL,
Was Racketted from Spring to Fall,
With so much heat and so much hast,
Time's arm for shame grew tyr'd at last.
Four Kings in CAMPS he truly seru'd.
And from his royalty ne'er sweru'd.
FATHER ruin'd, the SON slighted,
And from the CROWN ne'r requited,
Loss of ESTATE, RELATIONS, BLOOD,
Was too well Known, but did no good.
With long CAMPAIGNS and paines o'th GOUT,
He cou'd no longer hold it out.
Always a restless life he led,
Never at quiet till quite dead.
He marry'd, in his latter dayes,
ONE who exceeds the common praise ;
But wanting breath still to make Known
Her true AFFECTION and his OWN,
Death Kindly came, all wants supply'd
By giving REST which life deny'd.

This church possesses one of the best organs in the kingdom ; and its peal of bells, ten in number, is among the finest in England.

The arrangement of the interior of the church is tasteful and appropriate. The work of renovation was begun in 1849, when the galleries were swept away, and the pewing made low, open, and uniform. Much care and judgment have been exercised, also, in restoring the stone-work where it had been concealed by paint or plaster. There is some antique carved oak; but it is not of much interest.

TRINITY CHURCH suffers somewhat in effect from its too close proximity to St. Michael's. With not a few faults in style, owing to the injudicious manner in which alterations and repairs have been made at different periods, it is nevertheless a handsome and imposing structure. Of its history comparatively little is known. Dugdale says that the first mention of it is its appropriation to the priory in the 44th of Henry III.— that is, in 1260. There have been alterations of greater or less importance at various periods; and the ecclesiologist will have no difficulty in distinguishing these from the more ancient parts of the building. This church is well endowed; its various estates yielding a revenue of about £1000 a-year.

The church consists of nave and aisles, with two small chapels on the north side, transepts, chancel with side aisles, and tower surmounted by a spire rising from the intersection to an entire height of 237 feet. The original spire was blown down in 1664, and caused extensive injury to the body of the church. The new spire was erected, and the roof of the church restored, in the course of three years. The ancient stone pulpit is probably unsurpassed in the kingdom. The font will also attract the admiration of the antiquarian. An extraordinary fresco painting, representing the Last Judgment, was discovered in 1831 in the space above the western arch under the tower

The communion-table is an excellent specimen of antique carved oak-work. The east window is in memory of Richard Saurey Cox, Esq., who died in 1856. This gentleman left £12,150 for charitable purposes, about the half of the sum being for Coventry.

Among the monuments of Trinity Church there is one to Dr. Philemon Holland, the first translator of Camden's "Britannia." The tablet is affixed to the south wall of the choir, and bears a quaint Latin inscription written by himself. It runs as follows :—

Epitaphium

Doctoris Hollandi a seipso confectum, qui obiit 9 die Februarii 1636, et 85 ætatis suæ.

> Nemo habet hic, necnon ? hospes salveto, Philemon
> Holland hac recubat, rite repostus humo.
> Si quæras ratio quænam sit nominis, hæc est—
> Totus-terra fui, terraq.—totus ero ;
> At redivivus morte tua servabor, Jesu,
> Una Fides votis hæc est, via sola salutis.
> Hac spe fretus ego, culpâ, pœnâque solutus,
> Iamque renatus, et inde novo conspectus amictu,
> Cætu in sanctorum post redemitus ero.
> Claudicat incessu senior mea Musa, videsne ?
> Claudatur capulo mecum simul ipsa : valeto.

Holland was an indefatigable translator. In reference to his diligence in translation a contemporary wrote the epigram—

> " Holland with his translations doth so fill us,
> He will not let *Suetonius* be *Tranquillus*."

St. John's or Bablake Church is a chaste and interesting structure of the time of Edward III. It was erected by the members of St. John's Guild, and dedicated in 1350. On the union of St. John's Guild with that of the Holy Trinity, it became the property of the united Guilds, and so continued till their suppression. After experiencing much neglect, it was at length, in 1734, by Act of Parliament, made the rectorial church of the parish of St. John. Though bearing some marks of injury from neglect and modern alterations, it is still a noble edifice. It is cruciform, with a massive battlemented tower, turreted at the angles, rising in the centre. The interior consists of nave and aisles, chancel and aisles, and transepts. The magnificent west window is pronounced a splendid effort of genius. The church contains several square-headed windows much admired by antiquarians. A handsome font, said to be copied from that of St. Edward's Church at Cambridge, stands near the west window.

CHRIST CHURCH is a tasteful modern structure, in the early Decorated style, on the site of the Grey Friars' Monastery, the spire of which is incorporated with it. This is the third of "the three tall spires" of Coventry.

Of the other churches none call for special notice. The same may be said of the Dissenting chapels, with the exception of the ROMAN CATHOLIC CHURCH. This edifice is in the Decorated style, and its interior is richly and elegantly fitted up. The services are conducted by members of the order of St. Benedict; and a religious house, or "presbytery," for their accommodation, adjoins the church.

PUBLIC BUILDINGS.

Its churches are by no means the only attractions of Coventry. There is much in the style and architecture of many of the streets to delight the antiquarian. Many of the houses, with their projecting and timbered fronts, must wear much the same aspect, allowing for the effects of age, as in the time when Coventry was the "chamber of princes;" when Richard

the Second and his gallant array visited it just before
his fall; when Margaret of Anjou and her "holy
Henry" slept in the priory, and went in royal state
to St. Michael's; and when England's kings and
queens loved to resort to Coventry to find relaxation
in its plays and pageants. It is impossible to walk
through the ancient streets of Coventry without feeling
that the city "has seen better days," for the memorials
of former greatness are everywhere apparent. It cannot be denied, however, that though Coventry has
long lost the importance derived from the patronage
of royalty, it has gained by its energy in manufactures
and commerce a distinction much more real and valuable; of which fact the honours gained at the Great
Exhibitions by manufactures belonging to this city is
a sufficient proof. The remains of the city as it was
in the olden times have much to interest the tourist,
and are naturally preserved with care by the citizens.*

ST. MARY'S HALL is one of the most splendid and
remarkable buildings of Coventry. There are few, if
any, more magnificent specimens of ancient domestic
architecture in the kingdom. It is situated near St.
Michael's Church, and is in an admirable state of preservation. This hall was built about the year 1450,

---

* The citizens of ninety years ago did not exhibit the same regard
for the ancient architecture of their city, else COVENTRY CROSS
would have remained to this day. This structure was so celebrated
for its magnificence that a brief notice of it will doubtless be acceptable to the tourist. It stood in "Cross Cheaping," to which it
gave its name. It was erected in 1544 by Sir William Hollies,
Lord Mayor of London, and son to Thomas Hollies of Stoke, near
Coventry, and was 57 feet high, hexagonal in shape, and divided
into three storeys. Its pillars, pinnacles, and arches were exquisitely finished, and its numerous niches were adorned with statues
of English kings and saints. In 1669 it was thoroughly repaired,
and profusely decorated with gilding and painting. After this the
cross was wholly neglected, and rapidly fell into decay. In 1717 it
was wholly removed.

for the use of the Guild, some say, of St. Catherine. others of the Holy Trinity. On the dissolution of the Guild, it was bought by the mayor and corporation, and has been ever since used for purposes of civic ceremony and festivity.

The chief feature of the exterior is a noble window, the masonry of which is very fine. On the arch of the entrance to the courtyard are some basso-relievos of sacred subjects. From the courtyard a flight of stairs and an open gallery lead directly to the Great Hall. But by entering at a door under the gallery, the *Kitchen* may be first examined. This is a spacious room. Its liberal arrangements for cooking give one some idea of the hospitable spirit of the ancient Guilds.

The Great Hall is 76 feet 6 inches long, 30 feet broad, and 34 feet high. It is impossible, within the space which can be devoted to it, to do justice to this noble old hall, the different attractions of which antiquarians have delighted to describe at great length. The roof is richly adorned with carvings of angels. The great window at the north end of the hall is divided into nine compartments, and filled with old stained glass bearing figures of several of our monarchs, coats of arms, and other ornaments. Under this window, and extending the whole breadth of the hall, and 10 feet in depth, is a splendid piece of ancient tapestry. This admirable and elaborate work is divided into two tiers, one above the other, each consisting of three compartments. The first compartment, beginning at the left hand, contains the figures of Henry VI. and some of his principal courtiers. Henry is on his knees before a table, on which are placed his crown and a missal. Behind him is Cardinal Beaufort in the same attitude of devotion. The other personages are standing; among them may be observed the famous Humphrey, Duke of

Gloucester. In the compartment above are several of the apostles, with their appropriate emblems, and two Christian knights. In the second compartment of the lower tier is St. Mary in glory, surrounded by angels, and having the moon under her feet. On each side of her are, the twelve apostles in devotional attitudes. The compartment above this represents the opened heavens, and the angels round the eternal throne. The central figure of this bold design has been cut out, probably by some of the early Reformers, and a figure of Justice sewed in its place. The third compartment of the lower tier contains the noble figure of Margaret of Anjou, Henry's consort, with some of the chief ladies of her court. She is kneeling, like the king, with her missal on a table before her. In the compartment above are a number of female saints and martyrs. The divisions between the different compartments of this exquisite piece of tapestry, and the border round the whole, are tasteful and appropriate.

The east and west sides of the Great Hall have each three windows of stained glass of modern workmanship ; painted, however, with subjects of a most appropriate description. There is in this hall an ancient chair of state, a fine piece of oak-carving, which will be regarded with additional interest when it is remembered that more than one English sovereign sat in state upon it in the good old times when Coventry was the " chamber of princes." At the south end is the *Minstrel's Gallery*, at the front of which is some ancient armour used in the procession of Lady Godiva. The hall is adorned with some valuable paintings of royal personages, there being full-length portraits of Charles II., James II., William and Mary, George I., George II. and Caroline, George III., and George IV. On the east side of the Great Hall is the Mayoress's Parlour.

The Mayoress's Parlour has been considerably modernised, and is used as a police court by the city magistrates. Its walls are adorned with a whole-length portrait of Queen Anne, half-lengths of Queen Mary, Queen Elizabeth, Charles I., James. I., Sir Thomas White, founder of the "Four Pounds Charity" (210 of which are distributed annually to inhabitant householders, not being paupers), and the "City Fifties;" and a fine painting of Lady Godiva on horseback.

FORD's HOSPITAL, a singularly well-preserved specimen of the architecture of the 16th century, is situated in Grey Friars' Lane. It was founded in 1529 by William Ford, a merchant of this city : and its endowment was subsequently increased by other benevolent persons. It is timber-framed, and is extremely rich and elaborate in its decorations ; indeed it may be doubted whether a finer building of this style is to be found in the kingdom. Its annual revenues amount to upwards of £500. It was originally intended for the reception of aged married couples, but is now restricted to females, of whom there are about twenty, each receiving 3s. 6d. a-week and coals for use. About twenty-five women are out-door recipients of the same amount of money, and a ton of coals annually. Parties receiving parochial relief are not admitted into this hospital.

BABLAKE HOSPITAL is immediately behind St. John's Church, and with the school-houses forms three sides of a square, the church making the fourth. It was founded in 1506 by Thomas Bond, a draper, and mayor of Coventry, and was originally designed for ten poor men ; but subsequent donors having greatly augmented its funds, it now receives upwards of forty, resident and non-resident, each of whom has 6s. a-week.

This building, which had been allowed to fall into decay, was a number of years ago renovated and enlarged with much taste. The *School* adjoining was founded in 1560 by Thomas Wheatley, mayor of Coventry. It is devoted to the education of about fifty boys for a period of two years each. The boys are partially provided for the first year, and wholly the second ; and, on leaving, are apprenticed for seven years to such trades as their parents or friends may choose for them. The revenues are upwards of £900 a-year.

St. John's Hospital and Free School. The hospital, founded about 1155 by Lawrence, a prior of Coventry, for the sick and poor, was granted at the Dissolution to John Hales, who devoted its lands and possessions, along with other estates, to the foundation of a free school. John Hales died in 1573. The chief feature of the architecture of this school is its beautiful east window. The Free School is intended for the sons of freemen of Coventry. Its yearly revenue amounts to about £1000.

Others buildings deserving of notice are—*Drapers' Hall*, a neat building in the Grecian style, on the south side of St. Michael's Church, erected in 1832 ; the *County Hall*, built in 1785, a large and commodious building, with Doric columns in front ; the *Barracks*, in Smithford Street, opposite the Post Office, interesting as occupying the site of the famous " Bull Inn," where Henry VII. was entertained, and where subsequently the unfortunate Mary, Queen of Scots, was imprisoned for some time ; the *Coventry and Warwickshire Hospital*, etc. There are numerous schools, with more or less liberal endowments, which cannot be here noticed.

The *Coventry Cemetery* is beautifully laid out, after

a plan by the late Sir Joseph Paxton, and will repay a visit.

VICINITY OF COVENTRY.

The country round Coventry is rich in places of interest, to which the railway gives easy access. Five miles to the south is KENILWORTH ; 2 miles east from which is STONELEIGH ABBEY. Five miles farther south, on the line of railway, is the fashionable watering-place of LEAMINGTON, whence the ancient city of WARWICK is 2 miles distant by rail or road. Eastward is RUGBY, distant 11 miles. COMBE ABBEY, 5 miles distant, has received a separate description. Northward is NUNEATON, 10 miles distant, with various places of interest in its vicinity ; and a little farther away is the Roman *Manduessedum*. On the line westward to Birmingham there are various points whence the tourist can diverge to places of interest. From Hampton Junction; or from Berkswell Station, TEMPLE BALSAL, KNOWLE, and SOLIHULL may be included in a walk of about 7 miles.

GUY'S CLIFF.

In the VICINITY OF WARWICK.

HENLEY-IN-ARDEN

AND ITS VICINITY.

INNS : *The Swan* and *The Bear*.

From Bearley Station, 4 miles (Bearley from Warwick, 10 miles ; from Stratford-on-Avon, 6) ; Kingswood Station, 6 miles (Kingswood from Warwick, 10 miles).

HENLEY-IN-ARDEN is a quaint, straggling old place, its distance from the railway, which has absorbed most of the traffic that once passed through it, giving it a quiet, old-world aspect. That it is a town of much antiquity is evident from its name, which is compounded of the British words, *Hen*, old, and *Ley*, a place. " Arden" was the name of the great forest which in ancient times covered this part of the country. The first mention of the town is in records of the time of Henry II. After the battle of Evesham it was destroyed by fire, probably on account of the devotion of the inhabitants to the De Montforts, who were their great patrons. The town seems to have soon recovered from this calamity, as thirty years later we find it termed a borough. The present population is 1069.

THE CHURCH, originally erected in the reign of Edward III., is a plain and neat building with a battlemented tower, containing no monuments of any consequence. Several of the windows have recently been filled with stained glass.

THE MARKET CROSS, one of the few that have escaped the ravages of religious zeal of the times of the Reformation, stands in the main street. It is very much worn by the combined influences of the weather and rough usage, but seems now to be carefully preserved. The base, shaft, and capital consist of three separate stones, the shaft being morticed into the other two. The capital contains four niches with sculptured reliefs. Three of these pieces of sculpture represent the Rood, the Trinity, and St. Peter ; the fourth is too much mutilated to be known.

The district in which Henley-in-Arden lies contains various places interesting from either an antiquarian or a literary point of view. Walking from Bearley station, the tourist will, about a mile thence, pass on his right Edston Grange, and, a mile and a half farther on, the village of Wootton Wawen. In the immediate neighbourhood of Henley-in-Arden he will find the hamlet of Beaudesert ; and should he proceed to regain the railway at Kingswood, he may see the church of Lapworth. All these places are more or less interesting.

BEAUDESERT is only a few hundred yards from Henley-in-Arden. A strong castle was erected here by Thurstan de Montfort shortly after the Conquest, but completely destroyed in the wars of the Roses.

The Church is well deserving of a visit. It consists of nave, chancel, and embattled tower at the west end. The edifice is not without its incongruities, different parts displaying different styles, and the roof of the chancel being higher than that of the nave ; yet the remains of genuine Norman work in some parts, and the careful reproduction of it in others, cannot fail to please the enthusiast in church architecture. The original Norman work is in the east window and two windows in the north wall of the chancel. The east window has some zig-zag ornamentation inside. The "restored" Norman work consists of an elaborate doorway on the south side of the nave, consisting of a series of four receding arches, with zig-zag ornamentation, the three inner ones rising from circular columns ; and a lofty arch, in the same style, between the nave and chancel. These restorations, we understand, are the work of the Rev. Mr. Campbell, the present incumbent, who has strictly followed the details indicated by present remains and fragments of the old doorway discovered in the course of excavations. All such fragments have been reverently preserved and fitted into appropriate places in the restored arches. It is much to be desired that the restoration of the church could be thoroughly carried out in the same spirit. The pointed lights of the nave and south wall of the chancel may be tolerated, as they are small, and not much out of proportion with the Norman windows ; but the large Perpendicular west window, which throws such a flood of light into the church as all the other windows together do not produce, cannot fail to strike a tasteful observer as in the highest degree incongruous. There is a piscina in the south wall of the chancel. The church is very tastefully fitted up, and several of the windows are filled with stained glass.

Near Beaudesert was born, in 1715, Richard Jago, the author of "Edge Hill," and other poems. Jago was vicar of Snitterfield, near Stratford-on-Avon, where he died in 1781. He was an intimate friend of Shenstone, to whom several of his poems are dedicated.

LAPWORTH.—This hamlet, 4 miles to the north of Henley-in-Arden, possesses a finely-situated *Church*, with a detached tower, surmounted by a lofty spire. The interior is spacious, but contains no monuments of importance. There is a painted glass window to the memory of a member of the Lapworth family. The manor of Lapworth belonged to Sir William Catesby, who was taken prisoner at the battle of Bosworth Field, and beheaded by order of the conqueror. Catesby is immortalised by Shakspere in "King Richard III."

At Lapworth the tourist is two miles from Kingswood Station. Should he choose to walk on to Knowle Station, he may pass through the grounds of *Packwood House*, and see *Packwood Church*, which is a picturesque building, pleasantly situated.

WOOTTON WAWEN, two miles from Henley-in-Arden, is a scattered, pleasantly-situated village, with some interesting Saxon remains in its immediate vicinity.

The Church is a building of considerable antiquity, but has undergone a good deal of dubious reparation. It consists of nave with south aisle, chancel with south chapel, north and south porches, and square tower.

The north side of the church is almost wholly coated with plaster, and the upper part of the east window of the nave aisle, which is Decorated in style, has been filled with masonry.

The arches in the interior are pointed, with the exception of two somewhat perplexing ones, which are round. The east window is Perpendicular, of seven lights, and has some fragments of old stained glass. The church is rich in monuments. Outside the communion rails is an altar-tomb bearing the recumbent effigy of a knight in armour, with folded hands, a dog at his feet, and the fragments of his spear at his side. The date of this monument is 1415. It is supposed that it is in memory of an early proprietor of Packwood House. Within the rails is another altar-tomb, with the effigies in inlaid brass of a knight in armour, his lady, and their children (five boys and five girls). A Latin inscription running round the tomb states that it is to the memory of John Herwell and his wife Anna. John died in 1505 ; but the date of Anna's death is not filled in (a not uncommon omission in ancient monuments). The Herwells were possessors of a manor in the lordship of Wootton Wawen, which passed by purchase into the possession of the Smythe family, who were proprietors of the rest, and still retain it. An ancestor of this family is commemorated by a rather stately monument in the chapel on the south side of the chancel. This monument, which has no date, bears the effigy of Francis Smith, doubtless one of the earliest possessors of the hall. The figure is in armour, reclining on the right side, the head resting on a helmet. It has a long trimmed beard and a ruffle round the neck, and it is coloured in the style of monuments of the end of the sixteenth century. A canopy, supported by columns and adorned with coats

of arms, rises over the effigy. There are two modern
monuments deserving of notice. The one of these is
to the memory of John Phillips, Esq., formerly proprietor of Edstone Grange, representing a female
figure bending in an attitude of grief. The other is a
stately marble structure to the memory of Henry and
Henrietta Knight, son and daughter of Robert, Earl of
Catherlough, bearing the date 1710.

Wootton Wawen Hall is near the church. It is a
large building of little architectural pretensions. Behind it is a Roman Catholic chapel, the interior of
which presents the features of decoration usual in such
buildings. Externally it has nothing to show worthy
of notice. A small Roman Catholic cemetery on the
outskirts of the village contains an elegant stone cross.

Edston Grange, a handsome mansion, situated in a
well-wooded park, about a mile and a half from Wootton Wawen, was the birthplace, in 1692, of William
Somervile, author of "The Chace." He was a skilful
sportsman, and a useful justice of the peace, as well as
a man of letters. His death, which took place in 1742,
was hastened by habits of intoxication, to which he
gave way in consequence of the embarrassments re-
sulting from his extravagance. Alluding to this, his
friend Shenstone, who very much resembled him, remarks indignantly on the grievance of a man of genius
being asked to pay his debts, "For a man of high
spirit, conscious of having (at least in one production)
generally pleased the world, to be plagued and threatened by wretches that are low in every sense ; to be
forced to drink himself into pains of the body, in order
to get rid of the pains of the mind, is a misery."

KENILWORTH.

INNS.—*King's Arms, Castle, Bowling-Green, Globe.*
From Warwick, Leamington, or Coventry, 5 miles.

THERE can be no doubt that Kenilworth is a place of much antiquity. According to Dugdale, the name is derived from Kenulph, or his son Kenelm, Saxon kings of Mercia, its original possessors, and "worthe," signifying a dwelling-place. In many old documents of the time of Queen Elizabeth it is improperly called Killingworth. In the reign of Henry I. the manor was granted by the king to Geoffrey de Clinton, his chamberlain and treasurer, who founded the priory and church, and endowed them with a large portion of the estate. The castle was built by this Geoffrey de Clinton, and appears to have remained in his family to the fourth generation. The history of the town is simply that of its celebrated fortress, which will be given in the proper place.

Here, in the beginning of the fourteenth century, was born John of Killingworth, an eminent philosopher, astronomer, and physician. " He studied the stars so long," says Fuller, " that at last he became a star in his own sphere, and outshined all others of that faculty. He was father and founder to all the astronomers of that age."

The town consists mainly of one very long, straggling street, with various offshoots. The buildings have in general an air of neatness and comfort ; but though many of them are not destitute of elegance, there is nothing calling for notice in the architecture of the place.

At the census of 1871 the population of Kenilworth was 3335. This town does not seem at any period of its history to have been remarkable for its commerce or population. The manufacture of horn combs is carried on to some extent, and there are also some chemical works.

Besides its castle and its ancient parish church, Kenilworth possesses no public buildings of importance. A new church, dedicated to St. John the Evangelist, was erected in 1852, near the entrance to the town from the Warwick road. There are one or two Dissenting chapels.

KENILWORTH CASTLE

Is situated on a gentle eminence on the west side of the town. According to the commonly-received account, it was built by Geoffrey de Clinton, upon whom the manor of Kenilworth had been conferred by Henry I. After having been possessed by three of his descendants, it reverted to the crown. Henry III. bestowed the manor on Simon de Montfort, Earl of Leicester, and his wife Eleanor, the king's sister, for their respective lives. From this time Kenilworth begins to occupy a prominent position in history. When the earl took up arms against his sovereign, it became a great place of resort for the insurgent nobles. In the bloody battle of Evesham, August 1265, in which no quarter was given, the barons were defeated, and Montfort and his eldest son slain. His younger son, Simon de Montfort, and the remains of the rebel party, rallied at Kenilworth, which became the centre of their operations. In 1266 the king came against Kenilworth with a large force ; but for six months it resisted all his efforts. At length the garrison, being much reduced by sickness, surrendered on highly favourable terms. Henry bestowed

W HARVEY

J.KECK

KENILWORTH CASTLE (FROM WARWICK ROAD).

Kenilworth on his younger son Edmund, whom he created Earl of Leicester and Lancaster. In the reign of Edward I., while Kenilworth was in the possession of this prince, it was the scene of a splendid tournament. The chief promoter of this chivalrous festival was Roger Mortimer, Earl of March. The knights were one hundred in number ; and among them were many distinguished foreigners, who had come to England expressly for the occasion. The ladies were also a hundred in number. It is recorded by the chroniclers that the whole party dined at a *round table*—all difficulties regarding precedence being thus avoided. Edmund of Lancaster was succeeded in the possession of Kenilworth by his son Thomas, who was beheaded for joining in a rebellion against Edward II. That monarch, however, soon fell before the power of the barons, and was confined in Kenilworth till he abdicated in favour of his son, after which he was taken to Berkeley Castle in Gloucestershire, where he was murdered. Kenilworth was restored by Edward III. to Henry, brother of the late possessor, as a reward for his services in the rebellion which had placed him on the throne. By his marriage with Blanche, grand-daughter of this earl, John of Gaunt, son of Edward III. and Duke of Lancaster, became the possessor of the castle and estate. This nobleman made large additions to the fortress. When his son, Henry of Bolingbroke, was supplanted by Richard II., Kenilworth again became the property of the crown, and so continued till Elizabeth conferred it on her favourite, Robert Dudley, Earl of Leicester, who expended on the castle and the surrounding domains the sum of £60,000. Dudley built the entrance gateway and tower on the north side, and the part of the castle called Leicester's Buildings. He also rebuilt Mortimer's Tower and the Gallery Tower,

KENILWORTH RESTORED (FROM THE LAKE).

at the opposite ends of the tilt-yard. Queen Elizabeth visited Leicester at Kenilworth in the years 1566, 1568, and 1575. It is the last of these visits that Scott has immortalised. We quote part of his description of the castle as it existed at this period :—

" The outer wall of this splendid and gigantic struc·ture enclosed seven acres, a part of which was occupied by extensive stables, and by a pleasure garden with its trim arbours and parterres, and the rest formed the large base court, or outer yard of the noble castle. The lordly structure itself, which rose near the centre of this spacious enclosure, was composed of a huge pile of magnificent castellated buildings, apparently of different ages, surrounding an inner court, and bearing in the names attached to each portion of the magnificent mass, and in the armorial bearings which were there blazoned, the emblems of mighty chiefs who had long passed away, and whose history, could ambition have lent ear to it, might have read a lesson to the haughty favourite who had now acquired, and was augmenting he fair domain. . . . . The external wall of this royal castle was, on the south and west sides, adorned and defended by a lake, partly artificial, across which Leicester had constructed a stately bridge, that Elizabeth might enter the castle by a path hitherto untrodden, instead of the usual entrance to the northward, over which he had erected a gatehouse or barbican, which still exists, and is equal in extent, and superior in architecture, to the baronial castle of many a northern chief. Beyond the lake lay an extensive chase, full of red-deer, fallow-deer, roes, and every species of game, and abounding with lofty trees, from amongst which the extended front and massive towers of the castle were seen to rise in majesty and beauty." ("Kenilworth," chap. 25.)

Sir Walter Scott has faithfully as well as charmingly interwoven with his story the particulars of the "princely pleasures" with which Elizabeth's visit was celebrated. During the seventeen days of her stay the queen was entertained by a series of gorgeous spectacles, and by every species of amusement which the age could produce. As may be seen from the extracts from "Kenilworth Inventory" that are given by Sir Walter Scott, the furniture of the castle was of the most magnificent and costly description. Master Robert Laneham, whom Scott designates "as great a coxcomb as ever blotted paper," mentions as a proof of the hospitable spirit of the Earl, that "the clock bell rang not a note all the while her Highness was there; the clock stood also still withal; the hands of both the tables stood firm and fast, *always pointing at two o'clock*"—the hour of banquet! The quantity of beer drunk amounted to "320 hogsheads of the ordinary sort." The expense of the entertainments is said to have amounted to £1000 a-day.

Robert Dudley, dying in 1588 at Kenilworth, some say of poison he had prepared for others, left the castle and estate to his brother Ambrose, Earl of Warwick, for his life, and thereafter to his son, Sir Robert Dudley, whose legitimacy he had not publicly acknowledged. Sir Robert produced proofs of his legitimacy; but the castle and domain were nevertheless seized by the crown. Subsequently it was bestowed by Cromwell on certain of his officers, who demolished it for the sake of the materials, felled its timber, and drained its moat. Charles II., on his restoration, granted the castle and estate to Laurence Hyde, afterwards Earl of Rochester. Kenilworth after this passed by marriage first to the Earl of Essex, and then to Thomas Villiers, afterwards Earl of Clarendon, in whose family it still remains.

G

It has long been a complete though magnificent ruin.
The present Earl of Clarendon, we believe, makes it
his care to preserve this noble fabric as much as possible from further decay.

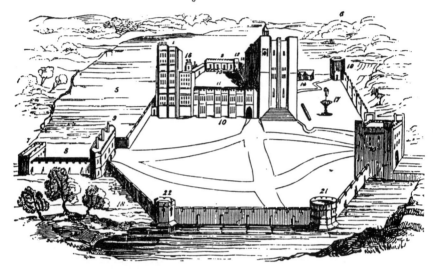

BIRD'S-EYE VIEW OF THE CASTLE RESTORED.*

The castle is approached by a pleasant green lane
diverging from which at a particular point there may
be heard a very fine echo.   The following description
takes up the different portions of the fortress in detail.
The ENTRANCE to the castle is by the GREAT GATE-

* We subjoin the names of the different parts of the castle, as indicated in this view, with a note of the pages at which they are
severally described :—

1. Leicester's Buildings, 91.	11. Inner Court, 86.
2. Cæsar's Tower, 86.	12. Strong Tower, 89.
3. Sir Robert Dudley's Lobby, 86.	13. The Three Kitchens, 87.
4. Base Court, 84.	14. The Pleasance, 93.
5. The Lake, 80.	16. The White Hall, 91.
6. Clinton Green, 83.	17. The Garden, 88.
7. Gallery Tower, 83.	18. The Orchard.
8. Tilt-Yard, 83.	19. Swan Tower, 93.
9. Mortimer's Tower, 93.	20. Great Gatehouse. 84.
10. King Henry's Lodgings, 86.	21. Lun's Tower, 93.

22. Water Tower, 93.

HOUSE, where a small charge is made (3d.), the proceeds being used to defray the expense of renovations. This gatehouse has been converted into a dwelling-house ; one apartment of which, on the ground-floor, is exhibited to visitors on an extra payment of sixpence. The apartment contains a carved chimney-piece, on which may be traced the arms and cognisance of Robert Dudley, Earl of Leicester ; otherwise the carving

GATEWAY.

is totally devoid of artistic handling or meaning, and not worth even the small charge made for its inspection. Proceeding onwards into the BASE COURT, a good view of the whole structure and of the inner court is obtained.

A careful study of the accompanying ground-plan of Kenilworth Castle will materially assist the tourist in finding the various parts of the ruins as they are noticed in the following description. Standing in the outer or Base Court, at the eastern side of the castle, the visitor has on his right Cæsar's Tower, and on his left Leicester's Buildings. The open space between

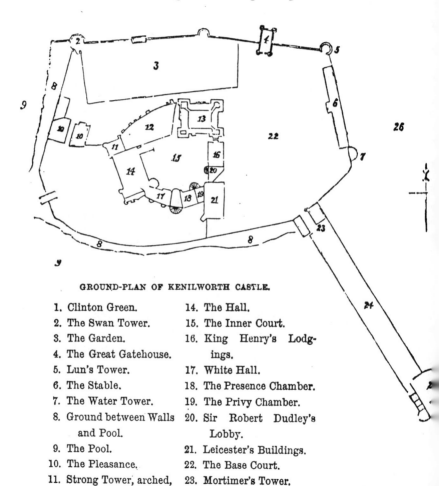

GROUND-PLAN OF KENILWORTH CASTLE.

1. Clinton Green.	14. The Hall.
2. The Swan Tower.	15. The Inner Court.
3. The Garden.	16. King Henry's Lodg-
4. The Great Gatehouse.	ings.
5. Lun's Tower.	17. White Hall.
6. The Stable.	18. The Presence Chamber.
7. The Water Tower.	19. The Privy Chamber.
8. Ground between Walls	20. Sir Robert Dudley's
and Pool.	Lobby.
9. The Pool.	21. Leicester's Buildings.
10. The Pleasance.	22. The Base Court.
11. Strong Tower, arched,	23. Mortimer's Tower.
three storeys.	24. The Tilt-yard.
12. The Three Kitchens.	25. The Gallery Tower.
13. Cæsar's Tower.	26. The Orchard.

them was originally occupied by Sir Robert Dudley's Lobby and King Henry VIII.'s Lodgings, which are

LEICESTER CHIMNEY-PIECE.

entirely destroyed. Between the latter of these parts of the castle and Cæsar's Tower was an arched entrance into the Inner Court. At the farther end of the inner court is the great banqueting-hall. Having made himself familiar with these points, the tourist can readily proceed to identify the other parts of this extensive and magnificent structure.

Cæsar's Tower, evidently the oldest part of the building, has been a keep of immense strength. The character of its architecture is so thoroughly Norman as to leave little doubt that it was erected by Geoffrey de Clinton. In some places its walls are not less than sixteen feet thick. Unlike other Norman towers, it has no dungeon. This massive keep has been square

in form ; but one side of it, the north, is entirely
demolished. Scott conjectures that it may have received its name from its resemblance to the one in the
Tower of London so called. In the south-east angle of

CÆSAR'S TOWER.

this tower is the well, now covered over. It was emptied
and examined in 1819, but nothing of consequence
found in it. Westward from Cæsar's Tower were the
KITCHENS, of which only a few crumbling ruins remain. The arched passage between the Kitchens and

Cæsar's Tower, built by Leicester, communicated with the GARDENS. There Scott represents Leicester as standing in the midst of a splendid group of lords

MERVYN'S TOWER.

and ladies, when Elizabeth, having discovered the Countess Amy in the grotto, dragged her towards him, saying, "Stand forth, my Lord of Leicester! Knowest thou this woman?" The scene that ensued is one of the most powerful in the novel. Beyond the Kitchens is the Strong Tower.

The STRONG TOWER, or, as Scott has named it, MERVYN'S TOWER, will be viewed with interest from the associations Scott has connected with it. Originally a very strong building of three storeys, it exactly answers the description given in "Kenilworth." "The floor of each storey," says Sir Walter, "was arched, the walls of tremendous thickness, while the space of the chamber did not exceed fifteen feet in diameter." It is here that the hapless Amy Robsart is represented as having found a brief refuge, when she came to Kenilworth, to make her appeal to her husband's love. The reader of "Kenilworth" will scarcely require to be reminded that it was here that she wrote her letter to Leicester, and fastened it with a braid of her hair in a "true-love knot;" that here occurred her interview with Tressilian, and the scene with Michael Lambourne and Lawrence Staples. The upper storey, which was Amy's chamber, is in ruins.

The GREAT HALL, which comes next in the line of building, now turning to the south, has been an apartment of most magnificent style and dimensions. This and several adjoining parts of the castle were built by John of Gaunt, "time-honoured Lancaster." The richly-ornamented portal shows the level of this noble room. Its floor rested on stone arches, the vaulted apartment below being probably used for stores. The hall has been 90 feet long by 45 broad. The windows are of great height and exquisite in design. On the south side of the great hall is a winding staircase, terminating in two vaulted apartments. In connection with this noble apartment, it will not be inappropriate to quote Sir Walter Scott's description of it when dignified by the presence of Elizabeth. It will help

THE GREAT HALL.

the visitor to realise to some extent what must have
been the grandeur of an apartment, the ruins of which

have still such an aspect of magnificence :—" The Queen . . . . at length found her way to the great hall of the castle, gorgeously hung for her reception with the richest silken tapestry, misty with perfumes, and sounding to strains of soft and delicious music. From the highly-carved oaken roof hung a superb chandelier of gilt bronze, formed like a spread eagle, whose outstretched wings supported three male and three female figures, grasping a pair of branches in each hand. The hall was thus illuminated by twenty-four torches of wax. At the upper end of the splendid apartment was a state canopy, overshadowing a royal throne, and beside was a door, which opened to a long suite of apartments, decorated with the utmost magnificence for the Queen and her ladies, whenever it should be her pleasure to be private."

Following the line of the building, which here turns to the east, the visitor finds the indistinct traces of the WHITE HALL, an apartment which seems to have measured about 50 feet by 25. It seems to have been erected at the same time as the Great Hall. Next in order to this apartment, according to Dugdale, were the PRESENCE CHAMBER and the PRIVY CHAMBERS —from the latter of which it is supposed that the chimney-piece already referred to, as exhibited in the gatehouse, was removed. These ruins possess no particular interest.

LEICESTER'S BUILDINGS complete the square. As the name implies, this stupendous pile was erected by the Earl of Leicester. Leicester's Buildings are less strongly and durably built than other parts of the castle. The stone of which it is composed is softer, and less able to resist the weather than that of the more ancient portions of the structure. From this cause it has even a more time-worn aspect than some parts of an earlier date. The floors have all fallen in ; but the visitor can readily mark the different storeys into which the gigantic pile has been divided, the remains of beams and disfigured fire-places rising above each other in the desolate walls. The ivy which so

LEICESTER'S BUILDINGS.

thickly covers this and the other parts of the castle, adding greatly to the picturesqueness of the various views, has, in some places, a trunk almost as thick as a man's body.

The surrounding country may be seen to great advantage from various points of the castle ; in particular from the windows of the Great Hall, and from the top of the Strong Tower.

The Outer Wall of the Castle, as has been already said, enclosed seven acres. The GARDEN was on the north side of the Castle. With it was connected the PLEASANCE, which was more to the west, adjoining the the Strong Tower. The Pleasance, it will be remembered, was the scene of the meeting of Queen Elizabeth

WATER TOWER.

and Amy Robsart. Several towers are connected with the walls. At the west corner of the north wall is the SWAN TOWER. To the eastward, beyond the Gatehouse, may be seen LUN'S TOWER, the STABLES, and the WATER TOWER, which are shut out from inspection, forming part of a farm-yard. The ruins of MORTIMER'S TOWER, at the beginning of the Tilt-Yard, and the

TILT-YARD itself, will not fail to excite the interest of the ·tourist, who will obtain a charming view of the castle from this side.

"We cannot but add," says Scott, concluding his general description of Kenilworth, "that of this lordly palace, where princes feasted and heroes fought, now in the bloody earnest of storm and siege, and now in the games of chivalry, all is now desolate. The bed of the lake is but a rushy swamp; and the massive ruins of the Castle only serve to show what their splendour once was, and to impress on the musing visitor the transitory value of human possessions, and the happiness of those who enjoy a humble lot in virtuous contentment."

Probably the bird's-eye view given on a preceding page may serve to give the tourist a better general idea of the castle as it existed in its integrity, than any verbal description.

At the south-eastern extremity of the Tilt-yard is the GALLERY TOWER.* Only the base and side walls of this tower remain; and these are so overgrown with underwood as only to be noticeable on a minute inspection. This was formerly the principal entrance to ·the castle. The reader of "Kenilworth" will re-

---

* "The entrance tower obtained the name of the Gallery Tower from the following circumstance :—The whole bridge, extending from the entrance to another tower on the opposite side of the lake, called Mortimer's Tower, was so disposed as to make a spacious tilt-yard, about one hundred and thirty yards in length and ten in breadth, strewed with the finest sand, and defended on either side by strong and high palisades. The broad and fair gallery, destined for the ladies who were to witness the feats of chivalry presented on this area, was erected on the northern side of the outer tower, to which it gave name."—(Scott's "Kenilworth," chap. xxvi.)

member that it was here the gigantic porter resigned
his club and keys on the approach of Queen Elizabeth:—

> " Dazzled and blind, mine office I forsake,
>   My club, my key.   My knee, my homage take,
>   Bright paragon ; pass on in joy and bliss ;—
>   Beshrew the gate that opes not wide at such a sight as this! "

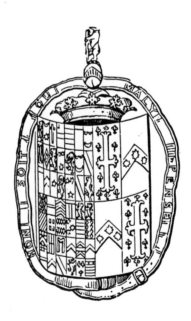

The PARISH CHURCH, dedicated to St. Nicholas, occupies a good position not far from the castle. It consists of nave, aisles, chancel with south aisle, and spire at the west end. The oldest part of the edifice is the fine Norman arch in the tower, forming the entrance. This is regarded as one of the finest of the kind in this country, and is supposed to have been originally the entrance to the abbey church, from which it was removed to the present position when that building was destroyed. This noble doorway consists of a series of receding arches, rising from circular columns, and ornamented with the diamond, embattled, zigzag, and beak-head mouldings. The picturesque spire-steeple which rises above the doorway is much more modern, as is also the body of the church, which is of various styles. The church underwent considerable restorations in 1865.

The interior is worthy of inspection. The east window is in the Second Pointed style, and was the

gift of the late Dr. Samuel Butler, then vicar of
Kenilworth and master of Shrewsbury school, afterwards bishop of Lichfield. It is filled with stained
glass, and contains the arms of the successive possessors
of the castle. It is to be regretted that the ancient
east window, the tracery of which was of a rare kind

should have been removed. This window, it is said,
now forms the entrance to a summer-house in the
vicar's garden. There are three sedilia on the south
side of the chancel. The south aisle has one of those
openings, regarding the use of which antiquarians are
not agreed. They are variously styled confessionals,
vulsre windows, and lychnoscopes. There is another
in the south-west wall of the chancel. The font, which
is octagonal, has the date 1664; but it is supposed to

be much older, and that that was the time at which it was reworked. The church contains a considerable number of monuments, none of them of much antiquity. The chancel contains a very beautiful one by Westmacott, to the memory of Caroline, the wife of Richard Gresley, Esq.

THE ABBEY, some remains of which may still be seen near the church, was of the order of St. Augustine, and endowed to the honour of the Virgin Mary. It owed its origin to Geoffrey de Clinton, the founder of the castle, who endowed it with all the woods and lands he had in the parish of Kenilworth, except the site of the castle and its park, and with other privileges. His descendants showed an equal interest in the prosperity of the monastery. At the general survey, taken in the 26th of King Henry VIII., its clear annual revenue was £533 : 15 : 4. When the abbey was surrendered at the Dissolution (1539), it had been in their possession more than four hundred years. Henry VIII. granted its site to Sir Andrew Flamock, whose granddaughter brought it in marriage to John Colburn, Esq. of Mareton Marrell, in this county, who was intimidated into parting with it on very easy terms to the Earl of Leicester. It is now, like the castle, the property of the Earl of Clarendon.

The most interesting part of the ruins is the old *Gateway*, which is in good preservation. This very picturesque object, viewed in connection with the rest of the ruins, makes it sufficiently evident that the building was of large extent and imposing architecture. The abbey has been of the Anglo-Norman style. Not far from the gateway already mentioned is another portion of this ancient structure, which has been converted into a cow-house or barn. At some distance there are several large and shapeless remnants of the old walls. Of the church originally in connection with the monastery there are no remains, with the exception of its arched entrance, which is supposed to have been removed to the present church close at hand. Some years ago, when the present churchyard was being enlarged, some portions of the foundations of the abbey were discovered, which are supposed to be the remains of the chapter-house; and some fine ornamental fragments of different periods and styles were found. Several stone coffin-lids with ancient carvings were also uncovered, and are still to be seen in the churchyard.

SEAL OF THE PRIORY.

KINETON AND ITS VICINITY.

From Stratford-on-Avon, 8 miles ; Fenny Compton Station (12 miles from Leamington), 5.

THOUGH not mentioned in Domesday Book, Kineton is a place of much antiquity. Henry I. gave the church, called then Chinton, to the monks of Kenilworth ; and there are records, but no remains, of a castle that existed here at a later period.

The *Church* dates from the reign of Edward II., and is a good specimen of the ecclesiastical architecture of that time.

About four miles to the south of Kineton is EDGE-HILL, a long elevated ridge, on the northern slope of which the battle that has made its name noted in history was fought, Oct. 23, 1642. Five hundred bodies were thrown into a contiguous pit, the site of which is marked by a clump of firs. Human bones and fragments of weapons are often turned up on the scene of the battle.

The edge of the hill is a beautiful natural terrace. On its summit are a tower and artificial ruins.

"From Edge-Hill," says Speed, "we may behold another Eden, as Lot did the plain of Jordan before that Sodom fell." To which Fuller adds : "But he might have put in, 'It is not altogether so well watered.'"

• The prospect from Edge-Hill, and the reflections to which it gives rise, form the subject of Richard Jago's chief poem, bearing its name.

The subject is pleasantly treated, but the poem seldom rises to a high pitch of excellence. "Edge-Hill" is included in all series of the British poets pretending to completeness.

On the eastern side of Edge-Hill is an ancient forti·
fication called *Nadbury Camp*, believed to be of Roman
construction.

COMPTON VERNEY, anciently called COMPTON MUR-
DACK, is about 2 miles west from Kineton. Originally
bestowed by the Conqueror on Henry de Newburgh,
Earl of Warwick, the manor came, in the reign of
Henry I., into the possession of Robert Murdack. In
the reign of Henry V. the estate was acquired by Sir
Richard Verney, who built a mansion on it, which was
in existence in the early part of the 17th century.
The present edifice was erected about a hundred years
ago from a design by Adams, and is surrounded by a
fine park, rich in wood and water. Its principal apartment is adorned with fine paintings on panels by Zucchero. There is a handsome chapel near the mansion.

COMPTON WINGATE, about 6 miles to the south of
Kineton, was the residence of Sir William Compton,
who, at the age of eleven, was appointed companion to
the second son of Henry VII., afterwards Henry VIII.
The members of this family were distinguished for
their loyalty. One of them, Spencer Compton, second
Earl of Northampton, was killed at the battle of Hop-
ton Heath, refusing to take quarter from "such base
rogues and rebels" as the Parliamentarians. The
most noted member of this family was Henry Compton,
Bishop of London.* The mansion, built by Sir Wil-

---

* Henry Compton, one of the most eminent prelates who ever
occupied the see of London, was born at Compton Wingate in
1632. Before entering the church he served for some time as
cornet in a cavalry regiment. In 1675 he was appointed to the
see of London, and entrusted with the education of the Princesses
Mary and Anne. To his influence is to be attributed the firm-
ness with which these princesses adhered to the Protestant religion.
When James II. ascended the throne he suspended Bishop Comp·
ton, but afterwards restored him to his office. Compton died in
1713, at the age of 81.

liam Compton in the reign of Henry **VIII.**, is an
irregular edifice of considerable extent, and has originally been surrounded by a moat. It is still the property
of the Compton family, but it is no longer inhabited
by them.

The *Church*, which had been destroyed by the
Parliamentarian soldiers in 1646, was rebuilt after the
Restoration.

TYSOE, a village 5 miles from Kineton, dates from
before the Conquest. The church is a building of
considerable antiquity. Under a monumental arch in
the north wall is a recumbent effigy much worn.

On the hillside, fronting the church, is cut in the
turf the gigantic figure of a horse. From the tint of
the soil it is called the *Red Horse*, and the low ground
below is called the *Red Horse Vale.* It is generally
supposed that the figure was cut to commemorate the
gallant conduct of Richard Neville, Earl of Warwick,
who, at the battle of Towton Heath, slew his steed, to
show his followers that he was prepared to share the
same dangers as the meanest soldier in the ranks. It
used to be a rustic custom to "scour" the figure every
Palm Sunday (the anniversary of the battle). Jago,
in his poem of "Edge-Hill," ascribes this figure to the
Saxons.

KNOWLE.

In the VICINITY OF SOLIHULL.

LEAMINGTON.

Hotels.—*Regent*, Lower Parade; *Clarendon*, Lansdowne Place; *Manor House*, within its own grounds, near N. and Gt. Western Station; *Crown*, High Street; *Bath*, Bath Street; *Angel*, Regent Street. Private Lodgings in all parts of the town.

From Warwick, 2 miles; Birmingham, 21; Coventry, 9¼; Rugby, 14½; London, 97; Edinburgh, 326.

THIS fashionable spa is pleasantly situated on the Leam, a tributary of the Avon. From a small obscure village it has risen in the course of forty years to be one of the most esteemed watering-places in the kingdom. The addition of "Priors" was made to its name in consequence of its being bestowed · on the monks of Kenilworth, and in order to distinguish it from the village of Leamington Hastang, several miles distant. The manor was one of the numerous possessions of Turchill, the last of the Saxon Earls of Warwick. After passing through various families, it was taken possession of by the crown on the dissolution of the monasteries by Henry VIII. It was conferred by Queen Elizabeth on Ambrose Dudley, the good Earl of Warwick, upon whose death, without heirs, it again reverted to the Crown, when it was bestowed in 1605 on the accomplished Fulke Greville by James I. Subsequently it was divided among various proprietors; but the manorial rights are vested in the Earl of Aylesford. Leamington owes its prosperity to its mineral waters. The first notice of them is by Camden in 1586. Afterwards they were mentioned by Speed, Dugdale, Fuller, and Dr. Thomas, the continuator of Dugdale. It was not, however, till the year 1784 that public attention began to be drawn to any extent to the waters of Leamington. In that year a saline spring was discovered by Benjamin Satchwell, the village shoemaker, to whose indefatigable exertions in bringing the various attractions of his native village before the public, its subsequent rise to prosperity is in a great measure to be traced. William Abbots, landlord of the "Dog Inn," zealously seconded the exertions of Satchwell, his friend and crony, establishing baths, now called the "Original Baths," and the "New Inn," now transformed into the *Bath Hotel*. The "Morning Chronicle" rendered good service to the infant spa by the publication of articles by Satchwell and others; and a treatise on the waters by Dr. Lambe of Warwick in 1794 had the effect of attracting considerable numbers of visitors. In the beginning of the present century several new springs were discovered, and some handsome suites of baths erected. The publication of Scott's novel of "Kenilworth," in 1818, had a great influence in attracting visitors to the locality, and bringing it into very general notice. Leamington is also under a deep debt of obligation to Doctor Jephson, whose liberality and untiring exertions for the promotion of the interests of the town are universally acknowledged.

The increase of its population within the last fifty years is a fair index of the remarkable growth of the prosperity of Leamington. In 1811 the population was 543; in 1821, 2183; in 1831, 6269; in 1841, 12,600; in 1851, 15,724; in 1861, 18,768, and in 1871, 22,730, showing an increase of 3962 during the ten years. The increase of houses is also shown by the following figures—1861, 3441; 1871, 4325. Fifty years ago, when the spirit of improvement was beginning to operate, the roads were miserable, the inns few and indifferent, and no stage-coach passed nearer than two miles. It was a small village, innocent of drainage, and possessing only a few buildings that could claim to be called fashionable. But in the course of these fifty years the public spirit and energy of the inhabitants and neighbouring proprietors have accomplished a wonderful change. Scarcely any traces of the old village remain. Leamington now boasts of " crescents," " squares," " terraces," and " parades," that need not dread comparison with metropolitan streets similarly named. In its neighbourhood are many handsome villas, and the number of these is increasing every year ; and with all the "appliances and means " of modern progress and comfort Leamington is now well supplied. It has hotels furnished and conducted in the most superior manner ; it is well supplied with vehicles of all kinds ; its roads are well kept ; it is accessible by railway from all parts of the country ; its public buildings are in general tasteful ; and its means of public amusement numerous. In 1838 the Leamington Spa was styled " Royal," with the sanction of Her Majesty, who had visited the town in 1830 when Princess Victoria.

THE MINERAL WATERS.—As it is mainly to its medicinal springs that Leamington is indebted for its importance, these naturally fall first to be considered in an account of the town. There are four springs, each differing a little from the other in the amount of their chemical constituents, yet not sufficiently so as to render it of much consequence to which the patient resorts. The two principal springs are saline, one of them being slightly impregnated with iron, and they are cathartic in their effects. The other two—the sulphureous and chalybeate—are not much patronised. Caution ought always to be exercised in commencing the use of saline waters if a medical man has not been consulted ; and this advice is particularly applicable to delicate persons and those unaccustomed to mineral-water drinking. They are regarded as efficacious in derangements of the digestive functions, diseases of the skin, and visceral obstructions. Long before and after their introduction to public notice by Benjamin Satchwell and his worthy coadjutor William Abbots, these waters were regarded as a potent cure for hydrophobia —a virtue not now insisted upon. The "season" for the use of the waters extends from May to October For a detailed account of their properties, and the manner in which they should be used, we must refer the visitor to the numerous medical papers and analyses that have been published. The following hints as to the use of the waters are derived from the treatises of Drs. Middleton and London, and other sources :—

Drinking.—The time required to give the waters a trial is a month or six weeks, though of course a much longer time will be required to experience their full virtues. The average quantity for adults is a pint. It is taken the first thing in the morning, one-half being reserved until twenty minutes' brisk exercise after the first dose. It should if possible be drunk at the spring. The saline waters should not be used without consideration, as, when taken in undue quantities, they have a very irritating and hurtful effect on the bowels. The sulphureous waters are not likely to be beneficial, when, after a strict attention to the medical directions as to their use, they are found to produce headache and sickness, and unduly to excite any of the excretions. The chalybeate water is valuable as a tonic and diffusible stimulus. It is used in weak, lax, and pale habits, and is regarded as having a favourable influence in the cachexiæ.

Bathing.—The warm saline bath is of great service for diseases of the skin, stiffness of the joints, and paralytic affections. It should be taken once or twice a-week in conjunction with the drinking of the waters, and oftener if the patient do not use the water internally. The cold

bath should be taken, in cases where it is desirable, in
the usual manner. Shower, tepid, medicated, and other
baths, may also be had at the various establishments.
Our space will not allow of a detailed account of the
analyses of the different springs. The following view
of their average contents (without decimal fractions)
will be found sufficiently accurate for general information. An imperial pint contains—

Sulphate of soda	35 grains.
Chloride of sodium	30 „
Chloride of calcium	23 „
Chloride of magnesium . . .	11 „

and in minute proportions—Silica—Peroxide of Iron
—Iodine, and Bromide of sodium.

At No. 6 High Street, near the railway viaduct, is a
well with sulphureous water, and in the same neighbourhood a chalybeate spring, but neither of them is of
importance.

The principal pump-rooms and baths require a brief
notice. The original spring is that called *The Old
Well*, in Bath Street, at the head of Spencer Street.
It was enclosed in 1803 by the Earl of Aylesford, lord
of the manor, who granted the use of it in perpetuity
to the poor. The present building was erected by his
grandson. There is an attendant here, but water may
be taken free in small quantities from the outside pump.

The ROYAL PUMP-ROOM AND BATHS were designed
by Mr. C. S. Smith of Warwick, and erected at a cost
of £25,000. The front facing the road is 106 feet in
length, and 30 feet high. At either end is a wing
appropriated to baths, which are twenty in number ;
and the whole is surrounded with a colonnade of
duplicated pillars of the Doric order. The Pump-
Room is well-proportioned and elegantly ornamented ;
the baths are furnished with every convenience, and

the adjoining grounds afford pleasant promenades. The *Swimming Baths* and *Hot Baths* (not mineral) are situated at Oldham's Mill, Mill Walk, Leam Terrace. The *Sulphurous* Springs and Baths, of which Mr. Hudson is proprietor, are situated at No. 6 High Street.

The Free Fountain or ORIGINAL SPA, in Bath Street, at the head of Spencer Street, was founded in 1786 by Thomas Abbots. The present building, which is of a tasteful character, is of a more recent date. Among the objects with which its interior is adorned is a portrait of Dr. Jephson.

The terms for drinking and bathing vary at the different establishments. Drinking for the season, from £1 : 1s. to 7s. 6d., for one person, and £2 : 2s. to £1, for a family; for a week, from 3s. 6d. to 1s. 6d. for one person, and 5s. to 4s. for a family. The average prices for baths are—warm, 1s. 6d.; cold or shower, 1s.; warm, 1s. 6d., cold, 1s. ; douche, 2s. 6d. ; medicated sulphur, 3s. ; chlorine, 4s. ; iodine, 4s. ; camphor, 3s. 6d. ; ammonia, 4s. ; hot air, 2s. 6d. ; vapour, 2s. 6d.

Leamington salts, produced by the evaporation of the mineral waters, may be obtained from any of the chemists in the town.

CHURCHES. — Leamington is well provided with places of worship.

ALL SAINTS' CHURCH is at the south side of Victoria Bridge. There can be no doubt that a church—or rather a chapel, for the building was subordinate to the neighbouring parish church of Leek Wootton—existed here at an early period. It underwent some repairs about the year 1524 ; but the date of its original foundation does not seem to have been preserved. In 1816 the great increase of population led to the enlargement of the sacred edifice ; and fresh additions

were made at subsequent dates. The partial reconstruction and enlargement of the church was commenced in 1843 by the Rev. John Craig, M.A., vicar
of the parish, and carried out at a cost of upwards of
£15,000. It is a handsome edifice, but not likely to
obtain unqualified praise from the ecclesiologist, not
being throughout of one order of architecture—a defect
as inexcusable as it is avoidable in a modern church. It
consists of nave, aisles, transepts, chancel, and spire.
The nave and its aisles are Perpendicular, the transepts
and chancel Decorated. There are no monuments of
importance in the interior. The west window is of
five lights, and is forty-two feet high and twenty wide.
It is filled with good stained glass, representing a series
of events in the history of our Saviour. This window
is said to be the largest, perhaps the finest, in the
county. The chancel has an apsidal end, and is
lighted with five good windows filled with stained
glass, the three inner ones being in memory of three
sisters of the name of Manners Sutton. There is a
fine rose window, said to have been copied from one
in the cathedral of Rouen in the north transept.

In the churchyard are interred Benjamin Satchwell
and William Abbots, the two men who gave Leamington
the impulse that carried it on to prosperity. Satchwell's monument, which is the more imposing of the two,
has a lengthy poetical inscription, bidding the reader

> " Hail the unassuming tomb
> Of him who told where health and beauty bloom ;
> Of him whose lengthened life improving ran—
> A blameless, useful, venerable man."

The churchyard was closed some years ago.*

* A CEMETERY was opened in 1852 in the southern extremity of
the parish. It is well drained and tastefully laid out. There are
two handsome little chapels, in the Early Decorated style, for the
performance of funeral service—one being for the use of Dissenters.

THE EPISCOPAL CHAPEL, in the centre of Beauchamp Square, was erected in 1826. It is in the Norman style, but, like many modern efforts in the same line, displays more of the heavy and sombre than of the impressive and majestic character of that order of architecture.

TRINITY CHAPEL, also in Beauchamp Square, is a cruciform building in the Decorated style. It was opened in 1847.

MILVERTON CHAPEL, on the New Warwick Road, erected in 1835, has a Doric front. Its only recommendation seems to be the amount of accommodation it affords.

ST. MARY'S DISTRICT CHURCH, near the Warneford Hospital, at the east end of the town, opened in 1839, is a good building in the Perpendicular style. The east window and several of the others are filled with stained glass. There is a handsome modern font, octagonal, and sculptured with emblems of our Saviour's passion.

ST. LUKE'S EPISCOPAL CHAPEL is in Augusta Place, but is of no architectural interest. It was opened in 1850.

DISSENTING CHAPELS are numerous, most of the sects being represented. The *Mill Street* (Lady Huntingdon's) *Chapel* was once the property of the Rev. Rowland Hill, who is commemorated by a tablet in the interior. The Rev. Octavius Winslow, D.D., well known to the religious public by his numerous works, was minister of the *Baptist Chapel*, Warwick Street. None of the Dissenting places of worship have any claim on the attention of the ecclesiologist.

PUBLIC BUILDINGS.—The public buildings of Leamington are on the whole worthy of its prominent position as a 'fashionable watering-place.

The ROYAL ASSEMBLY ROOMS, at the corner of the Lower Parade, were erected in 1813, at a cost of £10,000. This building, as its name implies, is used for balls and assemblies, etc. The principal hall, or ball-room, is 86 feet long, 36 wide, and 23 high. The building comprises a public billiard-room, refreshment-rooms, etc.

The ROYAL MUSIC HALL, originally called the Parthenon, is in Bath Street. It was erected in 1821, but has undergone many improvements and embellishments since that date. Externally and internally it is a handsome structure. The ground floor is occupied by the public reading room.

The TOWN HALL, High Street, erected in 1831 for municipal and police purposes, and the PUBLIC HALL, Windsor Street, erected in 1854 for public meetings, are good and commodious buildings, not calling, however, for special description.

The LEAMINGTON PROPRIETARY COLLEGE, Binwood Crescent, a handsome brick building, faced with stone, in the style of the time of Henry VIII., was founded in 1847, for the education of sons of the nobility, clergy, and gentry, in connection with the Established Church. It has been recently remodelled, and is now the property of shareholders in the town. The restriction as to the social position of the scholars is now disregarded, and the school is well managed under the new regime.

There are several excellent institutions for the education of young ladies. The ordinary day and Sunday schools are numerous and respectable.

The WARNEFORD HOSPITAL, so named in honour of the Rev. Dr. Warneford, rector of Burton-on-the-Hill, Gloucestershire, to whose munificence its establishment is mainly owing, was erected in 1832, for the gratuitous supply of medical assistance and baths to the poor. At various periods, through the liberal donations and bequests of benevolent persons, the hospital has been enlarged and rendered more efficient.

Leamington possesses ample provision for the amusement and recreation of the visitors and inhabitants.

The JEPHSON GARDENS occupy a charming position on the bank of the Leam, not far from the parish church. A fine marble statue of Dr. Jephson by Mr. Hollins of Birmingham, said to be an admirable likeness, stands in a little Corinthian temple on an elevated spot near the middle of the grounds. The gardens are vested in trustees, who have laid them out with ·great taste. These grounds contain charming and varied walks, an archery-ground, and other attractions. During "the season" an instrumental band is engaged to play in the grounds, which it is needless to say are a favourite resort of beauty and fashion.

The following are the terms of admission to the Jephson Gardens :—For the day, 3d. each (6d. when the band is playing) ; week, 1s. 6d. for one person, 3s. for a family ; month, 4s. for one, 7s. for a family ; three months, 7s. 6d. and 14s. ; year, 10s. 6d. and 21s. Opposite the gardens is the Public Park.

The TENNIS COURT, in Lower Bedford Street, is a favourite place of amusement. Besides the court which gives it its name, this building has billiard-rooms, racket-courts, and a refreshment room.

The THEATRE, in Clemens Street, is now used as an Independent Meeting House, the stage and other fittings being retained. Amateur theatricals occasionally take place in the Music Hall.

There is abundant provision for promenades, balls, and concerts during the season. A free public library was established some years ago in Bath Street. There are also circulating libraries and reading-rooms in connection with several of the booksellers' shops. Lists of the visitors are published weekly in the local newspapers, the " Leamington Spa Courier," and the " Leamington Advertiser."

ENVIRONS OF LEAMINGTON.*

The country round Leamington is rich in localities of interest. The railway is available for approaching many of these places, while others are within easy walking distance by the highways or footpaths through the fields. " The chief enjoyment of my several visits to Leamington," says Nathaniel Hawthorne, in " Our Old Home," " lay in rural walks about the neighbourhood, and in jaunts to places of note and interest, which are particularly abundant in that region. The high-roads are made pleasant to the traveller by a border of trees, and often afford him the hospitality of a wayside bench beneath a comfortable shade. But a fresher delight is to be found in the footpaths, which go wandering away from stile to stile, along hedges, and across broad fields, and through wooded parks, leading you to little hamlets of thatched cottages, ancient, solitary farmhouses, picturesque old mills, streamlets, pools, and all those quiet, secret, unexpected, yet strangely familiar features of English scenery that Tennyson shows us in his idylls and eclogues. These by-paths admit the wayfarer into the very heart of rural life, and yet do not burden him with a sense of intrusiveness. He has a right to go whithersoever they lead him ; for, with all their shaded privacy, they are as much the property of the public as the dusty high-road itself, and even by an older tenure.

* See also the Vicinity of Warwick

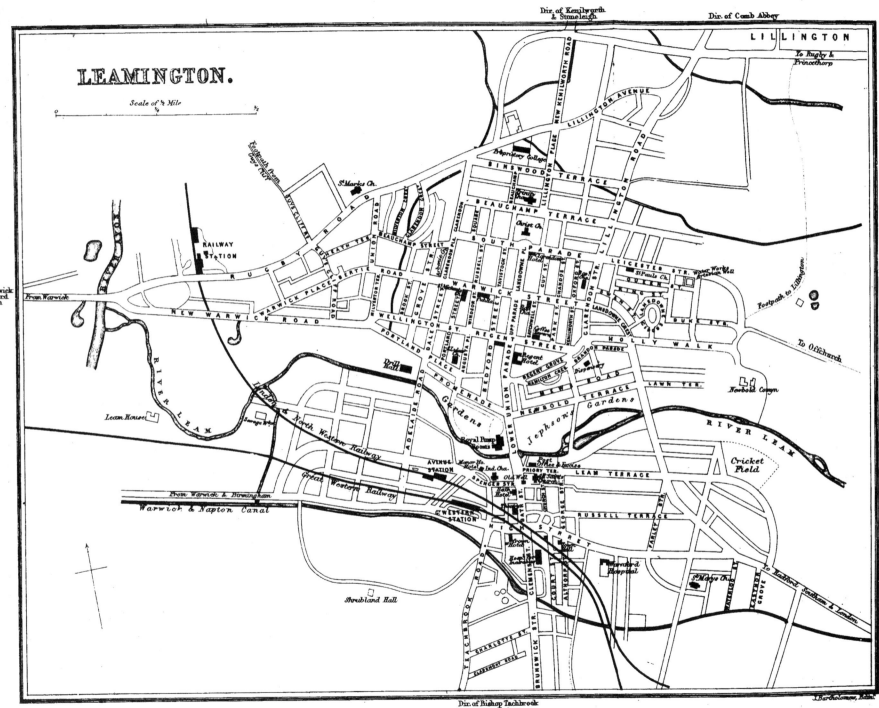

LEAMINGTON.

Scale of ½ Mile

"leir antiquity probably exceeds that of the Roman
ys ; the footsteps of the aboriginal Britons first wore
ay the grass, and the natural flow of intercourse
ween village and village has kept the tract bare
ver since."

BISHOP'S TACHBROOK.—This scattered and charm-
ingly-wooded village is about two miles to the south
of Leamington. Some of the houses have fronts of
timber and plaster. The *Church*, which is pleasantly
situated, consists of nave, aisles, chancel (with a vestry
clumsily built against its north side), and square tower
at the west end : the windows are mostly square-headed,
with two trefoil lights. The chancel has been rebuilt.
A Norman doorway in the wall of the north aisle has
been built up, and the wall is propped by three huge
buttresses without any ornamentation.

The interior is worthy of inspection. The east
window, which is new, and Decorated in style, is filled
with good painted glass representing the Ascension.
On the right of the chancel is a stately marble monument to the pious memory of Sir Thomas Wagstaffe,
who died in 1708, and Dame Francis Wagstaffe, his
wife, who died in 1706. On the left of the chancel is
a plainer one, to the memory of Combe Wagstaffe, who
died in 1667. A carved stone pulpit stands in the
nave.

At Bishop's Tachbrook the tourist is about 3 miles
n the Roman camp of CHESTERTON.

.KENILWORTH is 5 miles distant (p. 75.)

LILLINGTON, a pleasant hamlet about a mile from
Leamington, may be reached by a footpath through the
fields. The church, which originally belonged to the
monks of Kenilworth, is an ancient edifice, recently
restored and enlarged. and occupying a good site. It
has a good east window of painted glass. A stone in

the churchyard, to the memory of a man of the name of John Trees, has this quaint and touching inscription :—

> " Poorly lived,
> And poorly died,
> Poorly buried,
> And no one cried."

OFFCHURCH.—The small and picturesque village of Offchurch, about three miles east of Leamington, is said to derive its name from Offa, king of the Mercians, who had a residence here. In the time of Edward the Confessor it was part of the extensive possessions of Earl Leofric, who bestowed it upon the monks of Coventry. At the Dissolution, Offchurch was granted by Henry VIII. to Sir Edmund Knightley, in whose family the manor remained, till, by the marriage of Miss Knightley, the last representative, with Lord Guernsey, it came into the possession of that nobleman. *Offchurch Bury* is a fine old Gothic mansion, in the style of various periods, the earliest portions belonging to the time of Henry VIII. It is pleasantly situated on the banks of the Leam, and is surrounded by a park and grounds which harmonise well with its imposing and venerable appearance. A majestic chestnut tree, before the Gothic porch of the mansion, is an object of general admiration. Its spreading branches are capable of sheltering at least three hundred persons. The village church is pleasantly situated on an eminence. Adjoining it is the parsonage-house, a picturesque residence, with its grounds charmingly laid out.

PRINCETHORPE, between 5 and 6 miles from Leamington, on the Rugby road, is the site of a Roman Catholic nunnery. This is a large building, containing 200 apartments, and indicating taste in its construction and arrangements. The grounds are pleasingly laid out. The nuns, who are of the Benedictine order, took refuge in this country at the time of the French Revolution. At first they located themselves at Heath Hall in Yorkshire, then at Orrell Mount in Lancashire, and subsequently they purchased the ground at Princethorpe, where they erected the present structure. This institution has among its objects that of educating young ladies of the Roman Catholic faith.

At *Stretton-in-Dunsmore*, a mile beyond Princethorpe, there is a beautiful modern church, designed by Rickman.

STONELEIGH is about 4 miles to the north of Leamington, and 2 miles from Kenilworth. Before the Conquest, and down to the time of Henry II., Stoneleigh was held in demesne by the crown. In 1154 an abbey of Cistercian monks was founded here, the monks removing to this place from Radmore in Staffordshire. In subsequent reigns many privileges were conferred on the monastery, among which were a weekly market, annual fair, and free warren. At the time of the survey in the reign of Henry VIII. the annual revenue of the abbey amounted to £151 : 3 : 1. On the Dissolution it was bestowed on Charles Brandon, Duke of Suffolk, but subsequently passed by purchase to Sir Thomas Leigh, alderman of London, the first of the Leigh family who possessed this estate. Sir Thomas erected a mansion on the site of the abbey, incorporating with it some of the monastic buildings. The modern mansion was built by Edward, Lord Leigh, about the middle of last century. A considerable portion of the ancient dwelling-house has been preserved. Lady Alice Leigh, the wife of Sir Thomas, founded a range of almshouses for ten poor people— five men and five women, unmarried. Sir Thomas Leigh, great-grandson of the first Sir Thomas, was

created a baron of the realm by Charles I. for his
faithful service. The line of the first Lord Leigh
terminated about the beginning of the present century.
The title was, however, revived in 1835, in the
person of Chandos Leigh, Esq., who was created Baron
Leigh of Stoneleigh, and whose son is its present
possessor.

The VILLAGE, which is richly embosomed in wood,
is situated on the bank of the small river Sow, a little
above its junction with the Avon. The *almshouses*,
already referred to, are kept in a state of efficiency and
neatness, due, we believe, to the benevolent attention
of the present Lady Leigh.

The *Church* is large and picturesque, and contains
many remains of its original Norman architecture.
The highly-enriched doorway is a fine specimen of the
Norman style, and the architectural decorations of the
chancel, discovered in the course of alterations, and
judiciously preserved, are of the same order. The
church contains several monuments to members of the
Leigh family. The most important of these is a
marble altar-tomb, erected by the Duchess Dudley
(daughter of Sir Thomas Leigh, and wife of Sir Robert
Dudley, son of the Earl of Leicester, who received the
title of Duke from the Emperor Ferdinand II.), to herself and her daughter. It bears their recumbent figures
beneath a canopy. When her husband went abroad on
failing to get his legitimacy acknowledged, the Lady
Alicia remained in England. Sir Robert did not go
alone on his travels ; for, as Dugdale informs us,
"Elizabeth, the daughter of Sir Charles Southwell, a
very beautiful lady, went with him into Italy, in the
habit of a page, and there married him." The Lady
Alice died at the age of ninety. Sir Robert never
returned to England. He is described as a man of

great learning, as well as accomplished in knightly achievements.

In the chancel there is a curious old font, said to have been brought from Maxtoke, adorned with the carved figures of saints.

The ABBEY, the seat of Lord Leigh, is delightfully situated in a fine park, through which the Avon flows, with its usual beauty and more than its usual breadth. As has been said, it occupies the site of the ancient abbey. Of that edifice a very interesting relic still remains, in the old gateway near the house. It was erected by Robert de Hockele, the sixteenth abbot, who died in 1349, and has on an escutcheon over the arch the arms of Henry II., the founder of the abbey. The family mansion has undergone changes and improvements at different times; and it is enough to say that it is admirably in keeping with the noble park in which it stands. The gardens and pleasure-grounds are laid out with great taste.*

The various apartments correspond in their style and attractiveness with the beauty of the exterior. The *Hall* is a splendid room, supported by eight Corinthian pillars, four on either side, and ornamented with alto-relievos of the labours of Hercules. The *Chapel*, which is profusely ornamented with plaster-work, contains a fine altar-piece of white marble, with a painting of the Descent from the Cross. Among the valuable paintings with which this mansion is adorned, are portraits of Lord and Lady Leigh, by Hayter; Henry VIII., a valuable picture, by Holbein; Lord Byron, by Philips; Charles I., by Vandyke; the King and Queen of Bohemia, by Gerard Horst; two old portraits of monks, probably inmates of the abbey; and specimens of Albert Dürer, Rembrandt, Cuyp, Wouvermans, Teniers, etc.

* There is a footpath across the fields from Kenilworth Station to the Abbey.

The *Park* contains many magnificent oaks, and is well stocked with deer and other game. A handsome bridge of one arch across the Avon forms a fine approach to the house.

WHITNASH, a village about a mile to the south of Leamington, has an ancient church with two old brasses and some other monuments in the interior. There is a rather interesting old house, with timber and plaster front in the village. A visit to Whitnash may be combined with one to Bishop's Tachbrook, previously described.

MANCETTER.

In the VICINITY OF ATHERSTONE.

RUINS OF PRIORY—KENILWORTH.

NUNEATON AND ITS VICINITY.

INNS.—*Newdegate Arms, Castle, Bull.* From Birmingham, 29 miles; Coventry, 10; Rugby, 14; Tamworth, 13.

NUNEATON is a market town of considerable antiquity.
A convent of nuns was founded here, in the reign of
King Stephen, by Robert, Earl of Leicester, who
liberally endowed it. At the Dissolution the site was
granted to Marmaduke Constable, who still lies in
effigy in the parish church. The population of the
town amounts to nearly 5000. Silk in 1861 gave
occupation to 1758 women and 562 men; and ribbons
to 398 women and 240 men in the town and neighbourhood. Coal is plentiful in the district, and employs 212 men.

The town is well built, though somewhat irregular.
The CHURCH is a handsome building in the Decorated
style, with a lofty tower, containing a number of good
monuments. A well-endowed FREE SCHOOL, founded
in the reign of Edward VI., is the only other public
building calling for notice.

The ABBEY stands in a field about two or three
hundred yards to the south of the Midland station.
Its remains are small, consisting of part of the arches
which supported the central tower of the Abbey Church,
with a few other fragments. From records still in
existence it appears that this church was built early in
the reign of Henry III.

From Nuneaton the tourist may conveniently visit
Arbury Hall and Astley Castle.

ARBURY HALL is rather more than a mile from the
Stockingford * station. This fine mansion is on the

* STOCKINGFORD is a small hamlet, possessing a church which is
mostly modern. There is a circular doorway in the tower.

site of a monastery, founded for monks of the order of St. Augustine in the reign of Henry II., and suppressed, like all other institutions, in the reign of Henry VIII. The site and possessions being purchased, in the reign of Queen Elizabeth, by Sir Edmund Anderson, that gentleman, as Dugdale informs us, " totally demolished the whole fabric of the house and church, built out of their ruins a fair structure, in a quadrangular form, and having done so, passed it away, in exchange for other property, to John Newdegate, Esq." Sir Roger Newdegate, a descendant of the last-named person, by his numerous alterations and improvements, gave the mansion its present elegant appearance. Arbury Hall has been called the " Strawberry Hill of Warwickshire." Like Horace Walpole's famous villa, it has been altered to the Gothic style, the architectural style and ornaments being copied from ancient ecclesiastical edifices of that order. It stands in the centre of a noble park, finely ornamented with wood and water. The approach on the north is through a magnificent avenue. The four fronts are different in design, but each is consistent with the plan of the whole. The principal apartments are exquisitely ornamented in the Gothic style. The ceiling of the *Dining-Room* is enriched with pendant ornaments, and supported by taper pillars. This room is further adorned with fine casts from the antique, under elaborate Gothic canopies, and with the top of a Roman sarcophagus. The *Drawing-Room* contains several whole-length family portraits, and the ceiling is adorned with armorial bearings. The *Saloon* has a ceiling which is an elaborate imitation of that of Henry VII.'s Chapel, Westminster, the finest of the kind in this country. The large bay window of this apartment looks into the gardens, which are extensive and tastefully laid out. A room adjoining the Saloon contains a very curious and interesting painting, an engraving of which is given in Dugdale's "Antiquities of Warwickshire." It represents the achievements of John de Astley, and consists of two central compartments and eight smaller ones, four on each side, and displays two combats (in both of which he was victorious), one in Paris, in 1438, with a French knight, in the presence of Charles VII., the other in London, in 1446, before Henry VI., with a Spanish champion. This ancient painting was removed to Arbury from Astley Castle, which is also the property of the Newdegates of Arbury.

ASTLEY CASTLE, about a mile from Arbury, was long the seat of the ancient and powerful family of Astley. One member of this house fell at Evesham, fighting against Henry III.; two were taken prisoners at Bannockburn; and John de Astley, the subject of the old painting described above, was knighted by King Henry VI., and rewarded with a pension, and subsequently with the order of Knight of the Garter, for his military services. Sir William de Astley was the last male of the family. With his daughter the estate passed to the family of Grey. Sir John Grey, a member of this family, was the husband of Elizabeth Woodville, who, after his death, became the Queen of Edward IV. Thomas, son of Sir John and Elizabeth Woodville, was, through his mother's influence, created Marquis of Dorset. Henry, his grandson, third Marquis, married Frances, eldest daughter of Charles Brandon, Duke of Suffolk, by Mary, daughter of Henry VII., and Queen Dowager of France. Thus was brought into the Grey family the claim of Mary to the English throne, after the death of Edward VI., in the failure of the male issue of the Brandons. This Marquis was raised to the dukedom of Suffolk by right

of his wife on the failure of heirs-male. The result of
the unfortunate insurrection of the Duke of Suffolk and
Sir Thomas Wyatt, with the view of raising Suffolk's
daughter, Lady Jane Grey, to the throne, is sufficiently
well known. For some time after its suppression he
lurked in concealment in the woods of Astley, but was
at length betrayed by a forest-keeper for the sake of
the reward offered for his apprehension. He was
executed on Tower Hill, 1554.

The castle is surrounded by a moat overshadowed
with fine trees. The remains of the original structure
are picturesquely mantled with ivy. For a long time
this interesting building was much neglected, being
used only as a farm-house. It was, however, afterwards carefully fitted up, and is now an elegant and
aristocratic residence. The castle contains some old
armour, and several paintings, among which is a portrait of the last Duke of Suffolk.

The *Church*, though scarcely half its original size, is
a building of some interest. It contains several ancient
monuments considerably defaced.

RUGBY.

HOTELS.—*George, Eagle, Royal, Three Horse-shoes.*

From Birmingham, 30 miles ; Leamington, 15 ; Coventry, 11¼ ; London, 83 ;
York, 137.

RUGBY is situated on a slope above the south side of
the Avon, not far from the eastern border of the
county. In Domesday Book it is called *Rocheberie ;*
roche, as Dugdale remarks, signifying a rock or quarry
of stone, and *berie*, a court or habitation of note.
Whatever may have been its consequence in earlier
times, it seems to have been of little importance at the

Conquest, when it belonged to Turchill de Warwick. Near the town is an eminence called Castle Mount, from its having been formerly the site of a castle. Dugdale is of opinion that this was one of the fortresses erected by King Stephen when threatened with invasion by the Empress Matilda (daughter of Henry I. of England, and widow of Henry V., emperor of Germany), whose crown he had usurped. The castle was probably demolished by order of Henry II.

The town is well built, and exhibits many signs of growth and prosperity. In 1831 the population amounted to only 2501; while it now amounts to 8385, the inhabited houses numbering 1527. There are no manufactures of importance. Important fairs are held here for the sale of horses, cattle, and sheep.

RUGBY SCHOOL was founded in 1567 by Laurence Sheriff, a grocer of London, a native of the neighbouring village of Brownsover, who endowed this school and some alms-houses with estates in the neighbourhood of Rugby and London. It was not till 1653 that the full endowment was obtained. The original building was taken down in the beginning of this century and the present structure erected. It is in the Elizabethan style, from a proper regard to the period of its original erection and the memory of its founder, and is constructed of white brick, the angles, cornices, and dressings being of Attleborough stone. The principal front, which is towards the south, extends 220 feet. Of Rugby School as it was in the days of Dr. Arnold, a graphic account has been supplied in "Tom Brown's School Days." It has been recently greatly improved and extended. New Schoolrooms with their various offices were built in 1868, and form two sides of the Quadrangle, of which the chapel and the "Old Big School" fill up the other two. The accommodation is ample, and includes a sick-house, a covered racquet court, and a collection of Eton five courts, a cricket pavilion, a school workshop, and a gymnasium. The chapel, with the exception of two bays and the porch at the west end, has been entirely rebuilt. The structure now extends to 132 feet in length. Double-transepts have been thrown out on each side, and a tower 105 feet high and 22½ feet square, terminating in an octagonal lantern, with a timber spire, has been built above the choir space. The east window, which originally belonged to a monastery in Flanders, and was gifted to the chapel by Dr. Arnold, has been fitted into the new edifice. Its stained glass, by Albert Durer, represents the Adoration of the Wise Men. Four windows have been filled up in memory of the late Dr. Cotton, bishop of Calcutta.* Various memorial windows of the old chapel have been preserved and inserted in the new one. Two, called respectively the " Crimean " and the " Indian," have been erected in honour of

* Rugby School can boast of a long list of illustrious men educated within its walls. Among the twenty-five gallant Rugbeians commemorated in the windows mentioned above are Sir J. W. Adams, who was killed at Inkermann, and Hodson of " Hodson's Horse," who fell in the Indian mutiny. Of an earlier period are Field-Marshall Lord Combermere ; Major-General John Mansel, and his son Major J. C. Mansel—the former of whom was killed in 1794, while leading his heavy brigade to storm a French battery, and the latter wounded and taken prisoner in the same charge ; Sir Ralph Abercrombie, the victor of Alexandria ; Major-General Skerratt, who fell while leading the storming party of Bergen-op-Zoom in 1814, and General the Earl of Carysford, who distinguished himself in the same bloody struggle ; Colonel Miller, who led the Enniskillens at Waterloo ; and Captains Holbeche and Biddulph, who charged side by side with him. Many other noted names of soldiers might be mentioned did our space allow of it. In the navy occur the names of Admiral F. W. Fane, and Captains Lord Proby and the Hon. Harry Gray.

There is a goodly array of men of letters :—Edward Cave, originator of " The Gentlemen's Magazine ;" Thomas Carte, the historian ; John Parkhurst, author of a valuable Hebrew Lexicon, and

Rugbeians who fell in the Crimean and Indian wars. A marble slab in the pavement marks the grave of Dr. Arnold. Several mural and other monuments have been erected in the interior.

Among the eminent head-masters of Rugby School, Dr. Arnold is universally held in the highest estimation. He was elected in 1827, and—though appointed Professor of Modern History at Oxford, 1841—continued at Rugby until his death in 1842. Among his successors may be named the Rev. Dr. Archibald Campbell Tait, Archbishop of Canterbury ; the Rev. Frederic Temple, D.D., Bishop of Exeter, etc.

The annual revenue of the school from its endowments amounts to about £5650, of which sum £255 : 3s. are bestowed on the tenants of Lawrence Sheriff's almshouses. The total sum divisible between the headmaster and the assistant-masters is a little over £20,000. The head-master's salary from all sources is said to average £2957. The salaries of the classical assistants range from £1617 to £340 (five having over £1400, and the eight remaining ranging downwards from £870). The mathematical assistants have £1412, £647, and £586 ; and the modern language assistants £1234 and £286.

The usual number of boys in the school is from 400

other works ; William Bray, a distinguished antiquarian, joint author with Oliver Manning of the "History of Surrey ;" Walter Savage Landor ; Thomas Hughes, author of "Tom Brown's School Days"— an interesting and faithful account of Rugby under the late Dr. Arnold. Four Rugbeians have become bishops—Dr. Legge and Dr. Bagot of Oxford, Dr. Otter of Chichester, and Dr. James of Calcutta ; and from the lengthy list of clergymen it is sufficient to select the names of Archdeacon Churton and Canon Stanley. Among physicians few names of their time will rank higher than those of Sir Henry Halford and Sir Charles Locock. In the legal profession we find the names of Mr. Justice Coltman, Mr. Justice Vaughan, and Sir Roundell Palmer. To the list of eminent Rugbeians must also be added the name of W. C. Macready, the celebrated actor.

to 500. Of these 50 or 60 are upon the foundation. About 70 pupils board in the school-house under the superintendence of the head-master ; the others board with the different masters, or with friends in the town.

No boy above sixteen can enter, unless qualified for the upper fifth form ; and no boy is allowed to remain after completing his nineteenth year. The necessary expenses of a boy attending Rugby School amount to £5 : 5s. entrance-fees, and £90 : 18 : 9 for board and education annually. There are certain optional charges for private tuition in mathematics (£10 : 10s. annually, entrance £1 : 1s.) ; modern languages and laboratory instructions (each £6 : 6s.) ; natural philosophy (£5 : 5s.) ; drawing, music, drill (each £4 : 4s.) ; and dancing (variable). A foundationer pays about £19 less than the above charges ; and, should he not board at the school, there is the further deduction of the boarding-house charge (£58 : 14 : 3).

The management is vested in twelve trustees, who are gentlemen connected with the district. The benefit of the foundation was originally confined to Rugby and the four neighbouring parishes. In 1777, how-ever, an Act of Parliament was obtained to extend it to places within five miles.

In the same year seven exhibitions of the annual value of £40 each were established. By 1826 these exhibitions had increased both in number and in value, there being then twenty-one of the yearly value of £60 each, tenable for seven years at either Oxford or Cambridge. Important alterations were in 1854 made in the arrangements connected with these ex-hibitions. Under the sanction of the Charity Com-missioners, the term of their tenure was limited to four years, and their value varied to correspond with the varying merits of the candidates to whom they are awarded. Five of these are now given annually, the highest being £80, and the lowest £40. They are open to the competition of all members of the school without preference to any part of the United Kingdom. The exhibitions are awarded to the boys most proficient in divinity, classics, mathematics, and history. The examiners are appointed by the vice-chancellors of the universities. There are also scholarships of £30 and £20 for three years instituted by the masters. The system of fagging exists in this school, but to a limited extent, and under proper control.

St. Matthew's Church is near the centre of the town, and is more venerable than elegant in its aspect, having undergone a great deal of tasteless patching and alteration. There are no monuments of importance in the interior. It is said that this church was partly built of stone taken from the ruins of the castle already referred to. In the churchyard may be seen some quaint epitaphs.

Trinity Church, a tasteful modern structure, stands on the border of the town on the way to the station. It consists of nave, aisles, transepts, chancel, with aisle on the south side, and a handsome tower rising from the intersection. The interior is very elegantly fitted up. The east and west windows are Decorated, the former being filled with stained glass. The reredos under the east window is a fine piece of illumination and painting, representing the Lamb of God and emblematical figures of the four Evangelists. The south transept has a large circular window, Decorated in its upper part, and below it three early English windows, all filled with painted glass. The north transept has a large Decorated window of four lights. The pulpit and font are both of stone, elegantly sculptured.

Lawrence Sheriff's Almshouses are opposite the

parish church. The original endowment was for the benefit of four poor men, two of Rugby, and two of Brownsover ; but the number of persons benefited by the charity has been increased with the increase of the revenues.

RUGBY also possesses a *Charity School* and *Alms-houses*, founded and endowed by Richard Elborow, Esq., in 1707.

VICINITY OF RUGBY.

BILTON is about 2 miles from Rugby. On the picturesque village-green may be seen the stocks, in excellent condition. Beside them is part of a stone pillar, much defaced—perhaps the pillory.

The *Church* is a handsome edifice, with a graceful spire. The daughter of Joseph Addison is interred in the chancel, but without any monumental inscription.

Bilton Hall has been rendered classic by the residence of Addison, who purchased it and the estate in 1711, in anticipation of his marriage with the Countess Dowager of Warwick. On his taking up his residence here the poet Somervile addressed to him a complimentary epistle in verse, in which the following couplet occurs :—

" When panting virtue her last efforts made,
You brought your Clio to the virgin's aid."

Dr. Johnson remarks that this couplet is " written with the most exquisite delicacy of praise ; it exhibits one of those happy strokes that are seldom attained."

Addison was married in 1716. The union was not, a happy one, owing to the proud and irritable temper of the Countess. He died in London in 1719, and was buried in Westminster Abbey. He left one child, a daughter, who resided at Bilton Hall, and died unmarried at the age of 79.

The mansion is spacious but irregular. In construction it is of different periods, the oldest and largest portion bearing marks of the style of architecture common about the time of James I. The remainder of the building, being of the style which prevailed in the beginning of the eighteenth century, may have been erected by Addison himself.

The gardens retain much of the old formal character, being laid out principally in straight lines. A long walk on the north side is called "Addison's Walk," there being a tradition that this was his favourite retreat.

CHURCH LAWFORD is a small village, 4 miles north-west from Rugby. The *Church* has some Norman work. This parish is worthy of the attention of the geologist on account of the discovery in the diluvial deposit of many bones of the elephant and rhinoceros, as well as some of the hyæna. "The diluvial bed," observes Dr. Buckland, "is immediately incumbent on stratified beds of lias, and is composed of a mixture of various pebbles, sand, and clay, in the lower regions of which, where the clay predominates, the bones are found at the depth of fifteen feet from the surface. They are not in the least mineralised, and have lost almost nothing of their weight or animal matter."

A short distance from Church Lawford is the hamlet of NEWNHAM REGIS, or KING'S NEWNHAM, where there is a weak chalybeate spring, extolled for its virtues by both Camden and Speed, and still in some request.

At LITTLE LAWFORD, in the parish of NEWBOLD-ON-AVON (the church of which has some monuments to members of the Baughton family), about a mile from King's Newnham, stood till 1790 a residence of the Baughtons. This mansion was the scene of the murder of Sir Theodosius Baughton by his brother-in-law,

K

Captain John Donellan, in 1780. This murder, which excited a great sensation at the time, is the foundation of one of Mr. G. P. R. James's novels.

CHURCH OVER, 4½ miles north-east from Rugby, has near it a large tumulus, by the side of the Watling Street, which here forms the eastern boundary of the county. There can be little doubt that the tumulus is Roman.* The *Church* has in its interior several monuments of the Dixwell family.

CLIFTON, two miles east from Rugby, was the birthplace, in 1686, of Thomas Carte, a distinguished antiquary and historian. He died in 1754. The *Church* is a good building, well situated.

The hamlet of NEWTON, about a mile distant, was the birthplace (1691), of Edward Cave, the designer and original publisher of the " Gentleman's Magazine." The magazine, which was commenced in 1728, and at once achieved a remarkable success, is now the oldest in the kingdom. Cave died in 1754.

DUNCHURCH, two miles to the south of Rugby, possesses a handsome *Church* in the Decorated style, with a well-proportioned tower. There is an ancient porch on the south side of the building. The east window was restored and filled with fine painted glass, about thirty years ago, by Lord John Scott, the proprietor of the manor. The village also contains a *Free School*, founded in 1707 by Francis Baughton, of Causton House, in this neighbourhood; and *Almshouses*, founded by Thomas Newcomb, printer to Charles II., James II., and William III.

WILLOUGHBY, three miles from Dunchurch and five from Rugby, possesses a saline spring, which is much

* Two miles farther south on the same road, but on the Northamptonshire side of the boundary, are the extensive remains of the Roman station of *Tripontium* (Dowbridge, near Lilbourne).

resorted to. Roman coins, Mosaic pavements, and other relics, have been discovered here from time to time.

SHOTTERY.

In the VICINITY OF STRATFORD-ON-AVON.

SOLIHULL AND ITS VICINITY.

INNS: *George, Lion, Mason's Arms.*
From Birmingham, 7 miles; Warwick, 14½.

SOLIHULL is a pretty, quiet country town, picturesquely irregular in arrangement, and pleasant in situation, but presenting nothing remarkable in its architecture. Before the Conquest it bore the name of Uverlei or Wolverley, and possessed a church, no vestiges of which now remain.

The CHURCH, the most important building, is large and handsome, consisting of nave, aisles, chancel, transepts, and spire. It is of different dates and styles, but possesses sufficient features of interest to repay examination. The spire is a not very happy imitation of the original one, which was blown down in 1745. A chantry, now used as a vestry, was built in the reign of Edward I. Beneath it there is a groined crypt. The principal monument sets forth in a long Latin inscription the history and virtues of the family of Holbeche.

Solihull possesses several good schools. It was here that the poets Shenstone and Jago received their education under the tuition of the Rev. Mr. Crumpton; and here commenced that friendship which lasted throughout their lives.

At Solihull the tourist is within walking distance of Knowle and Temple Balsall, which may be visited in the same excursion. Two miles to the north is the hamlet of OLTON, where are the extensive earthworks and moat of a castle, said to have been erected by Ralph de Limesie, one of the ancient possessors of the manor of Solihull. There are similar traces of a castle built by the Arden family near HAMPTON-IN-ARDEN, $3\frac{1}{2}$ miles distant, to the east.

KNOWLE is three miles from Solihull, on the War-wick road. The country through which the road lies is in some places very picturesque, this being particularly the case in the neighbourhood of Malvern Hall, which is passed on the right shortly after leaving Solihull. Knowle is a small and irregular, but pleasant village. Its *Church*, a building of considerable beauty and antiquity, is well worthy of a visit. The style and ornaments of the exterior argue a considerable antiquity, but it is the interior which chiefly interests the visitor. Among the objects deserving of attention are—a splendid carved oak screen, several *sedilia* within embellished recesses, and some oak stalls with grotesque carvings. In the entrance porch the poor's box is recommended to notice by a somewhat curious allegorical group, the gift, as an inscription states, of Antony Holbeche, 1717. "The Midland Counties" Asylum for Idiots, founded in 1872, forms one of the most striking erections at Knowle.

TEMPLE BALSALL is about a mile and a half from Knowle. This is a place of great interest to the antiquarian, its old church remaining nearly in the same state in which it was left by its founders, the Knights Templars. Balsall, or Temple Balsall, is a hamlet and chapelry in the extensive parish of Hampton-in-Arden. In the reign of Henry II., it was bestowed by Roger de Mowbray upon the Knights Templar. These re-ligious knights originally had their residence near the

temple of Jerusalem, and devoted themselves to the
protection of Christian pilgrims who visited the Holy
Land. Coming to England in the reign of Henry II.,
they built their principal mansion in London, where it
is still known by the name of the Temple. The
knights obtained valuable grants of land in various
parts of this county, as well as elsewhere. They erected
a church in this place, and a preceptory, or cell, to
their principal mansion. The church is in good preservation; and part of the hall is incorporated with a
barn, and encased in brick. The Knights Templars
were formally dissolved in the reign of Edward II.,
and their estates bestowed on the Knights Hospitallers,
who remained in possession of them till the Dissolution.
Queen Elizabeth bestowed the manor on her favourite,
Robert Dudley, Earl of Leicester. Lady Catherine
Leveson, Leicester's grand-daughter, by her will devoted
the manor to the foundation of a hospital for indigent
females—a charitable institution now in a prosperous
condition.

The *Church*, an admirable specimen of the Decorated
style, is 104 feet long, 39 wide, and 57 high, and is
an entire and undivided apartment, without aisles or
galleries. The chancel differs from the body of the
church merely by being three steps above its level.
The great east window is very lofty, and consists of
five lights, the mullions being adorned with exquisite
carvings. On either side of the church are three
windows, enriched with beautiful tracery, the two in
the centre being the finest. There is also a very lofty
window of five lights at the west end, surmounted by a
fine marigold window of twelve compartments. The
entrance to the church is under this window; and here,
below the cornice, is a row of ten heads of excellent
workmanship. In the chancel there are three sedilia,

displaying some delicately-carved foliage. An octagonal piscina, now placed in the centre of the church,
is used as a font. The exterior is interesting. The
present roof is evidently lower than the original, and
the square bell-tower at the north-east corner is,
partly at least, more modern than the rest of the building. The mouldings of the doorways and windows,
and surmounting the base tablet, display much expres-
sion and beauty.

The *Hall*, or *Refectory*, of the Knights Templars
(near the church), though now reduced to a large barn,
still contains some interesting traces of its ancient
possessors. It has been 140 feet long, and seems to
have been framed entirely of timber. An apartment
called the Parlour is adorned with emblazoned shields,
probably taken from the roof of the hall, or of some
ancient building now destroyed.

The *Almshouses*, endowed by Lady Catherine Leveson, are near the church. Agreeably to the will of its
founder, this institution is devoted to the reception of
indigent widows or unmarried females of fair character.

STONELEIGH.

In the VICINITY OF LEAMINGTON.

STRATFORD-ON-AVON.

HOTELS : *The Shakspere; The Falcon.*
From Warwick, 13¼ miles (by rail); 8 by road; Birmingham, 20½;
Oxford, 47¼; London, 111.

STRATFORD-ON-AVON,* the birthplace of Shakspere, is situated on the south-western border of the county, on a gentle ascent from the river Avon. Attractive as a quiet and pleasant old English town, it is naturally in the birthplace and grave of Shakspere that all interest is here concentrated—an interest which yearly draws hither crowds of travellers from every part of the civilised world. The " visitors' books" in Shak-

---

* The name is derived from the highway (London to Birmingham) on which it stands ; *stræte* or *stret* being the Saxon word for a road, and *ford* evidently referring to the passage through the Avon.

spere's house, in Stratford church, and in the principal
hotels, contain many of the most distinguished names
in this country and America, and not a few of those
most famous on the Continent. Before passing on to
these, however, it may be interesting to notice that so
far back as three centuries before the Conquest a
monastery existed here, which remained under the
bishops of Worcester till the year 1549, when it was
made over to John Dudley, Earl of Warwick, in exchange for some lands in Worcestershire. That nobleman was beheaded for high treason, and ultimately
the manor of Stratford was conferred by Charles II.
on the Earl of Dorset and Middlesex, in whose family
it, and the patronage of the vicarage, still remain.
During the Parliamentary wars an unimportant conflict
took place in the neighbourhood, in which Lord Brooke
first put the royalists to flight, but had in his turn to
retire on their returning in great force, with Henrietta
Maria, queen of Charles I., at their head. The queen
on this occasion resided at New Place, the former abode
of Shakspere, and the home, at this time, of Shakspere's
grand-daughter. The only other notable events in the
history of Stratford are the famous jubilee of 1769,*

---

* The idea of the jubilee originated with David Garrick, who, on
being asked to give a benefit at his theatre for the raising of funds
for the erection of a statue of Shakspere in the niche in the north
front of the town hall, just rebuilt (1768), entered into the proposal
with enthusiasm. The idea of celebrating a jubilee at Stratford
occurred to him ; and being thoroughly approved of by the corporation, it was fixed for the autumn of the following year. Prepara-
tions of the most magnificent kind were made for the festival,
which took place in September 1769. Stratford and the surrounding villages could scarcely afford accommodation to the multitudes
of persons of rank and genius who repaired hither. The jubilee
lasted three days. In a magnificent amphitheatre, erected on the
banks of the Avon, capable of holding at least a thousand spectators,
the company dined together, and held assemblies, a masquerade, and
other entertainments.

originated and directed by David Garrick; the purchase of Shakspere's house for the British nation in 1847; and the tercentenary jubilee held in 1864.*

The particulars of the life of WILLIAM SHAKSPERE, so far as it has been possible to ascertain them, are too well known to require to be recounted here. It is sufficient for our purpose to mention the leading dates and facts. He was born in the little house in Henley Street on the 23d April 1564. About the year 1571 he was sent to the endowed Grammar School of his native town, where there can be no doubt he received a good education. That he was a precocious and adventurous youth is evidenced by the fact that he married in his eighteenth year, the licence being dated 28th November 1582. Anne Hathaway, Shakspere's wife, was eight years older than her husband. Susanna, the poet's favourite daughter, was born in 1583. The following year, twins, a son and a daughter, named Hamnet and Judith, were added to his family. In 1585 or 1586, Shakspere, having excited against himself the anger of Sir Thomas Lucy by his poaching adventures and his scurrilous verses, went to London, where, in 1589, we find him a joint-proprietor of Blackfriars Theatre. His progress to fame and fortune was rapid and uninterrupted Malone assigns his

* The three-hundredth anniversary of Shakspere's birthday was by common consent celebrated throughout Great Britain and her colonies, and indeed more or less throughout the civilised world. Special prominence was naturally given to the event at Stratford, where the jubilee was in many of its features analogous to that of 1769. The late Earl of Carlisle presided at the banquet, and delivered an eloquent address. The proceeds of the jubilee, which were to have been devoted to the erection of a monument to Shakspere and the founding of scholarships in the grammar school, unfortunately did not meet its expenditure. The idea of the monument (a very unnecessary thing anywhere, most of all in Stratford) is not, however, abandoned, and will probably be accomplished at no very distant date.

first play to so early a date as 1589, while other commentators are of opinion that his first attempt was made in 1592. In 1597 he purhased New Place, in his native town, and again in 1605 he made another considerable purchase of property. It is not precisely known at what date he terminated his connection with the stage, but probably it was about the time of the latter of these purchases. The concluding years of his life were spent in plenty. He died in his house, New Place, on his birthday, April 23, 1616, in the fifty-third year of his age   On April 25th he was buried in the chancel of Stratford church. His son Hamnet had died in 1596, and his daughters Susanna and Judith inherited his property, the former receiving the larger share, including New Place. Susanna, in 1607, married Dr. Hall—" medicâ celeberrimus arte," as his tombstone tells us. She had only one child, Elizabeth, who, by her second marriage, became the wife of Sir John Barnard. On the death of Lady Barnard, without issue, the property was in part sold, and in part bequeathed to Thomas Hart, the grandson of Shakspere's sister. Judith, Shakspere's second daughter, married Thomas Quincy, a substantial tradesman, styled " gentleman " in the Stratford Register. She left no children.

Among other notable persons born in this town may be mentioned John Stratford, archbishop of Canterbury in the reign of Edward III., who died 1348 ; Ralph Stratford, his kinsman, who was consecrated bishop of London in 1339, and died in 1355 ; Robert Stratford, brother of the archbishop, bishop of Chichester, and chancellor of Oxford and of all England, died 1362 ; and Hugh Clopton, mercer, and lord mayor of London, builder of the stone bridge over the Avon at Stratford.

The population of Stratford, at the census 1871, was 3863, and the inhabited houses 817. These numbers exhibit an increase of both persons and houses since the year 1851—a growth probably to be attributed to the extension of railway communication and the consequent improvement of trade. Stratford had, in point of commerce and population, been almost at a standstill for many years. The woollen manufacture, for which it was formerly noted, is now entirely gone ; and the malting trade has considerably diminished. The occupations of the inhabitants are mostly agricultural. The town is well built, and still possesses a few picturesque old houses.

SHAKSPERE'S HOUSE.—The birthplace of Shakspere is naturally the first spot in Stratford to which the tourist turns his steps. It is a small building, of humble but ancient appearance, situated in Henley Street. Originally an old faded inscription on a board over the projecting window on the ground-floor bore this inscription—" The immortal Shakspere was born in this house ;" but among other improvements this signboard has been removed. The house, humble though it may appear now, must have been one of some importance at the time of its erection. Like many other ancient houses, it was subdivided, though the exact date when this was done has not been clearly ascertained. One half of the building was known as the " Maidenhead Inn" as early as 1642. Its name was subsequently changed into the " Swan," and more recently into the " Swan and Maidenhead." The other half was long used as a butcher's shop, and was divided, previously to 1807, into two parts, the shop and a dwelling-house. It is the half originally used as a butcher's shop which, according to the universal tradition of the town, and in the opinion of almost all writers on the subject, was the birthplace of William Shakspere. The early history of this property has been investigated with great diligence by the various commentators of Shakspere. It descended to Shakspere from his father. In his last will and testament, the poet bequeathed " the house, with the appurtenances, in Stratford, wherein she dwelleth, for her natural life," to his sister Joan, the wife of William Hart. This evidently refers to the part of the building subsequently used as a butcher's shop. The whole property was conveyed by his will to his eldest daughter Susanna Hall, whose daughter, Lady Barnard, dying without issue, left it to the descendants of William Hart, with whom it remained till 1806, when it was sold to Thomas Court, the landlord of the Maidenhead. The birthplace of Shakspere was again exposed for sale in 1847, when, in consequence of a powerful appeal made to the feelings of the nation by the public press, prompt and vigorous measures were taken to raise funds to secure for the nation this inestimable relic. On the evening preceding the day of sale, the national agents offered a bidding of £3000 ; and on the day of sale it was eventually knocked down to them for a little more than that sum. Thus, on the 16th of September 1847 Shakspere's house became the property of the *British nation*. The trustees elected to take charge of the property were, the late Earl of Carlisle (then Lord Morpeth), the late Mr. Amyot, Mr. Payne Collier, and Dr. Thomson of Stratford. In connection with the history of Shakspere's house it is perhaps worthy of note that John Shakespeare, Esq. of Langley-Priory, near Ashby-de-la-Zouch (who thought he was related collaterally to the poet), devised £3000 to secure the preservation of the house, but the bequest was annulled by law. This object has, however, been accomplished by a Shakespeare Fund, established 1861

SHAKSPERE'S HOUSE (CIRCA 1807), PREVIOUS TO ALTERATIONS.

The admission fee is 6d. each person for the house, and 6d. for the museum. It is open every day, except Sunday, from 9 till 7. In winter it closes at dusk.

On entering Shakspere's house, the tourist first examines the apartment on the ground-floor, which has a very ancient and somewhat dreary aspect. It has the ample fireplace of the olden times. The stranger seldom lingers long to inspect this apartment, and the small room that it opens into behind, for he is informed that in the room up-stairs, reached by a wooden winding staircase, Shakspere was born. It is little changed from the time when the poet first opened his eyes on the light within it. Everything is ancient, and everything is preserved with the most scrupulous care. The furniture is old, but evidently not so old as Shakspere's time; but the room itself has all the marks of the antiquity which is claimed for it. The ceiling is low and its walls rough and bare; its fireplace, too, can scarcely be of a later date than the time of Queen Elizabeth. Probably this apartment had an air of much greater comfort when it was the residence of John Shakspere and his descendants, for the walls of the higher class of houses were frequently covered with heavy arras. The walls and ceiling are dark with a million pencilled autographs. Pilgrims of all countries and all ranks have here inscribed their names; and these signatures, as Washington Irving observes in his charming paper in the "Sketch-Book," "present a simple but striking instance of the spontaneous and universal homage of mankind to the great poet of nature."* Among other names scratched on the glass

* Some lines written on the wall of this apartment by Washing-

of the window may be seen that of Sir Walter Scott. The tourist will be able to find in the "visitors' book," and on various parts of the walls where they are not yet obliterated by vulgar names, the signatures of many of the most illustrious men and women of the age. In the room adjoining that in which Shakspere was born is a fine oil-painting of the poet, presented by the late Wm. Oakes Hunt, town-clerk of Stratford. This is supposed to be a genuine portrait. A part of the house has been set apart as a *Museum* of Shaksperian relics, including everything illustrative of the life of the poet and of the time in which he lived. The bibliographical collection is general, embracing copies of the oldest folio editions of his works extant, and of all books bearing on the subject of Shaksperian literature.

The tourist, on leaving Shakspere's house, should step into the garden, which is carefully kept, and ingeniously planted with the particular flowers alluded to in the poetry of Shakspere.

STRATFORD COLLEGIATE CHURCH.—The spot which next claims the notice of the tourist is the grave of Shakspere, in the parish church. This sacred edifice, dedicated to the Holy Trinity, is picturesquely situated on the bank of the Avon. The approach to it is through a beautiful avenue of lime-trees. The church, which is of large dimensions and unusual beauty, consists of nave, aisles, transepts, and chancel, a square

ton Irving in 1821, but long ago obliterated, have been preserved by a correspondent of the London "Standard:"—

"Of mighty Shakespeare's birth the room we see,
    That where he died in vain to find we try ;
Useless the search—for all immortal he,
    And those who are immortal never die.
—WASHINGTON IRVING. Second visit, October 1821."

tower, adorned with battlements and pinnacles, and surmounted by a graceful spire rising from the intersection to a height of 163 feet. Dugdale says regarding this church that it is " of a very ancient structure, little less than the Conqueror's time, as I guess by the fabric of the tower steeple ; but part thereof besides hath been rebuilt at several times." We have the records of some of these alterations. John de Stratford, archbishop of Canterbury, rebuilt the south aisle at his own expense, in the reign of Edward III. This same prelate had, in 1332, founded a chantry in the chapel of Saint Thomas the Martyr, adjoining the south aisle. His nephew, Ralph de Stratford, bishop of London, subsequently erected a large and commodious dwelling for the residence of the chantry priests, on the west side of the churchyard. This was named the COLLEGE, whence the church presently obtained the title of *Collegiate*. At the Dissolution, in the reign of Henry VIII., the College was suppressed, like all similar foundations. The building itself, which was granted to John Dudley, Earl of Warwick, passed through several hands, until, in 1796, it came into the possession of Mr Edward Battersbee of Stratford, who pulled it down in 1799, when it was still " capacious, handsome, and strong." No remains of it are now to be seen. The act of vandalism by which Stratford was deprived of this interesting old building is exceedingly to be regretted. The College had been, since the Dissolution, the residence of various families of note, particularly of the Combes. John à Combe, Shakspere's friend, resided here, and there can be no doubt that the bard often partook of his hospitality within the building thus ruthlessly destroyed.

Other alterations were made on the church in the reigns of Edward IV. and Henry VII. The present spire was erected in 1764, and replaced a timber steeple covered with lead, and about 42 feet high, which had been taken down the preceding year. Of late years the church has undergone various minor but important improvements.

The church is in various styles; but happily the incongruity between them is not such as seriously to mar the effect of the building as a whole. The chancel is Perpendicular, possessing a good east window in this style, of seven lights. On either side it has five windows of four lights each. The transepts have two Early English windows on their east and one on their west sides. Their large windows are Decorated, and of five lights. The tower has on each side two Early English lights within a circular-headed recess, and in the course above a round window, the tracery of which is mostly gone. In the north side of the tower there is a small round-headed arch in the range below the Early English lights. The windows of the north aisle of the nave, five in number, are Decorated, the two next the transept being uniform in size and ornamentation; the third similar in style, but not so high; and the fourth still smaller, and less graceful in its tracery. The fifth window on this side has been almost obliterated by the porch. The windows of the south aisle, also, are not uniform in size or style. The three farthest west are of the same size and style, the middle one being somewhat different in its tracery; the next is nearly round-headed, with three trefoil lights rising close to its arch; the other is much smaller. There is a fine clerestory range of twelve windows on either side. The west window is of nine lights, and is a fine specimen of the Perpendicular style.

The interior of the church is in all respects worthy of the exterior. The principal entrance is by the porch at the north-west end of the church, approached by the fine avenue already mentioned. The *Nave* is separated from its aisles on either side by six pointed arches, rising from graceful hexagonal columns. Above these arches, again, are the clerestory range, both sides having twelve Decorated windows of three lights each. In the *North Aisle*, which is referred by some writers to the reign of Edward I., are some interesting monuments, chiefly of the Clopton family. These occupy the space at the east end of the aisle which was formerly a chapel dedicated to the Virgin Mary. The most ancient of the tombs is an altar-shaped one, under a pointed arch on the south side of this chapel, and having no vestige of either effigy or inscription. This is supposed to be the tomb of Sir Hugh Clopton, Lord Mayor of London in 1492, who bestowed upon Stratford its fine stone bridge. Opposite this is another altar-tomb, bearing the recumbent effigies of William Clopton, and Anne his wife. The male figure is in armour, with a lion at his feet. The magnificent tomb of George Carew, earl of Totness and baron of Clopton, and of Joice his countess, eldest daughter of William Clopton already mentioned, is between these tombs, and against the east end. The figures of the earl and his countess, fashioned of alabaster, and coloured after life, lie under a Corinthian canopy, highly ornamented. An inscription on the tomb gives an account of the services and honours of this earl. He held office under Queen Elizabeth, James I., and Charles I., and died without issue in 1629.

The *South Aisle* has also had its chapel and altar at its east end, dedicated to St. Thomas à Becket. In the wall here are three sedilia, the canopies of which were restored about twenty years ago in accordance with their original design.

In the *Transepts* there are several monuments that
may be mentioned. The south transept has an altar-
tomb against its west wall to the memory of Richard
Hill, alderman. The date of the death of this worthy
is not recorded on his tomb, but the register shows it
to have been in 1593. The inscription on this monument is in Hebrew, Greek, Latin, and English. The
English verses may be quoted :—

> Heare borne, heare lived, heare died, and buried heare,
> Lieth Richarde Hil, thrise bailif of this borrow ;
> Too matrones of good fame he married in Godes feare,
> And now releast in joi, he reasts from worldlie sorrow.
>
> Heare lieth intomb'd the corps of Richarde Hill,
> A woollen draper beeing in his time ;
> Whose virtues live, whose fame dooth flourish stil,
> Though hee desolved be to dust and slime.
> A mirror he, and paterne mai be made
> For such as shall suckcead him in that trade ;
> He did not use to sweare, to glose, eather faigne,
> His brother to defraude in barganinge ;
> Hee woold not strive to get excessive gaine
> In any cloath or other kind of thinge ;
> His servant, S. I. this trueth can testifie,
> A witness that beheld it with mi eie.

The Latin inscription to the memory of Nathaniel
Mason, an eminent attorney of this town, was composed by the poet Somervile.

The *Chancel* is regarded as the most perfect and
beautiful part of the fabric. It was erected by Thomas
Balsall, D.D., Dean of Stratford, between 1465 and
1491. Dean Balsall died in the latter year, and a
curious but sadly defaced monument in the altar shape,
within the communion-rail, marks his tomb.

But that which gives a world-wide interest to this
chancel and to the church is THE GRAVE OF SHAK-
SPERE. It is a few paces from the wall in front of his
famous monument, which is about five feet from the

ground, and nearly over Dean Balsall's tomb, already
mentioned. It is covered by a plain flagstone, and
bears the often-quoted inscription—

GOOD FREND, FOR IESVS SAKE FORBEARE,
TO DIGG THE DVST ENCLOASED HEARE ;
BLESE BE Y^E MAN Y^T SPARES THES STONES,
AND CVRST BE HE Y^T MOVES MY BONES.

Though this stone does not bear the name of Shakspere, there can be no doubt that it covers the spot
consecrated by his ashes. We have Sir William
Dugdale's testimony to this effect, in his "Antiquities
of Warwickshire," first published in 1656, only forty
years after the death of Shakspere. There are other
ancient testimonies to the effect that this is the exact
site of the poet's resting-place. There is abundant
internal evidence in the lines engraved on the tombstone that Shakspere could not have been their
author. Mr. De Quincey observes truly that they
are "below his intellect no less than his scholarship."
The *Monumental Bust*, the only really trustworthy and
original representation of the poet, is placed under an
arch, between two Corinthian columns of black marble.
The entablature contains the arms of Shakspere, and
various monumental devices. Mr. Britton gives the
following description of the bust :—"The bust is the
size of life ; it is formed out of a block of soft stone,
and was originally painted over in imitation of nature.
The hands and face were of flesh colour, the eyes of a
light hazel, and the hair and beard auburn ; the doublet
or coat was scarlet, and covered with a loose black
gown or tabard, without sleeves ; the upper part of the
cushion was green, the under half crimson, and the
tassels gilt." The poet is represented with a pen in
his right hand, and his left resting on a scroll. On

MONUMENTAL BUST.

the tablet beneath the bust are the following inscriptions :—

Jvdicio Pylivm, genio socratem, arte maronem,
terra tegit, popvlvs mæret, olympvs habet.

STAY PASSENGER, WHY GOEST THOV BY SO FAST,
READ, IF THOV CANST, WHOM ENVIOVS DEATH HATH BLAST
WITHIN THIS MONVMENT, SHAKSPERE, WITH WHOME
QVICK NATVRE DIDE; WHOSE NAME DOTH DECK Y^S TOMBE
FAR MORE THAN COST ; SITH ALL Y^T HE HATH WRITT
LEAVES LIVING ART BVT PAGE TO SERVE HIS WITT
Obiit ano Doi. 1616. Ætatis 53, die 23 Ap.

The sculptor of this monument was Gerard Johnson. The tradition of Stratford is, that it was copied from a cast after nature. It is mentioned by Digges in his verses prefixed to the first edition of Shakspere, in 1623 ; so that it must have been erected within seven years after the poet's death.* The original colours were preserved till 1793 ; when, at the request of Mr. Malone, the whole was covered with a coating of white paint. Malone's conduct in this matter has been often and deservedly condemned. We quote the severe lines which his bad taste induced a visitor to inscribe in the album :—

" Stranger, to whom this monument is shown,
Invoke the poet's curse upon Malone ;
Whose meddling zeal his barbarous taste betrays,
And daubs his tombstone as he mars his plays ! "

---

* An engraved head of Shakspere faces the title-page of an early folio edition of his works. It is by Martin Droeshout, a Dutchman, and has under it some lines by Ben Jonson, which seem to testify to its being a correct likeness—

" The figure which thou seest here put,
It was for gentle Shakspere cut ;
In which the graver had a strife
With nature, to out-do the life.
Oh ! could he but have drawn his wit
As well in brass, as he has hit
His face, the piece would then surpass
All that was ever writ in brass."

The engraving referred to resembles the Stratford bust as nearly as a picture, in the state of the art at that time, could be expected to resemble a statue. In any case, the Stratford bust has claims to be regarded an authentic likeness of our immortal bard, such as no other portrait or statue can possess.

In 1861 the white paint was removed, and the original colouring carefully restored ; so that the monument now presents the appearance it wore before Malone's ill-judged interference with it.

By the side of Shakspere, and nearer the north wall, lies his wife, Anne Hathaway, who died in 1623. Her tombstone bears the following epitaph :—

HEERE LYETH INTERRED THE BODY OF ANNE, WIFE OF WILLIAM SHAKESPEARE, WHO DEPTED THIS LIFE THE 6 DAY OF AVGV : 1623 BEING OF THE AGE OF 67 YEARES.

Vbera tu mater, tu lac, vitamq. dedisti :
Vae mihi, pro tanto munere saxa dabo.
Quam mallem Amoueat lapidem bonus Angels, orē
Exeat christi corpus imago tua :
Sed nil votA valent ; venias cito, Christe, resurget
ClausA licet tumulo mater, et AstrA petet.

On the other side is buried his favourite daughter Susanna Hall. She died in 1649, aged 66. Some verses originally inscribed on her tombstone, but obliterated to make room for the record of a certain Richard Watts, have been restored from the copy of them preserved by Dugdale. They give an engaging picture of the excellences of Shakspere's beloved daughter :—

Heere lyeth ye body of Svsanna wIfe to Iohn Hall gent : ye daughter of William Shakespeare, gent : Shee deceased ye ŋth of ȷuly A°. 1649, aged 66.

Witty above her sexe, but that's not all,
Wise to salvation was good Mistris Hall.
Something of Shakespeare was in that, but this
Wholy of him with whom she's now in blisse.
Then, Passenger, hast ne're a teare,
To weepe with her that wept with all ?
That wept, yet set her selfe to chere
Them up with comforts cordiall.
Her love shall live, her mercy spread,
When thou ha'st ner'e a teare to shed.

Here are also buried Judith, Shakspere's younger

daughter, and Dr. Hall, Susanna's husband, and Elizabeth, his only child and Shakspere's grand-daughter.

Another tomb in the chancel is deserving of particular notice. It is a splendid marble monument to the
memory of John Combe, the friend of Shakspere.
There is a tradition that this man was a great usurer ;
and some satirical lines are even recorded as having
been written on him by Shakspere. The whole story
is in itself exceedingly improbable. The majestic
figure reclining on this tomb cannot be that of a miser ;
and it is an absurd libel to suppose Shakspere guilty of
writing lines, which, it has been truly said, " would
have disgraced a Thames waterman."

The decorations and general arrangements of all
parts of the church evince the most correct taste. The
ranges of ancient stalls in the chancel are worthy of
notice on account of the grotesque carvings in wood on
the under part of the seats. The church contains a
fine organ.

Adjoining the chancel on the north side, and accessible by an ornamented doorway, was a capacious
vault, built in the plain Saxon style, supposed by some
to have been part of the ancient monastic institution.
It had formerly been used as a charnel-house, and contained an immense quantity of human bones. In 1800
the great collection of human fragments was carefully
covered over, and the building demolished.

This notice of Stratford church cannot be more appropriately concluded than by a few eloquent sentences
from Washington Irving's description, already referred
to :—" The mind refuses to dwell on anything that is
not connected with Shakspere. This idea pervades the
place : the whole pile seems but as his mausoleum.
The feelings, no longer checked and thwarted by doubt,
here indulge in perfect confidence ; other traces of him

NEW PLACE AS REPRESENTED BY IRELAND

(Said to have been copied from an old drawing by Robert Treswells, made in 1599 by order of Sir George Carew, afterwards Baron Carew of Clopton and Earl of Totness, and found in Clopton House in 1786, in the possession of Mrs. Partheriche of Clopton House, the last of the Clopton family).

may be false or dubious, but here is palpable evidence and absolute certainty."

NEW PLACE.—After visiting the two chief shrines of Stratford, the tourist will naturally turn his steps to New Place, the literary sanctum of Shakspere's later days. The mansion which existed here was purchased by him in 1597, when he was 33 years of age. It was a brick and timber building of the reign of Henry VII. "Any one," says Mr. Bellew, "who has visited Coventry, Chester, Shrewsbury, or the Mint at Bristol, will be able in his mind's eye to picture the general appearance of New Place, with its multiplied gables, its overhanging eaves, its barge-boards, etc. The house was then rather more than one hundred years old, and would probably be repaired and re-modelled ; but, whatever it was, no remnant nor draw-ing* of it remains. Here, however, it is known that he spent the latter eighteen years of his life, and com-posed the majority of his plays. Here also he died, April 23, 1616, his reputed birthday, and 53d year of his age, shortly after the house had been the scene of the wedding festivities of his daughter Judith. After this event, New Place became the property of his daughter Judith, then Mrs. Hall, from whom it passed to her only child, Lady Barnard. She dying without issue, it was sold, in 1675, to Sir Edward Walker, and thereafter passed by marriage into the Clopton family (the original owners, *circa* 1490) one of whom, Sir Hugh, pulled down Shakspere's house and built a new one in its place. This was about 1720-30, at which time therefore perished this most interesting edifice. The perpetrator of this irretrievable disaster

---

* Ireland's view given on the previous page is from his work upon the Avon, and was produced in 1814. It is unfortunately as entirely fictitious as it is unskilful in its paste-board like uniformity of frontage.

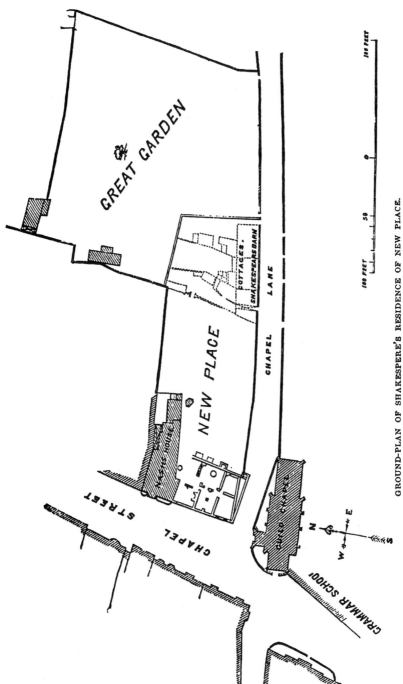

GROUND-PLAN OF SHAKESPERE'S RESIDENCE OF NEW PLACE.

died in 1751, and two years afterwards, 1753, the property was acquired by the Rev. Francis Gastrell, who, in a fit of spleen, or from some other barbarous motive, cut down the famous mulberry tree that grew in the garden, and had been planted by Shakspere's own hand. This tree was naturally a special object of curiosity, and under its boughs Sir Hugh Clopton had entertained Garrick and his friends in 1749. The greater part of the wood was bought by Thomas Sharp, a watchmaker of Stratford, who manufactured it into relics, which met with a ready and profitable sale. Among these is the Shaskpere chair, now in the possession of Baroness Burdett Coutts. Twelve rings made out of the wood were also manufactured for the Jubilee of 1769. Some years later (1759) Mr. Gastrell razed the New Place of 1720-30 to the ground, in consequence of a peevish umbrage he had taken at being too highly assessed for poors-rates. In 1759, as Mr. Wheeler relates, Gastrell "left Stratford in the dead of night, amidst the rage and curses of its inhabitants." Eventually, in 1861, the estate was secured by Mr. J. O. Halliwell Phillips by means of funds subscribed for the purpose, and it is now vested in the Corporation for behoof of the public. A few traces of the original foundations remain, and the surrounding ground is well kept.

THE CHAPEL OF THE HOLY CROSS, called also the Guild Chapel, is opposite New Place. This interesting edifice was founded in 1269 by Robert de Stratford, father of John de Stratford, archbishop of Canterbury, and Robert de Stratford, bishop of Chichester. The members of the Guild were originally of the rule of St. Austin ; but Henry IV. granted them the privilege of forming a fraternity " in honour of the Holy Cross and St. John the Baptist." Their first master was Robert de Stratford, and under his presidency the chapel was founded. No part of the original structure now remains. The chancel was rebuilt about the year 1450, and the rest of the edifice was taken down and rebuilt towards the end of the reign of Henry VII. by Sir Hugh Clopton. In 1804, during the repairs which the interior was undergoing, a series of paintings in fresco were discovered upon its walls. These were much injured, and could not be preserved on account of the nature of the repairs.* Those in the chancel represented the "Invention," or finding of the Holy Cross by the Empress Helena, mother of Constantine, and the "Exaltation" of the Cross, or Constantine's public entrance with it into Jerusalem. Over the arch at the east end of the nave were paintings of the Resurrection and the Day of Judgment; and at the west end were representations of the death of Thomas à Becket, and St. George and the Dragon. The building is in the Decorated style.

The GUILD HALL adjoins the chapel, on its south side. This building was erected at the same time as the Chapel of the Holy Cross, and for the use of the brethren of that guild, but has, like it, undergone many alterations since the date of its foundation. When this guild was suppressed at the Dissolution, the property was at first taken by the crown, but subsequently (1553) bestowed on the newly-incorporated borough of Stratford. The hall is used by the corporation for public business.

The GRAMMAR SCHOOL occupies the upper storey of the Guild Hall. This institution was founded in the reign of Henry VI. by Thomas Jolepe, a native of Stratford, and a member of the guild. The only

* They were copied in colours, and published in "Fisher's Antiquities of Warwickshire," with descriptions by Nichols.

qualifications for admission to this school are, that the boy be seven years old, able to read, and resident in Stratford.   There can be no reasonable doubt that Shakspere received his education here.   This being a "royal grammar school," the education would be of the fullest and most advanced kind.   The ignorant assertion, that Shakspere was possessed of an inferior education, has been abundantly refuted by those best qualified to pronounce a judgment on the subject.   The school-room probably presents much the same appearance that it wore when Shakspere was one of its scholars.   Part of a desk said to have been used by him is still preserved in *The Museum.*

Contiguous to the Guild Hall are the ALMSHOUSES, originally founded by the guild for twenty-four poor persons, and continued in their benevolent use by the corporation on becoming possessed of the property and revenues in 1553.   Twelve poor men and as many poor women are supported here.

The TOWN-HALL is in the High Street, not far from New Place.   It is of the Tuscan order of architecture, and was erected in 1768, on the site of an earlier building, which dated from 1633.   In 1769, the year of the jubilee, it was dedicated to Shakspere by Garrick, who presented to the corporation the fine statue of the bard which stands at the north end.   Shakspere is represented as leaning on a pillar and pointing to a scroll, on which are engraved his own beautiful lines in "Midsummer Night's Dream," descriptive of *the Poet.* The pedestal bears the equally well-known words from Hamlet—

> "Take him for all in all,
> We shall not look upon his like again."

The interior is adorned with portraits of **Shakspere,** **Garrick,** and the Duke of Dorset.

Besides the public buildings which have been de-scribed, Stratford possesses a market-house, a Wesleyan chapel, and other edifices—none, of them, however, of any interest.

SHAKSPERE'S CREST.

VICINITY OF STRATFORD-ON-AVON.

IT is scarcely necessary to say that the country round Stratford is rich in scenes of beauty and interest. Many of these, like the town itself, owe their highest attraction to their associations with Shakspere. The devout admirer of the poet will find many a spot which Shakspere's presence has made a shrine for all time. Even the scenes in this neighbourhood which no tradition associates with his name partake somewhat of the same charm ; for it was amid these scenes that Shakspere's boyish life was spent, and among them he wandered when, having achieved greatness and fortune, he returned to his native town to spend in peaceful retirement his closing years.

The AVON, independently of the associations which have made it world-famous, possesses features of quiet loveliness that would entitle it to notice. Seldom rapid, and never impetuous, it winds along through a rich and beautiful country, often expanding into broad glassy pools, and again gathering its waters into a narrower stream when it washes the base of some gentle but picturesquely-wooded acclivity. Above Stratford it is particularly remarkable for its aspect of peaceful beauty. Shakspere seems to have been referring to this, his native stream, in the following lines in " The Two Gentlemen of Verona," so accurately do they note the characteristics of the Avon :—

> " The current, that with gentle murmur glides,
> Thou know'st, being stopped, impatiently doth rage ;
> But, when his fair course is not hindered,
> He makes sweet music with the enamelled stones,
> Giving a gentle kiss to every sedge
> He overtaketh in his pilgrimage ;

And so, by many winding nooks he strays,
With willing sport to the wild ocean.
Then let me go, and hinder not my course :
I'll be as patient as a gentle stream,
And make a pastime of each weary step,
Till the last step hath brought me to my love ;
And there I'll rest, as, after much turmoil,
A blessed soul doth in Elysium."—(Act ii. scene 7.)

The banks of the stream are here shaded by fine old willows, which were doubtless alluded to by the poet in his account of the death of Ophelia, beginning—

" There is a willow grows ascaunt the brook,
That shows his hoar leaves in the glassy stream."
(" Hamlet," act iv. scene 7.)

" All the great natural features of the river," says Mr. Charles Knight, " must have suffered little change since the time of Shakspere. Inundations in some places may have widened the channel ; osier islands may have grown up where there was once a broad stream. But we here look upon the same scenery upon which he looked, as truly as we gaze upon the same blue sky, and see its image in the same glassy water."

The Avon rises at Naseby, in Northamptonshire, and flows, with many windings, in a south-westerly direction through Warwickshire and Worcestershire, till it joins the Severn at Tewksbury, on the northern border of Gloucestershire. In its course through this county, the Avon, besides the numerous picturesque villages which are scattered on its banks, flows through the noble park of Stoneleigh, expands into a beautiful lake-like pool at Guy's Cliff, washes the base of Warwick Castle, winds through the grounds of Charlecote, for ever classic from its associations with Shakspere ; then, after many a turning, it flows in a broad and placid stream past Stratford, lingeringly skirting the site of the poet's grave ; and, before passing from the county, wanders

M

beside some pleasant hamlets and secluded country nooks which tradition connects with the poet's name.

In the neighbourhood of Stratford is

ALCESTER [*Inns:* Angel, Swan], a small market-town situated near the western boundary of the county, at the junction of the Arrow and Alne, and about 7½ miles from Stratford. Its name, its position on the Ikenild Street, and the discovery of numerous vestiges of Roman art, make it sufficiently evident that this was a Roman encampment. Among the remains of the Romans found here are bricks, foundations of buildings, and coins. Urns have been frequently found, containing calcined human bones or ashes. It is recorded that a general synod was held here early in the eighth century. The manor was granted by Henry I. to Sir Robert Corbet, but subsequently passed into the possession of the Greville family. A monastery was founded here in 1140 by Ralph Boteler, on an insulated spot, surrounded partly by the river Arrow, and partly by a moat. The building has long disappeared, and only the moat and the name of the site, the "Priory Close," remain to tell where it once stood.

The principal source of employment in Alcester is the manufacture of needles—685 men and 600 women being at the time of last census engaged in this branch of trade. The population in the town and neighbourhood is 2128.

The *Church* contains several interesting monuments. The oldest of them bears the recumbent effigies of Sir Fulke Greville (father of the celebrated Lord Brooke) and his wife. A monument to the Marquis of Hertford bears his recumbent figure in Chantrey's best style.

In the *Market-Hall,* an ornamental building reared

on a colonnade (used by the market people), the Marquis of Hertford, as lord of the manor, holds his courts.

The other noticeable buildings are a Free School, founded in the reign of Elizabeth by Walter Newport, some almshouses, and a workhouse.

On the western bank of the Arrow, at a short distance from the town, a farm-house marks the site of Beauchamp's Court, the ancient seat of the Beauchamps and Grevilles. Here, in 1554, was born Fulke Greville, Lord Brooke, author of the *Life of Sir Philip Sidney*, and of many graceful poems, and a liberal patron of letters. He was murdered in 1628, and is interred in the chancel of St. Mary's church, Warwick, under a stately monument erected by himself.

Two miles north of Alcester is *Coughton Manor*, a building of considerable antiquity. The estate came by marriage into the Throckmorton family in the reign of Henry IV., and with them it still continues. The mansion was erected about the time of Henry VIII. The parish church is adorned with stained glass, said to have been brought from Evesham Abbey, and contains some interesting monuments of the Throckmorton family.

The Marquis of Hertford's noble seat of *Ragley Park* is about two miles south-west of Alcester. The house was built by Lord Conway, an ancestor of the present possessor, about the middle of last century, but considerably altered and improved by the late Marquis of Hertford, under the direction of Wyatt. The entrance-hall is splendid in its proportions, and exquisite in its embellishments. Different apartments contain fine portraits and other paintings, as well as other costly and elegant works of art. The park, which is extensive, contains majestic oaks and other wood, and is adorned with a large and picturesque lake. The gardens are probably unsurpassed in the kingdom.

About two miles to the south of Ragley Park is the village of BIDFORD, which has a church, with some remains of Norman work, picturesquely situated on the sloping bank of the Avon. There are the remains of an ancient cross in the churchyard.

BISHOPTON, two miles from Stratford, possesses a mineral spring which will form to valetudinarians an additional attraction of this interesting district. Though the virtues of this spring had been long known, an analysis of it having been published in 1744, it was not till the year 1840 that it was prominently brought before public notice. In that year, the pump-room and other buildings having been completed, the well was formally opened to the public. By permission of her Majesty it was named "the Victoria Spa." The following is Professor Daniel's recent analysis of an imperial pint of the water :—

Specific gravity, 1004·6.

Sulphuric acid -	-	-	-	14·38	grains.
Muriatic acid -	-	-	-	6·09	,,
Carbonic acid -	-	-	-	1·36	,,
Soda -	-	-	-	14·78	,,
Magnesia -	-	-	-	1·95	,,
Lime -	-	-	-	2·57	,,
				41·13	,,

Dr. Granville remarks, that "a course of the Stratford waters will be found useful in certain disorders of the stomach, in slighter affections of the liver, in cases of gravel, and those pseudo-rheumatic and gouty pains which persons with long-deranged digestion are so apt to have superadded to their other sufferings."

The position of this spa is pleasant and retired. The buildings include a range of baths of the usual kinds. There is here a modern chapel, erected on the site of a more ancient structure.

CHARLECOTE, indissolubly associated with the name of Shakspere, is four miles distant. Leaving Stratford by the great stone bridge, originally built by Sir Hugh Clopton in the reign of Henry VII., and taking the road which turns to the left, the tourist passes the pleasant villages of TIDDINGTON and ALVESTON—the latter of which Dr. Parry, on account of its salubrity, pronounced the *Montpelier of England.* Its church is modern; but in the old churchyard is a fragment of the original edifice, exhibiting some rude sculpture of a very grotesque description. Pursuing the main road past Alveston to a distance of nearly 4 miles from Stratford, a cross road, branching off to the left, skirts Charlecote Park, and affords a view of the ancient family mansion of the Lucys. The park is extensive, finely wooded, and well stocked with deer. The house was erected by Sir Thomas Lucy in the beginning of the reign of Queen Elizabeth. It continued with little alteration till the late George Lucy, Esq., made various improvements, which give evidence of a correct taste. The approach to the mansion is through a spacious but heavy gatehouse of brick, with small turrets at the sides. The house is a brick building in the Elizabethan style, and probably has much the same aspect which it had at the time of its erection.

Justly or unjustly, Sir Thomas Lucy has been dignified by Shakspere with an immortality of ridicule, as *Justice Shallow.* Shakspere, as the story runs, had on one or two occasions made free with the knight's deer, a fault for which Sir Thomas visited him with relentless persecution. The future poet revenged himself by a ballad, said to be his first effort in verse. Only one stanza has been preserved, and it is doubtful whether it is his production at all. It is, however, sufficiently curious to deserve quotation :—

> " A parliament member, a justice of peace,
> At home a poor scarecrow, at London an ass ;
> If lousy is Lucy, as some volk miscall it,
> Then Lucy is lousy, whatever befall it.
> He thinks himself great,
> Yet an ass in his state,
> We allow of his ears but with asses to mate ;
> If Lucy is lousy, as some volk miscall it,
> Sing lousy Lucy, whatever befall it."

The tradition adds that Shakspere attached this ballad to the park gates ; that he was compelled to leave Stratford to escape the vengeance of the enraged knight ; and that it was thus that, going to London, he at length became " the poet of all time."

There can be no doubt that there is some truth in this story, though doubtless it has been magnified and embellished ; it is told by early writers, and Shakspere's portraiture of Justice Shallow and his cousin Slender is such a merciless piece of satire, that it is not difficult to suppose that in depicting them he was revenging his own real or fancied injuries. As this matter is one of some interest, we add a couple of brief quotations from the " Merry Wives of Windsor " that seem to bear on it :—

Shallow. Sir Hugh, persuade me not ; I will make a Star-chamber matter of it : if he were twenty Sir John Falstaffs, he shall not abuse Robert Shallow, esquire.

Slender. In the county of Gloster, justice of peace, and *coram.*

Shal. Ay, cousin Slender, and *Cust-alorum.*

Slen. Ay, and *ratolorum* too ; and a gentleman born, master parson, who writes himself, *armigero ;* in any bill, warrant, quittance, or obligation, *armigero.*

Shal. Ay, that we do, and have done any time these three hundred years.

Slen. All his successors, gone before him, have done't ; and all his ancestors that come after him, may, they may give the dozen white luces in their coat.

Shal. It is an old coat.

Evans. The dozen white louses do become an old coat well ; it agrees well, passant ; it is a familiar beast to man, and signifies love."

The name of Lucy was first assumed by William, the son of Walter de Cherlecot, about the close of the twelfth century. The arms of the family exhibit *three luces* (pike fish) *hauriant d'argent*. The following extract from the same scene may perhaps refer to the offence Shakspere had committed, and the anger of the knight thereupon :—

Falstaff. Now, master Shallow, you will complain of me to the King ?

Shal. Knight, you have beaten my men, killed my deer, and broke open my lodge.

Fal. But not kissed your keeper's daughter.

Shal. Tut, a pin ! this shall be answered.

Fal. I will answer it straight : I have done all this—that is now answered.

Shal. The Council shall know this.

Fal. 'Twere better for you, if it were known in counsel, you'll be laughed at.

Shallow and his cousin Slender are also made to figure in the second part of " King Henry IV." It is right to state, in connection with the tradition just related, that, though the name of Sir Thomas Lucy must always be associated with Justice Shallow, there are some grounds for believing that the portraiture, if indeed intended by Shakspere as such, is unjust. An epitaph to the memory of his wife, in the church of Charlecote, if really written by himself, as it professes to be, would evince him to have been a man of a kind warm heart. Mr. Charles Knight has remarked regarding this epitaph, that it " is honourable alike to the deceased and to the survivor."

The interior of the house, should the tourist be so fortunate as to obtain admission, will be found to con-tain much that is highly interesting. The great hall is wainscotted with oak, and contains ancient and richly-carved furniture. Antique and valuable articles of furniture are in various apartments, among which may be mentioned a splendidly-carved cabinet. The house is enriched by a collection of paintings, the most important of which are, portraits of Charles I., Charles II., Archbishop Laud, Sir Thomas Lucy (in his youth), in the *Library;* Teniers' Wedding, purchased by Mr. Lucy for £1100, Landscapes by Hobbima, Cuyp, Berghem, and Paul Potter, Madonna and Child by Vandyke, and Marketing Parties going and returning by Wouvermans, in the *Drawing Room;* Battle of a Cock and Turkey by Ulnocbocker, Horses by Wouvermans, Cock and Gander by Jacob Jordans, in the *Dining Room;* St. Catherine and a Magdalene, Head of Christ, and a fine painting by an unknown artist, in the *Morning Room.* There are several fine busts in some of the rooms.

CHARLECOTE CHURCH was rebuilt by Mrs. Lucy in 1852, in the Decorated style. The interior is richly adorned. Adjoining the chancel, which contains ten beautifully-carved oak stalls, is the Lucy Chapel, containing some interesting monuments of the Lucy family. The figure of Sir Thomas Lucy on an altar-tomb, along with that of his lady, will especially attract attention. The face of the knight is certainly not such a countenance as we would assign to " Justice Shallow."

HAMPTON LUCY is on the opposite bank of the Avon from Charlecote, and about three miles from Stratford. If the Warrick road be taken from Stratford, the tourist will pass on his left WELCOMBE, the residence of John Combe and his brother William, the intimate friends of Shakspere. Of John Combe's dwelling there are no remains, the present house being quite a recent erection. Near Welcombe there are extensive earthworks and entrenchments, probably British. Rather farther away is CLOPTON, originally the property of a family of that name. William Howitt tells the sad story of a fair member of this family who was prematurely interred in a vault in Stratford Church.

Hampton Lucy, anciently called Bishop's Hampton, is one of the most picturesque villages in the county. Its church is an admirable example of the Decorated style, erected on the site of an ancient structure in 1826, after the designs of Rickman and Hutchinson, the whole charge, amounting to £11,050, being borne by the late Rev. J. Lucy.   This gentleman also built the iron bridge over the Avon.

From Hampton Lucy the tourist may conveniently visit Snitterfield, noticed below.

ILMINGTON, about nine miles from Stratford, and three from the station, has a strong chalybeate spring formerly in much repute.   In this parish, according to Anthony à Wood, was born in 1581 Sir Thomas Overbury, an elegant writer in prose and verse. Through the influence of the earl of Rochester and the countess of Essex he was imprisoned in the Tower of London, and there poisoned in 1613.

KINETON, about eight miles distant, has, with its interesting vicinity, been separately described.

SHOTTERY.—This pleasant hamlet is about a mile from Stratford.   The distance is shortened by a footpath through the fields on the left of the Alcester road, at the outside of the town.   There is a well-authenticated tradition that a cottage in this hamlet was the home of Anne Hathaway before she became the wife of Shakspere.   This cottage has an antique and picturesque appearance, having a timber and plaster front, and being roofed with thatch.   Its interior corresponds with its venerable exterior.   The kitchen, an ample and comfortable apartment, exhibits ancient oak wainscotting, low ceiling with heavy beams, and spacious fireplace.   The other rooms partake more or less of the

same character. There are some pieces of old furniture
and household linen, some of which were probably the
property of the Hathaway family at a period not much
after the time of Shakspere. Garrick purchased relics
out of this cottage ; and subsequently Samuel Ireland,
who published " Views on the River Avon," carried off
what was called " Shakspere's courting chair." The
genuineness, of these articles affirmed to have belonged
to Shakspere is more than doubtful, though nobody
very strongly disputes the truth of the tradition which
associates the bard so intimately with the cottage.
Probably the house still wears very much the same
aspect it bore when Shakspere repaired hither from
Stratford to woo Anne Hathaway.

From Shottery a walk of about a mile will bring
the tourist to the retired hamlet of LUDDINGTON,
situated on the bank of the Avon. It contains a very
neat Early Gothic church, "All Saints," erected in 1872,
and built of the blue limestone of the district, the
window traceries and dressings being of Corsham stone.
In the original church, which stood near the present
edifice, but has long since been destroyed, Shakspere is
said by local tradition to have been married. The architect of the new church was Mr. Cotton of Birmingham.

SNITTERFIELD is about 4 miles from Stratford, and
half that distance from the Bearley Station. This
pretty village is noted as the residence for many years
of the poet Jago, who was vicar of the parish. Jago
was born in 1715 and died in 1781. He is interred
in the church, which is a handsome building, having
some ancient wood-carving in its interior.

Samuel Ireland has suggested that FULBROKE PARKE,
about a mile distant, and not Charlecote, was the
scene of Shakspere's raid on Sir Thomas Lucy's deer.
This, though a mere conjecture, is not improbable,

There was no mansion in this park, and Shakspere may have been encouraged by this fact to regard the deer in the same light as other game rather than as the actual property of Sir Thomas.

TAMWORTH.

HOTELS : *The Castle, Peel Arms, White Horse.*
From Birmingham, 17¼ miles ; Rugby, 27 ; Coventry, 24.

THIS ancient town is pleasantly situated on the extreme northern border of the county—one-half of it, including the church, belonging to the adjoining county of Stafford. Tamworth dates from a period long anterior to the Conquest. Here the warlike Offa resided; and hence many of his charters to churches and towns were granted. Here many other of the Mercian kings held their court. In the Danish invasion the town was taken, and the palace laid in ruins. Ethelfleda, the heroic daughter of Alfred the Great, drove out the invaders from her paternal territories in this quarter, and raised and fortified the artificial mound which is now the site of Tamworth Castle, about the year 914. After Tamworth had ceased to be the seat of royalty, a mint appears to have been established there, some specimens of its coins being still to be met with. The town was incorporated in 1560, and two years afterwards returned two members to Parliament. Its subsequent history comprises no event of importance.

The population of Tamworth, at the census of 1871, was 11,502, and the inhabited houses 2356. The occupations are for the most part agricultural; but in the Tamworth district 470 persons are engaged in coal-mines, 150 in cotton manufactures, and 58 upon tape. There are also tanneries and ale-breweries. The borough returns two members to Parliament.

Tamworth is respectably, though not regularly, built. With the exception of its church and castle, it contains few notable memorials of ancient times. The King's Dyke, a wide and deep trench by which the town was formerly defended on the east, north, and west sides (the Tame and Auker being its defence on the south), may still be traced. The bones of men and horses, and warlike weapons, have been dug up in this trench.

The CASTLE, as has been already stated, is erected on the artificial mound raised and fortified by Ethelfleda. It was bestowed by William the Conqueror on Robert Marmion, the founder of the martial family whose name Sir Walter Scott has immortalised in his romantic "Tale of Flodden Field." In a note to "Marmion," Scott says :—"In earlier times, indeed, the family of Marmion, Lords of Fontenay, in Normandy, was highly distinguished. Robert de Marmion, Lord of Fontenay, a distinguished follower of the Conqueror, obtained a grant of the castle and town of Tamworth, and also of the manor of Scrivelby, in Lincolnshire. One or both of these noble possessions was held by the honourable service of being the royal champion, as the ancestors of Marmion had formerly been to the Dukes of Normandy. But after the castle and demesne of Tamworth had passed through four successive barons from Robert, the family became extinct in the person of Philip de Marmion, who died in twentieth Edward I., without issue-male. He was succeeded in the castle of Tamworth by Alexander de Freville, who married Mazera, his grand-daughter." In the reign of Henry VI. the family and possessions of Freville merged in the Earls of Ferrars. Subsequently Tamworth Castle passed to the Comptons, from whom it came, we believe by marriage, to the Marquis of Townshend, in whose family it now remains.

The artificial mound on which the castle is built is high and steep ; and the aspect of the building is very imposing. Unfortunately, from its not being inhabited by its owner, but let to various persons in succession, the interior has considerably suffered from neglect and decay. Latterly the castle has been more fortunate in this respect, the tenant having fitted it up in a tasteful and appropriate style. There is not space to particularise the various apartments ; nor, indeed, is this necessary, as the only original decorations they contain consist of coats of arms on the cornices, and some other antique details. Some of the apartments are of stately proportions, and must have presented a magnificent aspect when the castle was the residence of its noble owners. In one apartment, called "Queen Mary's Bedroom," the unfortunate Mary Queen of Scots slept while a prisoner in this castle. She was permitted, when she pleased, to ascend a staircase leading to the top of the square tower, or keep, to breathe the fresh air, and beguile the tediousness of her captivity by looking abroad on the surrounding scenery. The prospect from the summit is extensive and beautiful. In clear weather no fewer than forty-six churches can be counted with the naked eye.

The CHURCH, a large and handsome edifice, composed, however, of a soft friable stone, unfavourable to the preservation of the finer details of ecclesiastical architecture, consists of nave, aisles, chancel, north chapel, and a massive and lofty tower. Its architecture belongs to different periods. The oldest portion, exhibiting two Norman arches, with zig-zag mouldings, is probably part of a church erected by the Marmions shortly after the Conquest. Other portions of the edifice are in more recent styles ; and the restorations to which it has at several times been subjected have introduced still more modern features. The building is, nevertheless, very interesting, and will repay examination.

There are numerous monuments in the chancel and its chapel. On the south side is a stately marble tomb, with life-size kneeling figures on either side, to the memory of Sir John Ferrers of Tamworth Castle, who died in 1680, and his wife. On the north of the chancel, under one of the arches that separate it from its chapel, is an altar-tomb which has evidently had on it the inlaid effigies in brass of a king and his lady, with their children. The inscription running round its border has also been removed. Round its sides are the sculptured figures of angels, etc. Adjoining it, also under an arch, is another altar-tomb, with the mutilated figures of a knight and his lady. Probably this knight was a member of the Freville family, ancient possessors of the castle. Within an arched recess in the north wall of the chapel is a recumbent female figure, without any inscription, and considerably worn. There are many monumental stones in the floor, stripped of their brasses. The chancel has a handsome reredos in tabernacle work. There is a piscina in the south wall.

The church has accommodation for 3000 persons, and is comfortably fitted up. The tower is remarkable as having two staircases, the one winding over the other, and either having a separate entrance and exit. This feature is perhaps unique. The summit of the tower commands a magnificent view.

In a crypt beneath the church there is an immense collection of human bones.

Of other public buildings the chief are the MARKET HOUSE, founded in 1701 by Thomas Guy, the benevolent founder of Guy's Hospital, Southwark; a HOSPITAL, endowed by the same gentleman; a

GRAMMAR SCHOOL, founded by Queen Elizabeth in 1558; and a NATIONAL SCHOOL, founded by the late Sir Robert Peel. Sir Robert did a good deal to advance the prosperity of Tamworth by the establishment of manufactories. There is a monument to his memory here, consisting of a fine bronze statue on a pedestal bearing the following inscription :—" The Right Honourable Sir Robert Peel, Bart., born Feb. 5, 1788, elected, in the year 1830, Member of Parliament for Tamworth, which town he continued to represent until his death, July 2, 1850."

From Tamworth the tourist may visit Atherstone, Polesworth, and Seckington.

VICINITY OF TAMWORTH.

ATHERSTONE [*Inns;* Red Lion, dinner, 2s.; Angel, White Swan, Three Tuns. From Tamworth, 8 miles].— Atherstone is an irregular but picturesque market-town, situated on the Roman road called Watling Street, which here forms the eastern boundary of the county. Prior to the Conquest, Atherstone formed part of the vast possessions of the Countess Godiva of Mercia. After passing through many hands, the manor came in the reign of Elizabeth into the possession of Sir John Repington, from whom it passed to the Bracebridge family, who still possess it. Atherstone is noted in history as the scene of the conference between the Earl of Richmond and the disaffected nobles of Richard III. the night before the battle of Bosworth Field. Measures were concerted between Richmond and the two Stanleys, which resulted in the overthrow and death of the king. Richmond encamped with his troops, the night before the battle, in a meadow near the church. Bosworth

Field is 4 or 5 miles distant, in the neighbouring county of Leicester.

This town was the birthplace, in 1644, of Dr. Nehemiah Grew, a celebrated naturalist, author of "The Anatomy of Plants," and other works. He died in 1711.

The population of Atherstone at last census was 3877. The chief manufactures are hats, ribbons, and silk.

The *Church* consists of nave, aisles, and chancel, with a beautiful octagonal tower, ending in open work, rising between the nave and chancel. The chancel is walled off from the body of the church, and used as a school, a brick chimney rising through its roof. It is much to be desired that the chancel may be restored to its original purpose. The fine eastern window would greatly improve the appearance of the church.

The other notable public buildings are the *Town-Hall* and the *Endowed School*, both tasteful structures. There are many quaint old houses in different parts of the town.

The neighbourhood of Atherstone possesses much varied and richly-wooded scenery. Of the mansions in the surrounding district the most interesting is MERIVALE HALL, about a mile distant, to the west, noted as the residence of Sir William Dugdale,* author of the "Antiquities of Warwickshire." The hall, which is still occupied by his descendants, is well situated, and surrounded by fine grounds.

MANCESTER (pronounced and sometimes written MANCETTER), a mile and a half distant, is an extensive parish, including Atherstone, Oldbury, and Hartshill ; but the village itself has only 97 houses and 355 inhabitants. Its church is a little to the right of the

---

* Dugdale had also a seat at Shustoke.

Roman Road (Watling Street), which here forms the London highway Some two or three hundred yards beyond the point where a road branches off to Mancester church, the tourist will reach the site of the ancient Roman station of *Manduessedum*. A slight depression in the highway, which the quick eye of the antiquarian will detect and understand, indicates where the road crosses the foss, and in the fields on either hand the foss will be seen to be distinctly marked. The mean length of the level surface enclosed within the earthworks is 627 feet, and the mean breadth 438, the total contents being rather more than six acres. Roman coins and fragments of buildings are often dug up here and in the neighbourhood. The settlement had its outposts in various places in the neighbourhood, especially at Oldbury and Hartshill, which are noticed below.

A pleasant walk of three or four miles from Mancester will bring the tourist to Oldbury and Hartshill. Leaving the church, and taking the road on his right, after crossing the canal bridge he will find a footpath striking through the fields on his left, by which he may reach the places named. Thereafter, instead of retracing his steps, he may proceed by Ausley Hall through a picturesque country to the Arley or Whitacre station of the Birmingham and Leicester Railway. The churches passed on the way are generally worth turning aside to look at, though they are not individually of such interest as to repay a special excursion.

OLDBURY has the remains of an ancient Roman fort, on a commanding eminence, consisting of a quadrangular earthwork enclosed with high ramparts, which on three sides have been well preserved. This was the summer camp to the Roman station of Manduessedum. The area contains about seven acres. On the south side of the camp the nuns of Polesworth formerly had a cell. Within its area has been erected a handsome modern mansion, which, from its elevation, commands extensive prospects.

The hamlet of HARTSHILL, in the same neighbourhood, occupies part of the site of Manduessedum, and has been said to be the *Campus Martius* of the Romans. The site of this rural hamlet is pleasant and elevated. In clear weather, upwards of forty churches can be counted with the naked eye in the surrounding country. Here in 1563 was born Michael Drayton, author of the "Polyolbion," "Wars of the Barons," and numerous other standard poems. We find Drayton styled "poet-laureate" in 1626; but in those times the title was often a mere empty compliment, implying neither pension nor butt of canary. He died in 1631, and was buried in Westminster Abbey.

POLESWORTH, 4 miles to the south-east, is a village of considerable antiquity. A nunnery was founded here by King Egbert, for St. Modwena, an Irish virgin much reputed for her holy life. Dugdale makes this the first religious house established in this country; but the correctness of his opinion has been disputed. There can, however, be no doubt that a nunnery existed here at the Conquest. William bestowed Polesworth, among other possessions, upon Robert Marmion, who expelled the nuns, but afterwards, repenting of his harshness, reinstated them with additional endowments. The nunnery continued to flourish till the Dissolution, when it was in possession of considerable revenues. There are some fragments of the monastic buildings in the vicinity of the church. *The Church*, a handsome structure with a very massive tower, has some interesting features; and in its interior are two ancient monuments. There is a well-endowed *Free School*, founded in the reign of James I. by Sir Francis Nethersole, knight.

A short distance from Polesworth is *Pooley Hall*, a rather interesting specimen of ancient domestic architecture, erected in the reign of Henry VIII. by Sir Thomas Cokain.

SECKINGTON, 4 miles distant to the north-east, was, Camden informs us, anciently named Secandunum. The Roman name is considered to be corroborated by a large entrenched camp, situated near the church, probably, though not certainly, of Roman construction. The camp is circular, with an inner diameter of 300 feet, and is defended by a ditch about 12 feet deep and 20 feet wide. On its north side is an artificial mound, 42 feet high, either a tumulus or a watchtower.

TEMPLE OF BALSAL.

In the VICINITY OF SOLIHULL.

ENTRANCE TO WARWICK CASTLE.

WARWICK.

HOTEL: *Warwick Arms*, 5 minutes from Castle.
From Birmingham, 21 miles; Coventry, 11; Rugby, 17; Manchester, 106;
Liverpool, 88¾; London, 108; York, 151¼; London, 108.

THE county town is beautifully situated on elevated ground, near the bank of the Avon. John Rous dates its origin as far back as the beginning of the Christian era. According to this account, to which Dugdale gives the sanction of his name, it was founded by Gutheline, or Kimbeline, a British king, at the time of the birth of Christ. It was called by him Caerleon, the word being compounded of Caer (*civitas*), and his own name; Caer-Cuthleon being shortened into Caerleon. Another account makes its foundation considerably less ancient, attributing it to the Saxons. According to the antiquary already quoted, the town, having been destroyed by the Picts and Scots, was rebuilt by the great Caractacus, whose heroism in resisting the Romans for nine years has procured for him immortality on the page of Tacitus. Again it was destroyed, when it was rebuilt by Warremund, the first of the kings of Mercia, from whom it was named Warrewyk. Ethelfleda, daughter of king Alfred the Great, by the erection of a strong fortified building in 915, contributed very materially to its increase and prosperity. The Norman Conquest considerably benefited this town. William the Conqueror allowed Turchill, then vicecomes of Warwick, to retain his title and remain in possession of his estates, giving him orders at the same time to enlarge and fortify the castle, and strengthen the town with a ditch and gates. He afterwards created the earldom of Warwick, bestowing the title on Henry de Newburgh, one of his followers. From this time the town continued to prosper, the Earls of Warwick appearing to have in general administered its affairs in a manner tending to promote its welfare. In the reign of Edward I. Warwick was the scene of various knightly tournaments. In this and the following reigns various charters are mentioned as having been obtained by the earls, empowering them to levy taxes for the construction of the walls and other public purposes. A charter of incorporation was obtained in the reign of Mary and Philip. Queen Elizabeth visited Warwick in 1572, three years before the famous festivities at Kenilworth, and was received with due loyalty. James I, in one of his progresses, visited Warwick, when he was magnificently entertained in Leicester's Hospital, 4th September 1617. In common with other parts of the county, this town suffered during the civil war of the seventeenth century, the castle at one time sustaining a short siege from the Royalists. In 1694 the greater part of the town was destroyed by fire. The damage was estimated at the time at £90,600 ; but a sum of £120,000 had to be expended to repair the damage. Warwick is indebted to this occurrence for an improved style of architecture. William III. visited Warwick in 1695, when he was the guest of Fulke Greville, Lord Brooke, in Warwick Castle.

Two scholars of note were natives of this town. Walter of Coventry, the Benedictine monk, author of several works on English history, was born here about the middle of the twelfth century. John Rous, the zealous and laborious Warwick antiquary, after studying at Oxford, returned to his native county, and became a chantry priest at Guy's Cliff. His writings, which were more voluminous than valuable, have almost all perished. He died in 1491, and was interred in St. Mary's Church.

The earls of Warwick have in former times played so important a part in history, that a brief account of them may be appropriately given in this place. The first of note is the famous *Guy*, the hero of numberless legendary tales. After many wonderful exploits, the last and greatest of which was the killing of Colbrand, a Danish giant, he retired to Guy's Cliff, where he lived the secluded life of a " palmer poor," and died in 929. The Saxon earls, descendants of Guy, are enumerated by early chroniclers, but nothing in their history entitles them to mention. The earldom of Warwick, in the Norman line, was created by William the Conqueror, who conferred it on *Henry de Newburgh*, one of his followers, who died in 1123. The male line failing with the sixth earl of this family, the title and estates eventually passed by marriage into the family of the Beauchamps, barons of Elmley, in Worcestershire. *Guy de Beauchamp*, second earl of this house, distinguished himself in Scotland in the invasions of Edward I. In the reign of Edward II. he, in concert with the earls of Lancaster, Hereford, and Arundel, seized the person of Piers Gaveston, Earl of Cornwall, the king's worthless favourite, and beheaded him at Blacklow Hill, 1312. *Thomas*, his son, signalised himself in the campaigns of Edward the Black Prince. He died, 1370, at Calais, of which he was governor for many years, and lies buried in St. Mary's choir. *Thomas*, the second of that name, was the next earl. He also distinguished himself in the French wars, and proved himself a faithful servant of his country. Falling under the displeasure of the worthless Richard II., he was imprisoned in the Tower of London. Henry IV. restored him to liberty and to his estate. It was this earl who built Guy's Tower. He died in 1401. *Richard*, his only son, raised still more highly the

honour of the house of Warwick. He distinguished
himself in foreign wars and tournaments, vanquishing
the most renowned champions of Europe. His private
character was as estimable and irreproachable as his
public conduct was illustrious. The Emperor Sigis-
mund styled him " the father of courtesy ; " and Henry
V. of England committed to him the tutelage of his son,
afterwards Henry VI., till he should attain the age of
fifteen. He held the high office of regent of France
at the time of his death, which took place at Rouen
in 1439. His body was brought to England, and,
according to his own directions, buried in the Lady
Chapel of St. Mary's, under the magnificent tomb
already described. His son *Henry* was the last of the
Beauchamp line of earls of Warwick. He was high in
the favour of Henry VI., who created him duke of
Warwick, and afterward king of the Isle of Man.
Dying without heirs at the age of twenty-two, the estate
reverted to his father's sister, countess of *Richard
Neville*, Earl of Salisbury, upon whom the title of Earl
of Warwick was conferred. The name of Richard
Neville is one of the most prominent in the history of
the fifteenth century. The splendid delineation of
his character and actions by Shakspere in ", King
Henry VI.," from the time when, in the Temple
garden, he says—

> " I love no colours, and, without all colour
> Of base insinuating flattery,
> I pluck this white rose with Plantagenet,"

down to the battle of Barnet, where he died fighting
for Henry, whom he had dethroned a few years before,
is too well known to require more than a passing reference. The words which Shakspere puts into his
mouth as he dies on the field of Barnet, give an admir-

able picture of the character and power of the " king maker :"—-

"Thus yields the cedar to the axe's edge,
  Whose arms gave shelter to the princely eagle,
  Under whose shade the ramping lion slept,
  Whose top branch overpeered Jove's spreading tree,
  And kept low shrubs from winter's powerful wind.
  These eyes, that now are dimmed with death's dark veil,
  Have been as piercing as the mid-day sun,
  To search the secret treasons of the world.
  The wrinkles in my brow, now filled with blood,
  Were likened oft to kingly sepulchres ;
  For who lived king, but I could dig his grave ?
  And who durst smile when Warwick bent his brow ?
  Lo, now my glory smeared in dust and blood !
  My parks, my walks, my manors that I had,
  Even now forsake me ; and of all my lands
  Is nothing left me but my body's length !
  Why, what is pomp, rule, reign, but earth and dust?
  And, live we how we can, yet die we must."

Hume speaks of Richard Neville in the following terms :—" The undesigning frankness and openness of his character rendered his conquest over men's affections the more certain and infallible ; his presents were regarded as sure testimonies of esteem and friendship, and his professions as the overflowings of his genuine sentiments. No less than 30,000 persons are said to have daily lived at his board, in the different manors and castles which he possessed in England ; the military men, allured by his munificence and hospitality, as well as by his bravery, were zealously attached to his interests ; the people in general bore him an unlimited affection ; his numerous retainers were more devoted to his will than to the prince or to the laws, and he was the greatest, as well as the last of those mighty barons who formerly overawed the crown and rendered the people incapable of civil government." He was succeeded in the earldom by *George Plantagenet*, duke of Clarence, and brother of Edward IV., who had married his daughter. Clarence was murdered in the Tower of London, and his son *Edward*, who succeeded to the earldom, was beheaded, 1499, for being implicated with Perkin Warbeck in a plot for escaping from the Tower. After a lapse of forty-eight years the title was revived, and bestowed on *John Dudley*, Lord High Admiral of England, who rendered important services to the country under Henry VIII. and Edward VI., but was beheaded in the succeeding reign for espousing the cause of Lady Jane Grey. With his grandson *Ambrose*, "the good earl of Warwick," and brother of Queen Elizabeth's favourite the earl of Leicester, the title once more became extinct, 1589. The title, without the estates, was bestowed by James I., in 1618, on *Robert, Lord Rich*, in whose family it remained through seven descents. The second earl of this line was Lord High Admiral of England under the Long Parliament, and his grandson married the youngest daughter of Oliver Cromwell. Immediately on the extinction of the title in this family, it was conferred on *Francis Greville*, Earl Brooke, the possessor of the castle and estate, with whose descendants it still remains. The earls of Warwick of this line have not taken a conspicuous part in politics.

The population of Warwick, at the census of 1871, was 11,001, and the inhabited houses 2419. The borough returns two members to Parliament, and the constituency numbers about 650. The municipal government is vested in a council of twenty-four, consisting of six aldermen and eighteen councilmen. The mayor is elected annually by the council.

Commercially the town is of little importance. At one period it possessed manufactories for spinning and combing wool, for weaving cotton, and for making lace

and hats; but these branches of industry are for the
most part discontinued. There are one or two establishments in Warwick where wood-carving is carried
to a high point of perfection. Stained glass and ecclesiastical decorations are also produced here. The annual
value of real property assessed to income-tax in 1862
amounted to £52,398.

The town is mostly modern, the fire of 1694 having
swept away the great majority of its old houses; but
there still remain some interesting specimens of ancient
domestic architecture. Leicester's Hospital, the best
example of the old timber-framed style, will be noticed
in its proper place (p. 32). St. John's Hospital, erected
in the reign of Henry II., is now used as a seminary.
None of the private houses in which the timber-
framed style exists require to be specially mentioned
here.

St. Mary's Church is perhaps altogether the most
interesting ecclesiastical building in the county. This
is a noble structure on an imposing site, forming one
of the most prominent objects on a distant view of the
town. The time of its foundation cannot be precisely
ascertained; but it is certain, from the Domesday
survey, that a church existed on this site long before
the Conquest. The present building does not all belong to the same period. It was repaired by Roger de
Newburgh, second Norman earl of Warwick, in the
reign of King Stephen. Then, in 1394, it was restored by the first Thomas Beauchamp, earl of Warwick,
who founded the choir, which was finished by his son,
of the same name, who also rebuilt the whole edifice.
In 1694 it was almost wholly destroyed by the great
fire already alluded to; the choir, the lady chapel, the
chapter-house, the lobby, and the vestry on the north,
alone escaping the ravages of the flames. The new

church, "begun by public, was finished by royal piety, under the joyful auspices of Queen Anne, in the memorable year 1704." The architectural style of this church has often been severely commented upon. The design has been attributed to Sir Christopher Wren, but without any very tangible grounds. Though an incongruous mixture of styles is observable, it cannot be denied that the effect of the whole is grand and imposing. The fine proportions of the tower are particulary worthy of notice. From a base of 36 feet square, it rises from four groined arches to the height of 130 feet, above which again, at each corner, rise pinnacles to the height of 44 feet. Beneath the piers is a passage allowing of the transit of carriages. The extreme length of the church is 180 feet, and the breadth, measured along the transept, 106. The styles of architecture, as has been stated, are different in the ancient and modern parts of this structure. The lady chapel is an exquisite specimen of the Decorated style. The other parts of the building which escaped the great fire are of the same order. The more modern part was engrafted on the old walls : the result, as has been stated, is not very happy. The great windows have double rows of heavy arches, terminated by grotesque heads ; and the tower has a curious union of the round and pointed arch. The church has recently undergone various restorations externally and internally.

The church consists of the nave, aisles, transepts, chancel, lady chapel, with chantry and oratory, and a tower at the west end. The organ is situated at the west end, and is considered an instrument of some excellence. Originally there were many ancient monuments in the body of the church, but several of these were destroyed by the great fire in 1694. Among the monuments in the north transept worthy of notice, are

those of William Johnson, M.D., and Anne his wife ;
of Thomas Oken and Joan his wife—all of whom left
munificent bequests for the poor of this their native
town ; and of Francis Holyock, the lexicographer. In
the south transept is a brass plate to the memory of
Thomas Beauchamp, second earl of that name, which
is all that was spared by the great fire of a once
splendid monument. An engraving of the original
monument will be found in the work of Dugdale on the
antiquities of Warwickshire. The tomb, which was of
the altar kind, appears to have been richly adorned.

The *Choir* is entered from the termination of the
nave by an ascent of three steps, through wrought-iron
gates. The architecture is Decorated, of a remark-
ably pure and chaste character. The roof, which is of
stone, is lofty and beautifully ribbed. In the centre
of the ceiling are the arms of the founder borne by a
seraph. On each side are four windows, which unfortunately have lost the stained glass with which they
were formerly enriched. In the centre of the choir
stands a splendid monument to the memory of Thomas
Beauchamp, earl of Warwick, the founder, and Lady
Catherine Mortimer, his countess. This tomb, which
is of the altar kind, is asserted by Gough to be one of
the most elegant and beautiful of its kind in the kingdom. The tomb, which is composed of plaster in
excellent imitation of veined marble, is surmounted by
the effigies of the earl and his lady in a recumbent
position. The earl is habited in armour, his left hand
resting on his sword, but his right clasping the right
hand of his wife. The countess is dressed in mantle
and petticoat, with sleeves buttoned below the wrist.
At the head of each figure sits a female, as if in the
act of watching ; at the earl's feet is a bear, and at his
wife's a lamb. Round the sides of the tomb are thirty-

six figures, male and female, evidently meant to re-present the various relations of the deceased. Beneath these figures are armorial bearings more or less effaced. This earl distinguished himself, under the Black Prince, at Cressy and Poictiers ; and subsequently spent three years in Palestine fighting against the infidels. He died at Calais.

On the north side of the choir are three apartments, one of which, of an octagonal shape, will interest the tourist as containing the tomb of Fulke Greville, Lord Brooke. This apartment was originally the chapter-house, but was selected by Lord Brooke for his own monument, which he caused to be erected in his life-time. The monument is a sarcophagus, under a canopy supported by Corinthian pillars. The inscription, written by himself, is laconic, but very·significant :— " Fulke Greville, Servant to Queen Elizabeth, Coun-sellor to King James, and Friend to Sir Philip Sidney."

On the south side of the choir is the *Lady Chapel*, called also the *Beauchamp Chapel*, reached by a flight of steps, passing the oratory and chantry. It is con-sidered by the most competent judges one of the finest specimens extant of the purest Gothic style. Over the entrance door of this chapel is a fine arch, designed and executed in 1704, by a poor mason, a native of the town, whose name ought to have been preserved. This chapel was commenced in 1443, in conformity with the will of Richard Beauchamp, and was not completed till 1464. The total cost of its erection was £2481, a sum equal to at least £40,000 in the present day. The ceiling is of stone, richly carved, and adorned with shields bearing the arms of the old earls of Warwick single, and those of Warwick and Beauchamp (the founder) quartered. The flooring is of black and

white marble arranged lozenge-wise. On either side
are four rows of stalls, elaborately ornamented with
blank shields in quatrefoils, and with carvings of
lions, griffins, and bears, chained and muzzled. The
exterior has many beautiful and appropriate decorations, the great east window being especially conspicuous. The window contains the original glass ;
one of its subjects being a portrait of Earl Richard in
armour, kneeling, with his hands raised, in front of a
desk, on which lies an open book. Beneath a Gothic
canopy is a fine altar-piece, in bas-relief, of the Saluta-
tion of the Blessed Virgin, designed by Lightoler, and
sculptured by Collins. In the centre of this chapel is
the tomb of Richard Beauchamp, its founder, considered
the most splendid in the kingdom, with the single exception of that of Henry VII. in Westminster Abbey.
It is of the altar kind, and formed of grey marble.
On the sarcophagus is a full-length figure of the earl,
recumbent, clad in full armour of brass gilt, surmounted
by a hearse of brass hoops, also gilt. His head is uncovered and rests upon a helmet ; his hair is short
and his beard curled ; and his hands are elevated in
prayer. By his side are sword and dagger, and a
garter is on his left knee. A swan is at his head, and
a griffin and bear muzzled sit watching at his feet.
The sides and ends of the tomb are divided into fourteen beautifully-wrought niches, which are filled with
figures, weepers, in copper gilt, representing relatives
of the deceased. Each of these figures has its proper
arms. The following inscription runs round the
upper ledge of the tomb, giving an account of Richard
Beauchamp's death and burial. Figures of the bear
and ragged staff occasionally intervene :—

"Preieth devoutly for the Sowel whom god assoille
of one of the moost worshipful Knightes in his dayes

of monhode & conning Richard Beauchamp late earl of Warrewik Lord Despenser of Bergevenny & of mony other grete lordships whos body resteth here under this tumbe in a fulfeire vout of Stone set on the bare rooch thewhuch visited with longe siknes in the Castel of Roan therinne decessed ful cristenly the last day of April the year of oure lord god AMCCCCxxxix, he being at that tyme Lieutenant gen'al and governor of the Roialme of ffraunce and of the Duchie of Normandie by sufficient Autorite of oure Sou'aigne lord the King Harry vi. thewhuch body with grete deliberacon' and ful worshipful condiut Bi See Andby lond was broght to Warrewik the iiii day of October the yer abouesaide and was leide with ful Solenne exequies in a feir chest made of Stone in this Chirche afore the west dore of this chapel according to his last Wille And Testament therein to rest til this Chapel by him devised O his lief were made al thewhuche Chapel founded on the Rooch And alle the Membres therof his Executors dede fully make And apparaille By the Auctorite of his Seide last Wille and Testament and Therafter By the same Auctorite Theydide Translate fful worshipfully the seide Body into the vout aboueside Honrred be God therefore."

It is stated by Gough, that about the middle of the seventeenth century the floor of the chapel fell in, when the stone coffin containing the earl's body being broken, the body was found to be still fresh, though it rapidly decayed on exposure to the air. The ladies of Warwick profited by the circumstance, getting rings and other ornaments made of the earl's hair.

At the head of Earl Richard's monument is the tomb of Ambrose Dudley, the good earl of Warwick. It is of the altar kind, and has a full-size figure of the earl in armour, in a recumbent position. He died in

1589. He was brother of the famous earl of Leicester, whose monument is next noticed.

The tomb of Robert Dudley, earl of Leicester, favourite of Queen Elizabeth, stands at north side of the chapel. It is a splendid monument of the altar kind, bearing the recumbent figures of the earl and Lettice Knowles, his third wife, under a rich canopy supported by four Corinthian pillars. The earl is in armour, and deco-

TOMB OF EARL OF LEICESTER,

rated with the Order of the Garter and that of St. Michael. A Latin inscription gives him credit for virtues which history refuses to associate with his name. He died September 4, 1588, from the effects, it is said, of poison he had himself prepared for others.

O

The bill for his funeral amounted to £4000—an enormous sum for that age.

Against the south wall, and near the altar, is a fine monument to Robert, infant son to the earl of Leicester just mentioned. The tomb, which is of the altar kind, has a finely-sculptured figure of a child, seven or eight years old. An epitaph bears that the tomb contains the body of " the noble Impe, Robert of Dudley, Baron of Denbigh, sonne of Robert Earl of Leicester, and nephew and heir to Ambrose Earl of Warwick. He was born to the earl by his last countess, and died in 1584, when yet a child.

The *Chantry* is on the north side of the building. The tourist will be interested by its fine roof of pendant capitals, its floor of black and red glazed tiles, and its small piscina. The *Oratory*, or as some call it, the *Confessional*, is reached by an ascent of four steps from the north side of the chantry. The roof is fan-vaulted. At the east end is a seat, and beside it an oblique opening in the wall, through which confession is supposed to have been made. The place, however, in the opinion of some antiquarians, is a very unusual one for confession, being so near the choir and high altar. Below the choir, and entered from the churchyard, is a very interesting crypt, possibly part of the original church. At the north-eastern end is the burial-place of the earls of Warwick. In this crypt is preserved an ancient ducking stool. Among the monkish relics which were exhibited in the church before the Reformation were the following :—" Part of the chair of the patriarch Abraham ; of the burning bush of Moses ; of the manger in which Jesus was laid ; a thorn from His crown ; a piece of the cross ; part of the towel in which His body was wrapped by Nicodemus ; some hair of the Virgin Mary ; parts of her girdle and of her sepulchre ; part of the face of

St. Stephen; bones of Egidus, King Edward, St. Swithin, Alkemand, Rufus; bones of the Innocents; relics of St. James, St. George, St. Nicholas; and part of the penitential garment of St. Thomas, Archbishop of Canterbury."

St. Nicholas' Church is a modern structure, having been erected in 1799. A religious edifice occupying this site was destroyed by Canute the Dane in 1016, and rebuilt by Henry de Newburgh, the first Norman earl, whose son granted it to the canons of the collegiate church of St. Mary's, which he had lately founded. At the Dissolution it was granted by Henry VIII. to the burgesses of Warwick. In 1748 the ancient tower was taken down, and replaced by the present tower and spire; and in 1779 the body was rebuilt. It contains several monuments of some antiquity but no importance.

St. Paul's Church, Friars Street, erected in 1844 as a chapel of ease to St. Mary's, is of no architectural importance. Its east window, a good specimen of stained glass, is the production of a Warwick house.

Service is also performed in the chapel of St. James, over the West Gate, noticed below.

There are several Dissenting chapels, but they are architecturally unimportant. The first minister of the *Independent Chapel* Cow Lane, was the Rev. John Newton, the friend of Cowper, and author of the "Olney Hymns."

Leicester's Hospital, a fine example of the old half-timber style of building, stands at the western extremity of High Street. This structure originally belonged to the guilds of "The Holy Trinity and the Blessed Virgin" and "St. George the Martyr," and came after the Dissolution into the possession of the famous Robert Dudley, earl of Leicester, who endowed it as a collegiate hospital for twelve impotent men, and one master, a professor of divinity. The men admitted to this charity are called "brethren," and must wear a blue gown with Leicester's crest of a bear and ragged staff on the left sleeve, without which badge they are not allowed to appear in public. An Act of Parliament was obtained in 1813, modifying the original settlement. The allowance to each brother was made £80 a-year, while his patent cost £8; the master's salary was advanced to £400. The annual revenue of the institution is about £3000 per annum. In the appointment of brethren (which rests in the heir-general of the noble founder) the preference is given to those who have been maimed in the service of their country. Candidates must not have more than £50 a-year. The garden of the Hospital is very tastefully laid out, and commands a fine view of the adjacent country. In the adjoining CHAPEL OF ST. JAMES over the West Gate of the town, the brethren meet for daily prayer, except when there is service at St. Mary's, when they are required to attend there. This small chapel is neatly fitted up for the use of the master and brethren, and has a fine window of stained glass, and a good painting of the Ascension by Millar. It was in the Great Hall that James I. was entertained by Sir Fulke Greville, chancellor of the exchequer, and a tablet at the upper end commemorates the circumstance. In the kitchen there is preserved an old Saxon chair.

The PRIORY OF ST. SEPULCHRE stood on the north side of the town. It was founded in the reign of Henry I. by Henry de Newburgh, earl of Warwick, and his son, on the site of an ancient church. This religious house, which was instituted for regular canons in imitation of the order of the Holy Sepulchre at Jerusalem, prospered greatly under the fostering care of the earls of Warwick, and was possessed of many estates at the Dissolution. It was then bestowed on Thomas Hawkins, who pulled down the ancient edifice and erected the present building, which is a good specimen of the Elizabethan style of domestic architecture.

The COLLEGE SCHOOL, an antique edifice at the east end of St. Mary's churchyard, was built in the reign of Henry VI., by Richard Beauchamp, and endowed by Henry VIII., for the education, free of expense, of the native children of the town. Two exhibitions of the value of £70 each, for the space of seven years, are attached to this institution, for the education of young men at the university of Oxford.

There are several charitable institutions deserving of mention. SIR THOMAS WHITE'S CHARITY has the object of assisting young tradesmen, " inhabitants, being of good fame," by the free loan of £50 for nine years, on giving good security. The revenue of this charity is upwards of £800 a-year. The ALMSHOUSES are numerous.

THE TOWN GATES.—The ancient ornamental entrances to the town, called respectively the East and West gates, are in good though not appropriate repair, having been from time to time cased, without any pains to preserve their original character. They are situated at the opposite ends of the main street. The *East Gate* has over it the chapel of St. Peter, built in the reign of Henry VI.,· now used as a charity school. The *West Gate*, called also the Hongyng Gate, has above it the chapel of St. James. This chapel was given to the church of St. Mary by Roger de Newburgh, earl of Warwick. Subsequently it was bestowed by Thomas de Beauchamp, earl of Warwick, on the guild of St. George ; and eventually it came into the possession of Robert Dudley, earl of Leicester, who appropriated it to the use of the brethren of the neighbouring hospital founded by him. There is an oil painting of the Ascension above the communion-table.

Several other public buildings may be mentioned. The COUNTY HALL, erected about the year 1776, is a handsome edifice, with a front ornamented with Corinthian columns. The COURT-HOUSE, erected in 1730, is used for municipal business, town meetings, and occasional festive gatherings. The COUNTY GAOL is a large and substantial stone building, its front displaying little in the way of architectural ornamentation beyond columns of the Doric order. The MUSEUM in the Market-House contains some interesting objects. There is also a respectable PUBLIC LIBRARY.

WARWICK CASTLE.

WARWICK CASTLE, "that fairest monument," as Scott calls it, "of ancient and chivalrous splendour which yet remains uninjured by time," is situated at the south-east side of the town, on a rock, the base of which is washed by the Avon. It is one of the few real old baronial residences still kept up and inhabited; and whether on account of its antiquity, architecture, costliness of the objects of art which it contained, beauty of its grounds, or old associations, it has long claimed the particular attention of the tourist. We have previously alluded to the unfortunate fire which played such havoc at this fine old seat at the close of the year 1871. The foundation of this castle is attributed to Ethelfleda, daughter of Alfred the Great, in 915. The building erected by this lady was styled the Dungeon, and is supposed to have occupied an artificial mound of earth on the west side of the present structure. Turchill, who possessed it at the time of the Conquest, and added considerably to its fortifications by direction of king William, was shortly afterwards removed to make way for Henry de Newburgh, constituted the first Norman earl of Warwick. In the war with the barons, which embroiled the latter years of the reign of Henry III., the castle was surprised by the rebels, and, with the exception of the towers, levelled with the ground. It was restored and greatly strengthened by Thomas de Beauchamp, earl of Warwick, in the reign of Edward III. His son, of the same name, built Guy's Tower, in the north-east part of the building, in 1394. Various additions were made from time to time; and it is stated that the foundation of a new tower was laid by Richard III. Sir Fulke Greville, afterwards Lord Brooke, to whom the estate was granted by James I., restored the castle from the ruinous and dilapidated condition into which it had been suffered to fall. He expended the enormous sum, for that time, of £20,000 in repairs and embellishments, making it, as Dugdale remarks, "not only a place of great strength, but extraordinary delight; with most pleasant gardens, walks, and thickets, such as this part of England can hardly parallel; so that now it is the most princely seat that is within the midland parts of this realm." During the Parliamentary war an unsuccessful attack was made on the castle by the earl of Northampton, August 1642. On this occasion it was gallantly defended by Sir Edward Peyto, with a single piece of ordnance, until relieved by Lord Brooke. The castle and estate have continued down to the present day in the family of Greville. The title of Earl of Warwick, however, did not come into this family till 1759, when, on its extinction in the person of the last male representative of the house of Rich, earls of Warwick and Holland (with whom it had remained since 1618), it was conferred on the eighth Lord Brooke. George, second Earl Brooke and Warwick, grandfather of the present earl, expended vast sums in the adornment of the castle and grounds.

On entering within the principal gateway, the tourist will be invited to inspect the objects of interest contained in the PORTER'S LODGE. These consist chiefly of very imposing relics of the legendary Guy of Warwick. Here are shown Guy's sword, shield, breastplate, helmet, and walking-staff, all of enormous weight and size. The helmet weighs 7 lbs., the shield 32, the sword 20, the breastplate 52. The horse armour is of a later date, and of lighter construction. Conspicuous among the relics are Guy's porridge-pot and flesh-fork. The former of these is a large pot of bell metal, capable of containing 102 gallons, and produces a deafening sound when struck with the flesh-fork, which in dimensions resembles a pitchfork. The old woman who has charge of these relics informs the tourist that the porridge-pot is "now used as a punchbowl," she herself having seen it thrice filled and emptied on the occasion of the coming of age of the present Earl of Warwick. Other relics of Guy are an immense rib of the famous dun cow which he killed at Dunsmore heath, the pith of her horns, and one joint of the spine; the tusk and shoulder-blade of a wild boar; his lady's iron stirrups and slippers, etc. Besides these relics, the Porter's Lodge contains a Toledo sword, a Spanish halbert, maces, daggers, bar, chain, and spike-shot, found in the outer court; and a stone coffin found in the inner court.

The approach to the castle is by a winding road cut out of the solid rock, at the termination of which the majestic structure bursts at once on the view. The two lofty towers immediately arrest the eye. That on the left is Cæsar's Tower, the most ancient part of the building. On the right is Guy's Tower, so named in honour of the famous champion whose relics have just been examined. These will be noticed in a survey of the grounds and exterior features of the building.

The principal entrance to the castle is by a flight of steps through a Gothic porch on the south-east side of the inner court. This gives the visitor admission to the GREAT BARONIAL HALL, which along with the dining-room was entirely consumed by the recent fire, excepting the external walls. Previous to this calamity, the damages of which are being restored, this formed the first of a magnificent suite of apartments, the whole length of which could be taken in at a glance. The hall is 62 feet long, 40 wide, and 35 high. The ancient ceiling was removed in 1830, when an elaborately-wrought Gothic roof (designed by Poynter of London) was substituted, blazoned, not merely with the arms of the present noble earl, but also with the armorial bearings of the different earls and dukes of Warwick who have been knights of St. George, as well as the quarterings of the noble families with which the house of Warwick has been allied in different generations. The floor of the hall consists of polished squares of white and red Venetian marble, alternately arranged in lozenge fashion. This floor, which was expressly cut and prepared at Venice, has been seriously damaged wherever the richly-carved roof collapsed, and the ponderous beams fell from above. The apartment was lined with ancient armour, weapons, carvings, and other curiosities, nearly all of which have perished. Over the west door was suspended a large gun of curious workmanship, taken from a Spanish ship by Lord Archibald Hamilton, great-grandfather of the late earl.

Here, too, were preserved a helmet of Oliver Cromwell's, and the leathern doublet (spotted with blood) in which Lord Brooke, one of the generals of the Parliamentary army, was killed in 1643.

From the windows of the Great Hall, as indeed also from those of the other apartments, fine views are to be obtained. A hundred feet below flows the Avon, washing the castle's base. A bar, over which the stream has a tiny fall, as some of its water is diverted for the purpose of turning an old mill, and the remains of an ancient bridge in the middle of the stream, richly decked with shrubs, add very much to the picturesqueness of the scene. Farther up the stream is seen the New Bridge, a fine span of 105 feet. The more distant landscape is very fine, taking in the windings of the river for a considerable distance, through open and wooded country, the view being bounded in the far distance by the hills of Worcestershire and Gloucestershire.

Before leaving the Great Hall the visitor would do well to look down the long arched chapel passage, as from this point a splendid equestrian picture of Charles I. by Vandyke can be seen to great advantage. The king is mounted on a grey horse, and attended by his equerry, Mons. de St. Antoine, bearing his helmet. The effect is most life-like. It is said that Sir Joshua Reynolds offered 500 guineas for this painting.

The GREAT BANQUETING HALL, which almost entirely escaped the ravages of the fire, contains some fine antlers of the Irish Elk deer.

The "Kenilworth Buffet," an exquisite piece of decorative furniture, demands a distinct notice. It was constructed out of a colossal oak-tree from the grounds of Kenilworth Castle, measuring 10 feet in diameter, and containing 600 cubic feet of timber. It was executed by Cookes and Sons, cabinetmakers and decorative artists of Warwick, who very appropriately took the subjects for their carved relievos from Scott's novel of "Kenilworth." The buffet, or sideboard, was exhibited at the "world's fair" in 1851, and was regarded as one of the finest specimens of wood-carving displayed in the Exhibition. The carving on the centre panel represents Queen Elizabeth entering the castle in state ; that on the left is devoted to the well-known scene of Amy Robsart in the grotto casting herself on the protection of Elizabeth ; and that on the right has for its subject Leicester confessing his marriage to the Queen. This fine specimen of art was purchased for £1200, and presented by the county to the present Earl of Warwick, on the occasion of his marriage, March 10, 1852.

The DINING-ROOM, the floor of which was unburnt, enters off the Banqueting Hall. It is richly gilt, and adorned with representations of lions by Rubens.

Two large Etruscan vases here, and the busts of Augustus Cæsar, Scipio Africanus, and the Emperor Trajan, were also scarcely injured. This room was adorned with paintings of Frederick Prince of Wales, by Jonathan Richardson ; and of Augusta (his consort), and an infant (George III.), by Philips. And it is pleasant to know that almost all the valuable paintings in the various state apartments were saved, although many of them had to be cut from their frames.

The RED DRAWING-ROOM contains many exquisite and valuable paintings, and other objects of art. Above the chimney-piece, to the right, is a Dutch Burgomaster (Rembrandt) ; to the left, the wife of Snyder (Vandyke) ; opposite, Joanna of Arragon (Raffaelle) ; near the window, Thomas Howard, Earl of Arundel, collector of the Arundelian marbles (Rubens) ; near the door, on the left, Marquis of Spinola (Rubens) ; in the centre,

Margaret, Duchess of Parma (Paolo Veronese); opposite the window, a Lady and her Son (Vandyke). Some
beautiful urns and vases in marble and bronze adorn
the mantel-piece, tables, and buhl cabinets in this room.
A clock of curious and beautiful workmanship is over
the mantel-piece. The table of "pietra commessa" is
formed of precious stones tastefully fitted together,
among which are the amethyst, the onyx, the sardonyx,
the agate, and lapis-lazuli. This room, which was but
little injured by the fire, also contains some very rare
china.

The CEDAR DRAWING-ROOM is exquisitely furnished.
On every side the eye is charmed with objects of art,
rare for their antiquity or splendid workmanship. The
chimneypiece is unique, it being affirmed that the
marble of which it is composed is of a species not elsewhere to be seen in England. On the tables in this
room, all of which are of a beautiful and costly description, and one of which,* inlaid with marble, and lava
from Vesuvius, will attract attention, are placed, a
marble bust from the Justinian Minerva at Rome, two
fine Etruscan vases, a beautiful wax model of Venus,
and two fine busts of the late Earl of Warwick, and
the Countess of Warwick. The most interesting of
the paintings in this room are—Circe the Enchantress,
a noble painting by Guido; the Muse of Painting, by
William Patoun; the well-known half-length portrait
of Charles I., by Vandyke; James Graham, Marquis
of Montrose, and Don Ferdinand de Toledo, Duke of
Alva, both by the same artist; and Edward Wortley
Montague, by Rowney.

THE GREEN OR GILT DRAWING-ROOM.—The ceiling
of this room, which is magnificently gilt, attracts universal admiration. On the chimney-piece, which is of

* The other is in the Gilt Drawing-Room.

elegant workmanship, are fine vases, bronzes, and other antiques. A Florentine table, composed of precious stones valued at £10,000, bronze statues of gladiators, and a fine cinque cento figure, in white marble, of the Faun Marsyas, deserve notice. There is also a beautiful wax model of Venus. The paintings in this apartment are of immense value. That of Ignatius Loyola, opposite the fireplace, is one of the finest and most valuable pictures in the extensive collection of the Earl of Warwick. It is a full-length portrait by Rubens, and was painted for the Jesuit college of Antwerp, whence it was brought to this country soon after the French Revolution. Right and left of this picture are portraits by Vandyke, Lely, and Jansens. The following will be found deserving of special notice :—Mary, Queen of Scots, and her son James I. of England, over the mantel-piece ; two portraits of the Earl of Stratford ; portraits of Charles I. and Henrietta Maria, his consort ; Prince Rupert, whole-length, by Vandyke ; Robert Rich, Earl of Warwick, and Lord High Admiral of England during the Commonwealth, by Vandyke ; Thomas Howard, Earl of Arundel, a magnificent full-length portrait, by Rubens ; Robert Dudley, Earl of Leicester, the favourite of Queen Elizabeth ; and a Girl Blowing Bubbles, by Murillo.

THE STATE BED-ROOM.—The chief object of interest in this apartment is the bed of Queen Anne, an interesting relic of antiquity. The bed and its furniture are of crimson velvet, embroidered with green and yellow silk, and were presented to the great-grandfather of the present earl by George III. Queen Elizabeth slept in this room when on a visit to Warwick Castle. The walls are hung with curious tapestry, made at Brussels in 1604, and supposed to represent the gardens of Versailles. This room contains some rich buhl cabinets, vases, antique Indian bowls, small marble figures, and a very valuable pietra commessa table. There are portraits of Queen Anne by Kneller, full-length; Robert Devereux, Earl of Essex, by Zucchero; Marquis of Huntly, by Vandyke; Sir Robert Walpole.

LADY WARWICK'S BOUDOIR is a delightful retreat, at the west end of the castle, terminating this range of apartments. It is hung with pea-green silk and velvet, and the furniture and ornaments are of the richest and most tasteful kind. Its windows, too, command a fine and varied prospect. It would be impossible to enumerate here all the objects of *vertu* with which this exquisite boudoir is adorned. There are bronze casts, groups in terra cotta, crystal vases, ormolu, buhl, and marqueterie tables and stands, etc. There is also a large number of splendid paintings, many of which are of much historical interest. Here is the portrait of "bluff King Hal," a half-length, by Holbein, and one of Anne Boleyn, by the same artist; one of the Duchess of Cleveland, by Lely, as well as portraits of several others of the beauties of the court of Charles II.; a fine half-length portrait of Martin Luther, by Holbein; Henry IV. of France, by Patoun; a head of St. Jerome, and a Boar Hunt, by Rubens. There are also landscapes, figures, and sacred subjects, by Salvator Rosa, Teniers the younger, Gerard Dow, Vandervelde the younger, Vandyke, etc.

The COMPASS ROOM comes next. It has a fine window of painted glass, said to be the work of Rubens. Among the paintings are—Head of an Old Woman, by Rubens; A Reformer, by William Van Mieris; Storm at Sea, by Vandervelde the younger; a Bacchanalian group, by Rubens; Triton and Sea-Horses, by the same great master; and Napoleon I., by David.

The Chapel Passage, contains a beautiful bust in white marble of Edward the Black Prince ; the equestrian painting of Charles I., by Vandyke, already noticed. Mrs. Syddons, by Reynolds, and the Duke of Parma, by P. Veronese. The *Chapel* itself does not call for any special notice. It is tastefully fitted up ; its Gothic windows, *temp.* Elizabeth, being filled with painted glass. In the Armour Passage will be found a plaster cast of the face of Oliver Cromwell.

After completing the examination of the interior of the castle, the tourist may proceed to view the Towers and Grounds. *Cæsar's Tower* is evidently the most ancient part of the structure. The origin of its name is not known, the opinion which some writers have held that it was built by Julius Cæsar being utterly destitute of any reasonable grounds. It is octangular in form, of immense strength, and in excellent preservation. Beneath it is a gloomy dungeon, with inscriptions on its walls by some of the miserable wretches who have pined within it. This tower is 147 feet high. *Guy's Tower*, to the top of which the tourist may ascend, if he please, was built in 1394 by the second Thomas de Beauchamp. From the base to the battlements it measures about 130 feet, but looks higher and more imposing than Cæsar's Tower from being built on a more elevated part of the rock. On the walls of various apartments in this tower may be seen devices of various kinds, fleurs de lys, initials, names, and sentences in English or French scraped in relief, the work, doubtless, of long and weary hours of captivity.* A fine view is to be had from the summit

---

* The Earl of Lindsay wounded at Edgehill died here, in the 1st guard-room ; while in the 2d guard-room will be observed an inscription, evidently carved by a German prisoner, "Ich bin ein gefangene." Off the latter room, entrance is obtained to the Torture-Room, where there is a Latin inscription, the work of a captive priest.

of the Tower. The position of the ancient moat may be very distinctly seen below. Besides the smaller towers, which do not require any special notice, the tourist should not fail to visit the GREENHOUSE, which contains the famous Warwick Vase. This exquisite work of Grecian art was discovered in 1774, at the bottom of a lake near the Emperor Hadrian's Tiburtine villa at Tivoli, 14 miles from Rome, and purchased by Sir William Hamilton, then ambassador at Naples. It is of white marble, of circular shape, measuring, including the plinth, nearly seven feet in height; in circumference it is 21 feet; and it is capable of hold-ing 163 gallons. We copy the inscription:—

Hoc pristinæ Artis
Romanæ Q. Magnificentiæ Monumentum
Ruderibus Villæ Tiburtinæ
Hadriano Aug. In Deliciis Habitæ Effosum
Restitui Curavit
Eques Gulielmus Hamilton
A Georgio III. Mag. Brit. Rege
Ad Sicil Regem Ferdinandum IV. Legatus
Et in patriam transmissum
Patrio Bonarum Artium Genio Dicavit
An. Ac. n. CIƆDCCLXXIV.

Visitors are allowed to walk through the pleasure-grounds, which are charmingly laid out. Among the fine trees which adorn them the stately cedars of Lebanon will not fail to attract admiration.

VICINITY OF WARWICK.*

GUY'S CLIFF is rather more than a mile from War-wick, and is deservedly celebrated for its natural and artificial beauties. To this place, according to the old legends, Guy of Warwick retired, after renouncing war

* See also the VICINITY OF LEAMINGTON.

and love, and scooped for himself a cave out of the rock, in which he lived, and died, and was buried. There can be no doubt that there was a hermitage here from a very early period. Richard Beauchamp founded a chantry for two priests in 1422, and in pursuance of his will the chapel was rebuilt, and the statue of Guy erected in it. John Rous, the Warwick antiquary, was priest here in the reign of Edward IV. At the Dissolution the chapel and its possessions were bestowed upon Sir Edward Flammock. After various transmissions, it is now the property of the Hon. Mr. Percy.

Leland calls Guy's Cliff "the abode of pleasure, a place meet for the Muses;" Camden, "the very seat of pleasantness;" and Sir William Dugdale remarked that it is "a place this of so great delight, in respect to the river gliding below the rock, the dry and wholesome situation, and the fair grove of lofty elms overshadowing it, that to one who desireth a retired life, either for his devotions or study, the like is hardly to be found." The view of Guy's Cliff from the Coventry road, through a long and magnificent avenue of fir-trees, is universally admired. More comprehensive views are to be obtained from various parts of a foot-path through the fields to Leamington, past the church and village of Milverton. The view in particular from the old mill where the foot-bridge crosses the Avon, opposite Guy's Cliff, is extremely picturesque. The house is only shown to visitors when the family is not at home; but the views of scenery in the neighbourhood are so fine that the tourist will scarcely think his time lost, even though he may not have the opportunity of inspecting it.

The singular excavations in the rock which rises in the courtyard were probably the work of the hermits and

P

chantry priests of former times, perhaps undertaken in imitation of the devout Sir Guy. On the left hand is the *Chapel of the Magdalen,* built on the rock, containing a statue of Guy, eight feet high, much defaced.*

Guy's Cave will be viewed with interest. According to the old legend the cave was constructed by himself—

> " There with my hands I hewed a house
> 　Out of a craggy rock of stone;　*
> And lived like a palmer poor,
> 　Within that cave myself alone."

On one side of the cave are some traces of an inscription in Saxon characters, much too faint to be deciphered. *Guy's Well* is also shown, and a walk is named after the fair Phillis, who, as the legend runs, used often to give alms to the hermit, and to resort to him for his saintly counsel, never dreaming that the solitary man was her long-lost husband, whom she be-

* The engraving given above represents this statue as it existed in the time of Pennant, when it was still uninjured.

lieved to be dead, or a captive in the Holy Land. Guy was induced to betake himself to this life of penance and mortification from a deep feeling of remorse for having wrought so much mischief and bloodshed in the world for the sake of one woman, Phillis having, like the noble ladies of her time, required deeds of arms from her lover before she would yield to his affection. Guy made himself known to her when he was dying, and of course the story ends with their being buried in the same grave.

The house is comparatively modern, the principal part being built early in the eighteenth century by Samuel Greatheed, Esq. Various additions have been made more recently. The apartments shown to visitors contain many fine paintings and other objects of interest. Several of the pictures are by the late Mr. Greatheed, father of Mrs. B. Percy, and by his son, a youth of great talent and promise, who died in 1804, at the early age of twenty-two. The steps leading to the entrance-hall are ornamented in plaster. In a recess is a cast of the Venus de Medici. The *Small Drawing-Room* contains some family portraits, among them two of the earls of Lindsey. There are also pictures by Van Eyck, Van Steen, Biltius, Vander, Myn, Wovermans, etc. The *Library* contains a fine view in Venice, by Canaletti ; a portrait by Lauder of the Hon. C. B. Percy ; a Pot-House, by Brouwer ; a Pouting Child, by Sir Joshua Reynolds ; Jonah cast on the Dry Land, by Salvator Rosa, and one or two fine copies by the old masters. The *Drawing-Room*, besides family portraits (Duchess of Ancaster, by Sir Godfrey Kneller ; and Hon. Mrs. Percy and her daughter, from Cregan), contains several valuable pictures, the chief of which are :—A View on the River Maese, by Albert Cuyp ; View of Dort, by Van Goyen ; Cupid Blowing Bubbles, by Castiglione; the Angels appearing to the Shepherds, by Bassano; and a copy of the Madonna and Child, by Raphael, in the Dresden Gallery. The view from the window of this room is highly picturesque. In the *Vestibule* are Venus and Adonis by Ritscher; a Landscape by Ruysdale; Christ and the Woman of Samaria by Sebastian Ricci; and a painting by the younger Mr. Greatheed, already alluded to, having for its subject the Discovery by Atabualpa of Pizarro's Ignorance of Reading and Writing. In the arcade to which this room opens are some fine Italian vases. The *Dining-Room* contains a large picture by the younger Greatheed, the "Cave of Despair," as described in Spenser's "Faerie Queen," a subject which the young artist has treated with considerable power. There is here also a bronze equestrian statue of the Duke of Cumberland. The *Small Dining-Room* is adorned with pictures by the late Mr. Greatheed. The portrait of Napoleon was pronounced by the emperor's mother the most striking resemblance of her son that she had ever seen, yet Mr. Greatheed had only the means of seeing Napoleon at a public audience. There are three subjects from Shakspere:—King Lear and his Daughter, Macbeth and his Lady, and Shylock. In addition to these, there are copies, well executed, of the St. Jerome of Corregio, and of Diogenes, by Spagnoletto. This room also contains busts of John and Charles Kemble, and Mrs. Siddons and her daughter. Mrs. Siddons lived for some time at Guy's Cliff as waiting-woman to Lady Mary Greatheed.

A little beyond Guy's Cliff, on the opposite side of the Kenilworth road, is a small wooded eminence called BLACKLOW HILL, the scene of the summary execution of Piers Gaveston, Earl of Cornwall, the favourite of Edward II. Having surrendered himself, on a promise of safety, to the insurgent barons, he was conveyed to Deddington Castle, near Banbury; which place being attacked by Guy de Beauchamp, Earl of Warwick, the unhappy prisoner was, after a mere show of resistance, delivered up to him. Warwick bore a deadly hatred to Gaveston, having been branded by him with the epithet of "the black hound of Arden." Gaveston was carried off to Warwick Castle, and thence to Blacklow Hill, where he was beheaded. On the moss-grown rock on its side may be seen the inscription, nearly illegible: "P. Gaveston, Earl of Cornwall, beheaded here + 1311." A stone cross erected by the late Mr. Greatheed adds materially to the picturesque beauty of the spot. On its base is the following inscription: "On the 1st of July 1312, in the hollow of this rock, was beheaded Piers Gaveston, Earl of Cornwall, the minion of a hateful king; in life, as in death, a striking instance of misrule."

HATTON is three miles from Warwick, and five from Leamington, on the Birmingham road, and about a mile from the station of the same name. This small village is noted as having been the residence of Dr. Samuel Parr, who was curate of the parish for forty years. It is to Dr. Parr's liberality and taste that the *Church* is indebted for many of its decorations. The stained-glass windows are much admired. The east window has a representation of the Crucifixion, and the figures of the apostles Paul and Peter. The north and south windows of the chancel have for their subjects the Agony in the Garden and the Ascension. There are also, in painted glass, figures of the Twelve Apostles, of Faith, Hope, and Charity, and portraits of Archbishops Cranmer and Tillotson. The church contains numerous monumental inscriptions, some of which are the work of Dr. Parr. and exhibit that sententious and admirable classical style for which he was so distinguished. A tablet to his own memory is placed in the chancel. Dr. Parr was born in 1746 at Harrow-on-the-Hill, and died here in 1825.

On the way to Hatton from Warwick, about two miles from the latter place, the tourist passes on his right the *County Lunatic Asylum*, an extensive and elegant structure in the Tudor style. It was erected at a cost of £50,000. It has a frontage of 700 feet, and can accommodate from 300 to 400 patients.

About a mile south from the Hatton station are the small remains of *Pinley Abbey*, a Benedictine nunnery, founded shortly after the Conquest.

WROXHALL ABBEY is three miles from Hatton, and six from Warwick, on the Birmingham road. Dugdale tells a romantic legend regarding its foundation. Hugh de Hatton, who held the lordships of Hatton and Wroxhall from Henry, Earl of Warwick, was taken prisoner in the Holy Land, where he had been serving against the infidels, and confined there for seven years. The good knight at length bethought himself of his patron saint St. Leonard, who appeared to him in a vision, and after making him vow to erect a house of St. Benedict, transported him miraculously to Wroxhall woods, not far from his own house. He fulfilled his vow by erecting a nunnery here, and making two of his daughters become nuns. At the Dissolution the abbey and its possessions were granted to Robert Burgoyne, who erected a mansion on its site. This mansion is in the form of a quadrangle, the western front of which was raised from its foundation by Robert Burgoyne, and the southern and eastern sides adapted from the remains of the previous building. The north side is occupied by the church or chapel, which seems to have been originally part of the cloisters. The manor was purchased in 1713 by Sir Christopher Wren, the celebrated architect, with whose family it still remains. The *Church* is an ancient and picturesque building. Dugdale ascribes the date of its erection, or at least of its reconstruction, to the early part of the reign of Edward II. It is of the Decorated style, but without aisles. The ancient wood-carvings on the open seats and communion-chairs, and three carved stones, which have doubtless been brought here from some more ancient part of the buildings, will attract some notice. The tourist, however, will probably be most interested by the stained glass, which is of great antiquity and fair preservation. The large east window has lost all its original stained glass, and contains several shields of more recent construction. One very perfect window contains in the centre a figure of St. Benedict, with a crozier in his left hand, and holding up the right in benediction. At the bottom is an Agnus Dei, and on either side is a kneeling figure. A smaller window, also perfect, is filled with foliage. Two other windows contain fragments of ancient stained glass, one of them having a tolerably well-preserved representation of a male and female kneeling. There are no ancient monuments in the church, with the exception of a fragment of a monumental brass, representing a female figure with her hands joined in prayer. This is supposed to belong to the tomb of one of the abbesses, which was to be seen in Dugdale's time, and contained the following inscription :—" Domina Jocosa Breme, filia Johanis Breme, et Priorissa de Wroxhall, obiit xxi Junii, anno M. D. xxviii."

WOOTON WAWEN.

In the vicinity of HENLEY-IN-ARDEN.

INDEX.

Q

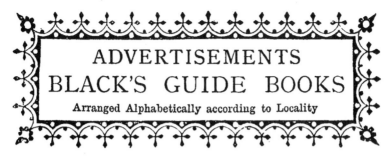

ABERDEEN.

MANN'S PALACE HOTEL,

UNION STREET AND BRIDGE STREET.

The Hotel 'Bus awaits the arrival of all through Trains.

THE PALACE is the most recently erected and only First-class Hotel in the City. The Management being under the direct and constant supervision of the Proprietor, who has had a long practical experience, and as *Chef de Cuisine* has had the honour of serving personally many of the Royal and Imperial Families of Europe, he trusts to merit the patronage of visitors.

LETTERS AND TELEGRAMS PROMPTLY ATTENDED TO.

Position, the most central and select, though only One Hundred Yards from the Railway Station.   CHARLES MANN, *Proprietor.*

FORSYTH'S HOTEL
90 TO 102 UNION STREET,
ABERDEEN.

M. & E. WALKER.

DEESIDE HYDROPATHIC ESTABLISHMENT,
HEATHCOT, near ABERDEEN.

THE Climate of Deeside is the healthiest in Scotland. Residents at this Establishment have the privilege of Salmon and Trout Fishing in the River Dee, which runs through the Estate of Heathcot.

The Turkish and other Baths are constructed with all the latest improvements necessary for the practice of Hydropathy. Terms, £2 : 10s. per week. For two in one Room, £2 each.

For Particulars, apply to Dr. STEWART, Medical Superintendent, Heathcot, near Aberdeen.

QUEEN'S HOTEL
ABERYSTWITH.

THIS Hotel is situated on the Marine Terrace, facing the sea, and contains several Private Sitting-Rooms, Coffee Rooms, Ladies' Drawing-Room, Library, and all its Bedrooms are pleasantly situated.

Table d'Hote at 6.30 during the Season.

Arrangements made for Families.

TARIFF ON APPLICATION.

W. H. PALMER, *Proprietor.*

ARDENTINNY.
ARDENTINNY HOTEL,
LOCH LONG.

M. FERGUSON, for many years head steward of the Loch Long and Loch Goil Steamers, has leased the above Hotel, which is beautifully situated on the banks of Loch Long, and at the entrance to the celebrated Glen Finart. This Hotel has been thoroughly repaired and elegantly furnished, and visitors are assured that every attention will be paid to their comfort.

CHARGES MODERATE.

Posting, with careful Drivers.   Fishing Boats.

AYR—LAND OF BURNS.

KING'S ARMS

FAMILY AND COMMERCIAL HOTEL.
(Under New Management.)

PRIVATE PARLOURS. LADIES' COFFEE ROOM.
COMMERCIAL ROOM.
LARGE STOCK ROOM. POSTING & LIVERY ESTABLISHMENT.
WM. SCOTT, Proprietor,
(*Late of* QUEEN'S HOTEL, AYR.)

BALLATER.

INVERCAULD ARMS HOTEL
Will be under

NEW MANAGEMENT

In connection with the Invercauld Arms Hotel, Braemar.

POSTING IN ALL ITS BRANCHES. : COACH TO BRAEMAR DAILY ON AND AFTER 1ST MAY,

THE

LOCHIEL ARMS HOTEL.
FRONT OF BEN NEVIS, BANAVIE.

REVISED TARIFF FOR 1881—

BED, 3s. each.	TABLE D'HOTE, 4s. 6d.
BREAKFAST, 2s. and 3s.	TEAS, 2s. and 3s.
LUNCHEON from 1s. to 2s. 6d.	ATTENDANCE, 1s. 6d. each.

Parties boarded, 12s. 6d. per Day; or £3:3s. per Week.

THE Situation is one of the finest in the Highlands, immediately in front of Ben Nevis, and the Views from the Hotel windows are unsurpassed.

ROUTE—*By David M'Brayne's Steamers from Glasgow, Oban, and Inverness, or by Coach from Kingussie.*

JOHN M'GREGOR, *Proprietor.*

GRAND
PUMP ROOM HOTEL

Is situated in the centre of the City, and connected with the finest suite of Mineral Water Baths in Europe,

IMMEDIATELY OPPOSITE THE GRAND PUMP ROOM AND ABBEY.

This Handsome Hotel is replete with every accommodation, and is especially adapted for those requiring the use of the Bath Waters.

The Wines are carefully selected, and the Cuisine is under an experienced Chef.

FOR PARTICULARS APPLY TO

C. W. RADWAY, *Lessee.*

BELFAST.
ROBINSON'S COMMERCIAL TEMPERANCE HOTEL,
82 DONEGALL STREET.

ESTABLISHED 1851.

A FIRST-CLASS Family and Commercial Hotel. Conducted on strictly Abstinence Principles. Comfort, Quiet, and moderate Charges.

Private Sitting Rooms and Show Rooms.

BETTWS-Y-COED.
ROYAL OAK HOTEL

THIS Hotel has an unrivalled situation, and is very suitable as a centre from which the most beautiful scenery in North Wales may be visited. It is near the Station, to which it has a private road. The coaches for Llanberis, Beddgelert, and Bangor, start daily from the Hotel.

AN OMNIBUS MEETS EVERY TRAIN.
FISHING TICKETS FOR ALL THE NEIGHBOURING RIVERS.
Billiards.   Lawn Tennis.   Archery.
POSTING IN ALL ITS BRANCHES.
David Cox's celebrated Signboard Picture.

E. PULLAN, *Proprietor* (Ten Years Proprietor of the Crown Hotel, Harrogate).

BETTWS-Y-COED, NORTH WALES.

THE GWYDYR HOTEL.

THIS Hotel, which is near the Railway Station, offers every comfort and attention to Families and Tourists.

Tickets for fishing may be had at the bar.

E. FAICHNEY, *Proprietor.*

BIDEFORD, DEVONSHIRE.
TANTON'S
FIRST-CLASS FAMILY AND COMMERCIAL HOTEL AND POSTING HOUSE.

THIS Hotel is pleasantly situated, facing the river Torridge, noted for its Salmon, Trout, and other fishing.

An Omnibus meets every train ; private Omnibuses and Carriages can be had at the shortest notice.

BILLIARDS.

N.B.—The Mail-Coach starts from this Hotel daily at 7.15 A.M., taking passengers, parcels, etc., for Clovelly, Hartland, and its neighbourhood.

CHAS. E. CLEMOW, PROPRIETOR.

and at ANDERTON'S HOTEL, Fleet Street, London.

BIDEFORD.
NEW INN FAMILY HOTEL.
HENRY ASCOT, *Proprietor.*

THIS old-established and commodious Hotel and Posting House is pleasantly situated in an elevated and central part of the town, and commands extensive views of the River Torridge and surrounding country, and is eleven miles distant from Clovelly.

PRIVATE SUITES OF APARTMENTS.

COFFEE, COMMERCIAL AND BILLIARD ROOMS.   POSTING AND LIVERY STABLES.

Omnibuses meet all Trains.

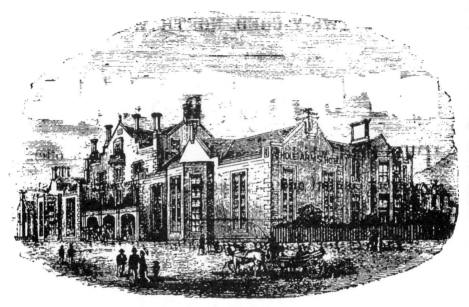

BLAIR-ATHOLE.
ATHOLE ARMS HOTEL.

Adjoining the Railway Station. No Omnibus necessary.

THE recently completed additions render this Hotel one of the largest and best appointed in the Highlands, while this year, by further refurnishing in the first style, no expense has been spared to enhance its reputation.

TABLE D'HÔTE daily during the season in the well-known magnificent Dining Hall, with which is connected *en suite* a spacious and elegantly furnished Drawing-Room.

Special terms for Board by the week, except during August.

Blair-Athole is much the nearest and most central point from which to visit Killiecrankie, the Queen's View, Loch Tummel, Rannoch, Glen Tilt, Braemar; the Falls of Bruar, Garry, Tummel, and Fender; the grounds of Blair Castle, &c.; and it is the most convenient resting-place for breaking the long railway journey to and from the North of Scotland.

THE POSTING DEPARTMENT is thoroughly well equipped.

Experienced Guides and Ponies for Glen Tilt, Braemar, and Mountain Excursions.

D. & P. T. MACDONALD, *Proprietors.*

BLAIR-ATHOLE.
THE TILT HOTEL.
Within Five Minutes' Walk from the Railway Station.
ALEXANDER STEWART, PROPRIETOR.

THIS HOTEL, under new Management, is beautifully situated opposite the entrance of famous GLEN TILT, BLAIR CASTLE GROUNDS, and within walking distance of the FALLS OF FENDER, THE SALMON LEAP, and other objects of interest.

Visitors and Tourists honouring this Hotel will find every attention paid to their comfort and convenience, combined with Moderate Charges.

POSTING IN ALL ITS DEPARTMENTS.

The Drives include Glen Tilt, the Pass of Killiecrankie, Queen's View, Loch Tummel, Loch Rannoch, Falls of Tummel, Falls of Bruar, &c. &c.

Letters and Telegrams for Apartments or Conveyances punctually attended to.

An Omnibus to and from the Station free of Charge.

Parties boarded by the week at a reduced rate except during August.

Guides and Ponies for Glen Tilt, Braemar, and other Excursions.

BLAIRGOWRIE.
QUEEN'S HOTEL.
Established — *Half a Century.*

THE above long-established and first-class HOTEL has recently been much enlarged and improved, so that Families, Tourists, and Commercial Gentlemen will find in it every comfort and attention. Blairgowrie is on the shortest and most direct route to Braemar and Balmoral, the drive to which is very grand, passing Craighall (Col. Clerk-Rattray), one of the most picturesquely-situated mansions in Scotland. Post Horses and Carriages of every description, with careful Drivers.

Charges strictly Moderate.

Coaches to Braemar early in July. Passengers booked at the Hotel.
An Omnibus waits all Trains. D. M'DONALD, PROPRIETOR.
Orders by Post or Telegram for Rooms, Carriages, or Coach seats, carefully attended to.

BLAIRGOWRIE.
ROYAL HOTEL.

FAMILIES, Tourists, and Commercial Gentlemen will find every endeavour being made to render this Hotel equal to its long-known reputation. Salmon Fishing on the Tay by the Day; or longer. FAMILIES BOARDED WEEKLY BY AGREEMENT.

A1 Stud of Horses and Vehicles.

Coach to and from Braemar daily in July; Seats secured by post or telegram.
'Bus meets all trains.

SHOOTINGS INSPECTED AND VALUED.
JOHN ANDERSON, *Proprietor.*

THE FIFE ARMS HOTEL
BRAEMAR, BY BALMORAL.
Patronised by Royal Family and Court.

MR. M'NAB begs respectfully to inform the Nobility, Gentry, and Tourists, that the extensive additions to the Hotel are now completed. The Hotel, as now constructed, comprises over 100 Bedrooms, a Dining Saloon (one of the largest and most elegant in Scotland), elegant Private Sitting-Rooms, Ladies' Drawing-Room, Billiard-Room, and Bath-Rooms.

Charges strictly moderate. Letters or Telegrams will receive the most careful attention. Posting in all its varied departments. Coaches during the Season daily from the hotel to Blairgowrie and Dunkeld, and twice daily between Ballater and Braemar.

Parties Boarded by the Week or Month.

NOTE.—*Gentlemen staying at the Hotel can have excellent Salmon or Trout Fishing.*

INVERCAULD ARMS. BRAEMAR. *J. T. Wimperis, Arcl*

BRAEMAR.

THE INVERCAULD ARMS,

The finest Hotel situation in Scotland.

Recently re-erected after Plans by J. T. WIMPERIS, Esq., Sackville St., London.

MAGNIFICENT DINING HALL, ELEGANT LADIES' DRAWING ROOM, AND NUMEROUS SUITES OF APARTMENTS.

POSTING IN ALL ITS BRANCHES.

Coaches during the Season to Blairgowrie, Dunkeld, and Ballater.
Excellent Salmon Fishing in connection with the Hotel.
Letters and Telegrams Punctually attended to.

A. M'GREGOR.

(IRELAND) INTERNATIONAL HOTEL, BRAY,
County Wicklow.

THIS FIRST-CLASS HOTEL is situated near the Railway Station, Sea-beach, and Esplanade, central to all the far-famed Scenery of the County of Wicklow.

Visitors to this fashionable place will find THE INTERNATIONAL HOTEL replete with every comfort, and the *Cuisine* and Wines of the best quality.

All Charges are fixed and moderate.

Boarding Terms per week may be had on application to the MANAGER.

C. DUFRESNE, *Proprietor.*

BRIDGE OF ALLAN.
QUEEN'S HOTEL.

This Hotel affords excellent accommodation for Tourists and Visitors.
The Hotel 'bus meets all Trains.

A. ANDERSON, *Proprietor.*

HYDROPATHIC ESTABLISHMENT.

BRIDGE OF ALLAN, NEAR STIRLING.

THE situation is high and dry, cool in summer and mild in winter. The House is well appointed, and the Baths are elegant and complete.

Terms, including all charges, £2 : 12 : 6 per week.

Applications to be addressed to MR. M'KAY, House Superintendent.

BUXTON, DERBYSHIRE.

CRESCENT HOTEL.

THIS FIRST-CLASS HOTEL for FAMILIES and GENTLEMEN forms the South Wing of the Crescent. It is only ONE MINUTE from RAILWAY STATIONS, and is *connected* by *Covered Colonnade* with the *Hot and Natural Baths, Drinking Wells,* and the *New Pavilion and Gardens,* where a splendid BAND performs Four Hours daily.

THE ASSEMBLY ROOM

in this Hotel, which has long been celebrated for its elegant proportions, has recently been redecorated in the first style, and is now converted into the

DINING-ROOM OF THE HOTEL.

Public, Dining, Drawing, Smoking, and Billiard Rooms.

SUITES OF APARTMENTS FOR PRIVATE FAMILIES.

TABLE D'HOTE AT 6 P.M.

FIRST-CLASS STABLING AND LOCK-UP COACH-HOUSES.

JOHN SMILTER, *Proprietor.*

CALLANDER.
THE M'GREGOR HOTEL.
ALEXANDER M'NAUGHTON, Proprietor
(For Ten Years Waiter at the Alexandra Hotel, Oban).

TOURISTS and Families visiting the above long-established and First-Class Hotel will have every comfort and attention, and the Charges will be found strictly moderate.

Salmon and Trout Fishing on several Lochs, also on three miles of the River Teith.

Letters and Telegrams for Rooms promptly attended to.

CARLISLE.
THE COUNTY AND STATION HOTEL,

FOR Families and Gentlemen, is connected with the Platform of the Central Railway Station by a covered way. Porters from this Hotel are in attendance on arrival of all Trains.

A Ladies' Coffee-Room.

CARNARVON, NORTH WALES.
THE ROYAL HOTEL
(LATE UXBRIDGE ARMS),
FIRST-CLASS FAMILY & COMMERCIAL ESTABLISHMENT
Beautifully situated on the Banks of the Menai Straits, and in close proximity to the Railway Station.

EDWARD HUMPHREYS.

An Omnibus will regularly attend the arrival of each Train at the Railway Station. Billiards in detached premises.

On and after June 19th, a Coach round Snowdon, after the arrival of the 9.25 a.m. train, via Beddgelert, Vale of Gwynant, and the Pass of Llanberis, arriving at the hotel for dinner, and in time for the train for Llandudno, Rhyl, &c.

CHATSWORTH HOTEL, EDENSOR,
DERBYSHIRE.

This Hotel is beautifully situated in Chatsworth Park, and within ten minutes' walk of the princely residence of the Duke of Devonshire.

The hotel is the largest in the neighbourhood, and its proximity to the Bowsley Station, on the Midland Railway, affords every facility to Tourists desirous of visiting the beauties of Haddon Hall, Matlock, the Mines at Castleton, Dove Dale, etc.

Omnibuses from the hotel meet all the principal trains at Rowsley Station.

A spacious Coffee-Room for Ladies. Private Sitting and well-appointed Bed-Rooms. Post-horses, etc.

HENRY HARRISON, Proprietor ;

IN CONNECTION WITH ST. ANN'S HOTEL, BUXTON.

Railway Station, Rowsley.   *Postal address*, Bakewell.

Day Tickets for the Chatsworth Fishery.

CHESTER.

THE GROSVENOR HOTEL.

FIRST-CLASS. Situated in the centre of the City, close to the Cathedral and other objects of interest.

A Large Coffee-Room and Ladies' Drawing Room for the convenience of Ladies and Families. The Bedrooms are large and handsomely furnished.

Open and close Carriages, and Posting in all its Branches.

Omnibuses attend the Trains for the use of Visitors to the Hotel. Tariff to be had on application. A Night Porter in attendance.

DAVID FOSTER, *Manager.*

CLIFTON DOWN HOTEL.
CLIFTON, NEAR BRISTOL.

THIS Hotel is within two hours and a half from London, by the Great Western Rail, per Flying Dutchman (the fastest train in the world). The situation of the hotel is unrivalled, being on the Downs, and facing the Suspension Bridge, St. Vincent's Rocks, and Nightingale Valley. Tourists should not miss seeing this truly grand and bold scenery. Visitors will find every comfort and Quietude ; and those proceeding to Ilfracombe should take Clifton on their route, and save the long and tedious journey by South Western. The hotel is noted for its extensive Wine List, and its Moderate charges. A private Omnibus meets all the express and principal trains.

N.B.—From this hotel the following TRIPS are easy, returning to the hotel the same day :—Chepstow Castle, the Wynd Cliff, Tintern Abbey, Wells Cathedral, Glastonbury, Tor, Bath, Weston-super-Mare, Clevedon, Portishead, Cardiff, Newport, and Channel Docks.

All communications address,

Clifton Hotel Company (Limited).   D. GITTINS, *Manager.*

CONWAY.

THE CASTLE HOTEL.

FIRST-CLASS. Beautifully situated in the Vale of Conway, and very central for Tourists in North Wales.

COLWYN BAY, NORTH WALES.

POLLYCROCHON HOTEL,

(Late the Residence of Lady Erskine).

THIS First-class Family Hotel is most beautifully situated in its own finely-wooded park in Colwyn Bay, commanding splendid land and sea views; there are miles of delightful walks in the adjacent woods. It is within a few minutes' walk of the Beach and ten minutes' of Colwyn Bay Station, and a short drive of Conway and Llandudno.

Sea-Bathing, Billiards, Posting.

J. PORTER, *Proprietor.*

CORK.

STEPHENS' COMMERCIAL HOTEL

(*Opposite the General Post Office, Cork*)

POSSESSES first-class accommodation for Tourists, Commercial Gentlemen, and Families.

It is very centrally situated, being opposite the General Post Office—close to the Bank, Theatre, &c. &c.

Charges extremely Moderate.

WILLIAM D. STEPHENS, PROPRIETOR,
From the West of England.

EXTRACT from a " Tour through Ireland," published in the *North Briton*, 1864:—

" When we arrived in Cork we took up our quarters at Stephens' Commercial Hotel, where we obtained excellent accommodation.

" What this Hotel lacks in external show is amply compensated by unremitting attention on the part of the Proprietors and their attendants to the comfort of their Guests. "

IMPERIAL  HOTEL.

CORK.

P. CURRY, Proprietor.

THIS long-established and well-known Hotel is conducted on the most approved and modern system. It possesses every requisite to promote the Comfort and Convenience of Tourists. The Hotel contains

OVER ONE HUNDRED BEDROOMS,

Three Coffee Rooms, Commercial Room, a Drawing Room for Ladies and Families, Suites of Private Apartments, Smoking and Billiard Rooms, Bath Rooms, &c.

TABLE D'HOTE DAILY AT HALF-PAST SIX O'CLOCK.

The Hotel adjoins the General Post Office; as also the Commercial Building, where Merchants meet on "'Change," and the earliest Telegraphic News is received, to the Reading Room, of which Visitors to the Hotel have free access. It has been patronised within the last few years by their Royal Highnesses the Prince of Wales, Duke of Connaught, Prince Alfred, Prince Napoleon, the Duc D'Orleans, the Comte de Paris, and the Count de Flandres, the successive Lords-Lieutenant of Ireland—Clarendon, Eglinton, Carlisle, Abercorn, and Marlborough—as well as by the Nobility, and most of the leading Gentry visiting Cork.

The Charges will be found most Moderate.

The Imperial Omnibuses attend the arrival and departure of each Train.

Extract from Sir CUSACK RONEY'S "Month in Ireland:"

"Judge Haliburton (Sam Slick) says, 'There are two things to be recommended to the notice of visitors to Ireland:—If you are an admirer of beautiful scenery, go to the Cove of Cork; if you want a good hotel, go to the Imperial.' The Hotel in question is situated in Pembroke Street, having an entrance also in the South Mall, through the Commercial Buildings, the splendid News Room of which is open to visitors to the Hotel. For convenience and comfort there is not a hotel superior to it in the Empire."

CRIEFF.
THE DRUMMOND ARMS HOTEL.

The only First-Class Hotel in Crieff. Families boarded by Week or Month. Large Posting Establishment.

PROMPT ATTENTION GIVEN TO ALL COMMUNICATIONS.

The Hotel Omnibus meets every Train.

D. MACKENZIE, PROPRIETOR.

DERBY.
THE ST. JAMES'S HOTEL,

IN the centre of the Town, facing the Post Office and Corn Market, is new and modern built, with every convenience for Families and Commercial Gentlemen. A Large Hall for Meetings, Wedding Breakfasts, Concerts, &c. Hot and Cold Baths. Stock Rooms.

THE NEW STABLING IS PERFECT AND EXTENSIVE.

J. WAGSTAFF, Proprietor.

DROGHEDA.
WHITE HORSE HOTEL.

JAMES J. KEPPOCH, Proprietor, begs to announce that, having greatly enlarged the above old Established Commercial and Family Hotel, he has now ample accommodation for all who may favour him with their patronage, and trusts, by strict attention to the comfort of his visitors, to merit a continuance of the support he has so long received.

Private Rooms.   Billiard Room.

Posting in all its Branches.   An Omnibus attends the Trains.

DUBLIN.
JURY'S HOTEL, COLLEGE GREEN.

In the centre of the City. Confidently recommended for cleanliness, convenience, and moderate charges.

LADIES' COFFEE ROOM AND DRAWING ROOM.

Table d'Hote at 3 and 6.30 p.m. daily, Sundays at 5.30 p.m. Two Night Porters.   Fire Escape, &c.

HENRY I. JURY, Proprietor.

DUBLIN.

SHELBOURNE HOTEL.

SITUATED in most central and fashionable part of Dublin, and is the great Tourist Hotel of Ireland. Contains magnificent Public Rooms, Elevator, Telegraph Office, &c. &c. First-Class. Charges Moderate.

JURY & COTTON, *Proprietors.*

DUBLIN.

SALT HILL HOTEL,

MONKSTOWN, CO. DUBLIN.

FIRST-Class Hotel for Families and Gentlemen. Pleasantly situated in its own grounds (twenty minutes by rail from Dublin). Elegantly furnished suites of apartments, spacious Coffee, Reception, and Drawing Rooms, facing the sea. An excellent Billiard Room, provided with a champion Billiard Table; Lawn Tennis and Croquet Grounds. Table d'Hote. Carriages in every variety. The whole under the personal superintendence of the Proprietor, WILLIAM PARRY.

N.B.—Special arrangements for families sojourning.

DUNKELD.

THE DUKE OF ATHOLE'S ARMS HOTEL.

D. ROBERTSON, *Proprietor* (late GRANT'S).

THIS Hotel, from its situation close to the beautiful Bridge of Dunkeld, commands an unrivalled view of the magnificent scenery on either side of the River Tay. The Apartments, both public and Private, are elegantly furnished and well aired.
Her Majesty the Queen, in her Journal of her Life in the Highlands, has been graciously pleased to take notice of this Hotel as being very clean, and having such a charming view from the windows. The Empress of the French, with her Son, the Prince Imperial, also visited this Hotel, and was pleased to express her entire approval of all the arrangements. EVERY ATTENTION IS PAID TO THE COMFORT OF VISITORS. *Job and Post Horses, with Careful Drivers. An Omnibus awaits the arrival of all the Trains.*
Seats can be secured at this Hotel for the Braemar Coach.

DUNOON.

THE CROWN HOTEL.

(Situated close to the Pier.)

THIS first-class Hotel has been lately enlarged and refurnished, and Tourists and Travelling Public will find every comfort, combined with moderate charges. Dunoon, by its mild climate, is recommended for a Winter Residence, and the " Crown " offers every comfort. Full Board, 50s, per week.

Hot and Cold Sea Water Baths. Table d'Hote Daily,

OSCAR TROEGER, *Proprietor.*

DUNBLANE HYDROPATHIC ESTABLISHMENT.

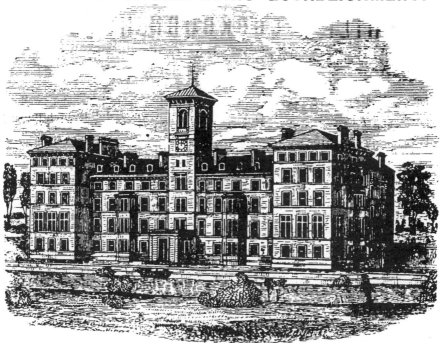

THIS Magnificent Establishment, built on a commanding eminence facing the Grampian Hills, and in close proximity to Dunblane Railway Station, offers to Tourists and Travellers all the Luxuries and Conveniences of a First-Class Metropolitan Hotel, and to parties requiring rest and change all the comforts and appliances (including the most skilled Medical Treatment) of the best English Hydropathic Institutions,—all combined with the most Moderate Charges.

Situated in the very centre of Scotland, at the entrance to the Highlands of Perthshire, Dunblane is an Important Railway Junction on the Main Line between England and the North of Scotland, about one hour from Edinburgh, Glasgow, Perth, or Dundee, and forms a most convenient stopping place for parties travelling to or from Perthshire, Argyllshire, Inverness-shire, and Aberdeenshire.

The Branch-line to the Trossachs, Killin, Oban, Inveraray, and the West Highlands, leaves the main line at Dunblane: and Travellers stopping at Dunblane can break the journey there without extra charge.

The Coupons issued by the Railway Company are accepted in the Establishment. Private Sitting-rooms, Superb Public Drawing-room, Ladies' Room, Dining-room, Billiard-room, and large Recreation-room 120 feet long, where Visitors may find amusement in wet weather.

A complete system of Baths free to Visitors.

An Omnibus meets the arrival and departure of all trains between 8 A.M. and 8.37 P.M.

The scenery around Dunblane is unsurpassed in Scotland, and the neighbourhood abounds in magnificent Walks and Drives. The following trips can be easily made, returning to the Establishment the same day :—The Trossachs, Loch Lomond, Edinburgh, Glasgow, Perth, Stirling Castle, Doune Castle, Field of Bannockburn, Castle Campbell, Rumbling Bridge, Roman Camp at Ardoch, the most perfect Roman Camp in Britain, &c. &c.

The charges for driving are very moderate, and the roads are free of Tolls.

EDINBURGH,
PHILP'S COCKBURN HOTEL,

Immediately adjoining the terminus of the Midland and Great Northern Trains, Waverley Bridge Station.

THIS commodious and well-known Hotel is beautifully situated, overlooking PRINCES STREET GARDENS, and commanding some of the finest views of the City.

(In connection with Philp's Cockburn Hotel, Glasgow.)

Excellent Turkish and other Baths in both Hotels.

Charges, including Attendance, strictly Moderate.

N.B.—Mr. Cook (of London) makes this Hotel his headquarters when in Scotland, where every information may be obtained of his Tourist arrangements, and Tickets for Highland and other Tours supplied.

GLASGOW.

PHILP'S COCKBURN HOTEL,
141 BATH STREET.

THE COCKBURN HOTEL, containing upwards of 100 Rooms, is specially planned and constructed with every Modern Improvement to meet the requirements of a First-Class Hotel. Situated in an elevated and quiet, but central and convenient part of the City; within easy access of the different Railway Stations and Steam-Ship Landings. Street Cars pass within a few yards to all parts of the City.

A Passenger Elevator to every landing.

Agent for Cook's System of Tours to the Highlands and Islands of Scotland, and Tickets supplied same as at the Edinburgh House.

Both Hotels conducted on the *same principles*.

OPPOSITE THE SCOTT MONUMENT

PRINCES STREET GARDENS.

(One of the finest Hotels in Europe.)

THE

ROYAL HOTEL

DONALD MACGREGOR, Proprietor,

53 PRINCES STREET, EDINBURGH.

The Royal Hotel is within a hundred yards of Railway Terminus, and occupies the finest position in the City.

PLACES OF INTEREST SEEN FROM HOTEL:— Arthur's Seat, over 800 feet high. Assembly Hall. Calton Hill. Edinburgh Castle. East and West Princes Street Gardens. Free Church College and Assembly Hall. Royal Observatory. Sir Walter Scott's Monument. Salisbury Crags. St. Giles's Cathedral. Parliament House. The Royal Institution. The Royal Scottish Academy and National Gallery. The Antiquarian Museum. From tower of Hotel are seen the Firth of Forth, Bass Rock, the Lomond, Corstorphine, and Pentland Hills, and a part of four or five of the neighbouring counties.

Charges Moderate. Rooms from 2s. 6d. Passenger Elevator. Night Porters.

CAUTION.—*Visitors intending to put up at the Royal must be careful to see that they are taken there, as mistakes have occurred causing great disappointment.*

CRANSTON'S OLD

WAVERLEY

TEMPERANCE HOTEL,

43 PRINCES STREET, EDINBURGH.

ROBERT CRANSTON, in returning thanks to his numerous Friends and the Public, begs to inform them that the above Hotel has been reconstructed, fitted, and furnished with all the most modern improvements which the present times can supply, and that, notwithstanding the great rise in the value of property in Princes Street, and the high prices of labour and material in the erection of his New Hotel, the charges for Bed-Rooms remain the same as they were 33 years ago. Hoping for a continuance of their kind patronage, R. C. will make it his constant endeavour to attend to the comfort, convenience, and interest of his Friends.

TO STRANGERS unacquainted with Edinburgh, R. C. begs to intimate that the situation of the OLD WAVERLEY is within one minute from the Great Central Railway Station, and commands the Grandest Views in the City; while the street itself is said to be the finest in the world. Immediately opposite the Hotel, and forming the south side of Princes Street, is the Garden Terrace, a public promenade, upon which stand the unequalled "Scott" and other noble monuments, while the gardens below form the valley betwixt the Old and New Towns. To the west, the grand old Castle, towering over the city; to the south, the romantic Old Town, with St. Giles's Cathedral and other prominent structures; and to the east, Arthur's Seat, Holyrood Palace, and Calton Hill, the view from the latter of which is said to surpass even that of the Bay of Naples.

Uniform Charges are made at the following Hotels, belonging to the same Proprietor:—

EDINBURGH	.	OLD WAVERLEY, 43 PRINCES STREET.
EDINBURGH	.	NEW WAVERLEY, 18 WATERLOO PLACE.
GLASGOW	. .	185 BUCHANAN STREET.
LONDON	. .	4 LAWRENCE LANE, CHEAPSIDE.

Breakfast or Tea . .	1s. 3d., 1s. 6d., 1s. 9d.
Public Dinner	2s.
Bed-Room	1s. 6d.
Private Parlours	3s.
Service	1s.

THE NEW WAVERLEY, Waterloo Place, contains numerous and commodious Stock-Rooms on the ground-floor, well suited for all kinds of Commercial Merchandise. Also a large Hall on the ground-floor, seated for about 700 people, for Public Meetings, Concerts, &c.

Recommended by Bradshaw's Tourists' Guide as "the cheapest and best Temperance Hotel they had ever seen," and by J. B. Gough as "the only HOME he had found since leaving his own in America."

EDINBURGH.

WATERLOO HOTEL,
WATERLOO PLACE, PRINCES STREET.

ROYAL BRITISH HOTEL,
(FAMILY AND COMMERCIAL), 22 PRINCES STREET.

BALMORAL HOTEL,
91 PRINCES STREET.

PALACE HOTEL
109 PRINCES STREET.

THESE FIRST-CLASS HOTELS

in the Principal Thoroughfare, overlooking the PUBLIC GARDENS, and opposite the CASTLE, command the FINEST VIEWS of EDINBURGH.

Cuisine Superb.   Luxuriously Furnished.   Prices Moderate.

Continental Languages spoken.

PATRONISED BY THE ROYAL FAMILY AND NOBILITY.

J. GRIEVE and J. FERGUSON,
Proprietors and Managers.

BEDFORD HOTEL,
83 PRINCES STREET, EDINBURGH.

Recently leased by Mme. Dejay (late of Dejay's Hotel), and under her own personal superintendence.   Unsurpassed for comfort, economy, and quietness.

Most moderate terms.   *Cuisine à la française.*
Coffee Room and Ladies' Drawing-Room.

This Hotel is situated in the best part of Princes Street, and commands a good view of the Castle.

EDINBURGH.

CALEDONIAN HOTEL,

115, 116, & 117 PRINCES STREET, AND 1, 3, & 5 CASTLE STREET,

Established 50 Years.

(Exactly opposite the Castle.)

R. B. MOORE.   LATE J. BURNETT.

THE SHANDON HYDROPATHIC

BEAUTIFULLY SITUATED ON THE GARELOCH, near HELENSBURGH.

Terms, £3 : 3s. per week, or 10s. 6d. per day.

THE FINEST HYDROPATHIC RESIDENCE IN THE KINGDOM.

WELL sheltered, salubrious climate, Highland Scenery, within easy drives to Lochlong and Lochlomond. The Conservatory, Vineries, Gardens, and Policies, with five miles of Enclosed Gravel Walks, are unrivalled. Large Salt Water Swimming, Turkish and other Baths, with every Modern luxury. Pleasure Boats, &c. Post and Telegraph Offices at the Entrance Lodge. Resident Physician—Dr. F. F. JAY. Omnibus awaits arrival of 10.40 and 4.5 Trains from Glasgow.

Apply to the Manager, West Shandon, by Helensburgh.

THE GRAND HOTEL,

CHARING CROSS, GLASGOW.

THIS magnificent Hotel, the comfort of which has been greatly increased by the extensive and costly alterations just completed, is now open for the reception of families and gentlemen under new and efficient management. This establishment offers unrivalled accommodation to visitors during their stay in Glasgow, whether for one day, or for a lengthened period.

The charges are strictly moderate, and the attendance all that can be desired.

Letters and Telegrams to be addressed to

W. G. DAVIDSON, *Manager*.

BLAIR'S HOTEL,

80 BATH STREET, GLASGOW.

THIS New First-Class TEMPERANCE HOTEL, situated within Four Minutes' walk of the Principal Railway Stations, is unsurpassed for Cleanliness, Quiet, and Comfort.

Private Parlours and Stock Rooms.

BREAKFAST,			DINNER,	BED ROOM,	ATTENDANCE,
1s. 6d.	1s. 9d.	2s.	From 1s. 9d.	1s. 6d.	1s.

THE ROYAL HOTEL,

GEORGE SQUARE, GLASGOW.

OPPOSITE THE GENERAL POST OFFICE.

All Communications to be addressed to the Manager.

c

TO TOURISTS.

Tourists will find a large variety of

STEREOSCOPIC, SCRAP, AND ALBUM

VIEWS OF SCOTTISH SCENERY,

GUIDE-BOOKS, MAPS, &c. &c.

AT

REID'S STATIONERY EMPORIUM,

144 ARGYLE STREET, GLASGOW, 144.

Fourth Shop West of Buchanan Street.

Visitors are innvited to **Inspect the Stock,** though they may not wish to Purchase.

GOLSPIE.

ROYAL SUTHERLAND ARMS HOTEL.

BEAUTIFULLY situated within a mile of Dunrobin Castle, the Grounds of which are open to the Public. Free Trout Fishing on Loch Brora for parties staying at the Hotel. Five minutes' walk from sea-shore. Horses and Carriages on Hire. An Omnibus meets Trains. Charges moderate. JAMES MITCHELL, Proprietor.

GREENOCK.

TONTINE HOTEL.

First-Class Family and Commercial

(*Nearly Opposite the Caledonian Railway Station*),

GREENOCK.

MRS. M'DERMOTT, *Proprietrix.*

GREENOCK.

WHITE HART HOTEL,

CATHCART SQUARE.

FAMILY AND COMMERCIAL.

Within Three Minutes' Walk of the Railway Stations and
Steamboat Wharves.

The Oldest Family and Commercial Hotel in town.

THE ISLAND OF GUERNSEY.

GARDNER'S

ROYAL  HOTEL,

FAMILY & COMMERCIAL HOUSE, ESPLANADE, GUERNSEY.

THIS Hotel is situated in the most commanding part of the Island, facing the
spacious harbours and the approaches thereto, also having a full front view of the
adjacent islands of Sark, Herm, Jersey, and Alderney. Visitors should be especially
careful on landing to ask for the "Royal." *Table d'Hôte.*

JAS. B. GARDNER, *Proprietor.*

GUERNSEY.

OLD GOVERNMENT HOUSE.

GARDNER'S PRIVATE HOTEL.

THIS establishment, being elevated above the town, commands a sea and panoramic
view of all the Channel Islands. Visitors should be particular in mentioning the
"Old Government House." *Table d'Hôte. Terms on application.*

J. GARDNER, *Proprietor.*

GUERNSEY, CHANNEL ISLANDS.

VICTORIA HOTEL,

FAMILY AND COMMERCIAL,

COMMANDS the finest sea view in the Island. The established reputation of this Hotel is the best guarantee that every attention is paid
to the comfort of its Patrons. Hot and Cold Baths always ready.

A Moderate fixed Tariff, including attendance. Private Sitting-Rooms
Ladies' Drawing-Room. Table d'Hote at six oclock. A Porter in attendance on the arrival of Steamers.

M. J. GREEN, *Proprietress.*

HARROGATE WELLS.

BARBER'S GEORGE HOTEL.

HELENSBURGH.

INNELLAN.

ROYAL HOTEL.

JOHN CLARK, in returning thanks to his friends and the Public for past patronage, begs to announce that the new additions to this already large and commodious Hotel are now finished, and include one of the largest and most handsome Dining-Room and Ladies' Drawing Room of any Hotel on the Firth of Clyde, also Parlours with suites of Bed Rooms on each flat.

The Hotel is within three minutes' walk of the Pier, and, being built upon an elevation, commands a sea-view of the surrounding country, including Bute, Arran, the Cumbraes, Ayrshire, Renfrewshire, and Dumbartonshire, making the situation one of the finest in Scotland. The grounds of the Hotel are laid out in walks and interspersed with shrubs and flowers, and are quiet and retired for families. There are also beautiful Drives in the vicinity. The Dining Room has a large Fernery, with water fountain which plays daily during the summer, making it cool and refreshing during the hot weather.

Steamers call at the pier nearly every hour for the Highlands and all parts of the coast. Tourists arriving at the Hotel the night before can have breakfast at *Table d'Hôte at* 9 A.M., and be in time to join the "Iona" at 10 A.M., for the North, calling at Innellan on her return at 4 P.M.

The Cuisine and Wines are of the finest quality. Large Billiard Room attached. Hot, Cold, and Spray Baths.

Horses and Carriages kept for Hire. Families Boarded by the Day or Week.

INVERARAY.

ARGYLL ARMS HOTEL

GENTLEMEN staying at the ARGYLL ARMS HOTEL can have excellent SALMON and TROUT FISHING on the Rivers Aray and Douglas, *Free of Charge.*

Ponies kept for ascending Duniquoich Hill.

D. MACPHERSON, *Proprietor.*

INVERARY.

CAIRNDOW HOTEL,
HEAD OF LOCH FYNE,

PARTIES staying at the Hotel can have excellent Salmon and Trout Fishing, free of charge, on the river Kinlass and Loch Restel. The Tarbet, Inverary, and Oban Coaches pass the Hotel daily during the Season.

Horses and Carriages on Hire.

WILLIAM JONES, *Proprietor.*

INVERNESS.

THE ROYAL HOTEL.

Opposite the entrance to the Railway Station.

J. S. CHRISTIE begs to solicit the attention of the travelling Public to this large well-known First-class Hotel, which has been greatly enlarged, and now comprehends, besides extensive First-class Bed-Room accommodation, a SPACIOUS and LOFTY LADIES' and GENTLEMEN'S DINING SALOON, with handsome DRAWING-ROOM *en suite*, and several elegant and handsomely furnished SUITES of PRIVATE ROOMS ; also SMOKING-ROOM, HOT, COLD, and SHOWER BATH ROOMS, etc.

Though immediately *opposite* and within a *few yards* of the Railway Station entrance, the Hotel is entirely removed from the bustle, noise, and other disturbing influences which usually affect the comfort of Hotels situated in close proximity to the Railway.

Table d'Hote daily, and Dinners à la Carte.

The Porters of the Hotel await the arrival of all trains, and an Omnibus attends the Caledonian Canal Steamers. Posting.

CALEDONIAN HOTEL

UNDER NEW MANAGEMENT.

Two minutes' walk from the Railway Station.

ALEXANDER M'FARLANE begs to intimate he has taken a lease of this well-known first-class Family Hotel, patronised by the Royal Family and most of the nobility of Europe; has recently undergone extensive additions and improvements. Handsomely refurnished throughout.

A LARGE DINING SALOON.

MAGNIFICENT LADIES' DRAWING-ROOM,
OVERLOOKING THE RIVER NESS.

SPACIOUS SMOKING & BILLIARD ROOM (Two Tables).

In point of situation, this hotel is the only one that commands a wide and extensive view of the Ness and the great Glen of "Caledonia."

Table d'Hôte daily.   Dinners à la carte.

AN OMNIBUS ATTENDS ALL THE CANAL STEAMERS.

The Hotel Porters await the arrival of all trains.

POSTING IN ALL ITS BRANCHES.

ALEXANDER M'FARLANE, *Proprietor.*

INVERNESS.

THE
IMPERIAL HOTEL,

OPPOSITE THE GENERAL STATION.

D. ROBERTSON.

WHEN YOU ARE

IN

THE HIGHLANDS

VISIT

MACDOUGALL & CO.'S.

ISLE OF WIGHT.

THE MARINE HOTEL,

PARADE, WEST COWES.

JAMES DROVER, PROPRIETOR.

PLEASANTLY SITUATED, FACING THE SEA.

The comfort of Visitors studied in every way.

N.B.—Board at low Rates during the **Winter Months.**

KENMORE.

PERTHSHIRE HIGHLANDS.

BREADALBANE HOTEL.

THIS comfortable Hotel is picturesquely situated at the east end of Loch Tay, quite close to Taymouth Castle, the princely seat of the Earl of Breadalbane. From its central position, it forms an admirable point from which to make excursions to the historic and romantic scenes with which the district abounds, while its quiet and retired situation eminently suits it for the invalid and lover of nature.

A large and commodious Billiard-room has been added to the Hotel.

Visitors staying at the Hotel are allowed the privilege of fishing for Trout and Salmon in the river Lyon free—and in Loch Tay for a specified charge.

Coaches run daily during the summer months to and from Aberfeldy and Killin, and the Hotel 'Bus awaits the arrival of the principal trains at Aberfeldy. There is a daily post to and from Aberfeldy and Killin.

Letters and Telegrams for Apartments, Conveyances, &c., punctually attended to.

N.B.—The Trout Fishing of Loch Tay, which is free to Parties staying at this Hotel, is considered one of the best in Scotland.

W. MUNRO, Proprietor.

KILLARNEY LAKES.

By Her Most Gracious Majesty's Special Permission.

THE ROYAL VICTORIA HOTEL

Patronised by H.R.H. THE PRINCE OF WALES ; by H.R.H. PRINCE ARTHUR ; and by the Royal Families of France and Belgium, &c.

THIS Hotel is situated on the Lower Lake, close to the water's edge, within ten minutes' drive of the Railway Station, and a short distance from the far-famed Gap of Dunloe.

TABLE D'HOTE DURING THE SEASON.

There is a Postal Telegraph Office in the Hotel.

Hotel open throughout the year. Boarding terms from Oct. to June inclusive.

JOHN O'LEARY, *Proprietor.*

LOCH TAY, PERTHSHIRE.

KILLIN HOTEL.

By Callander and Oban Railway, one of the grandest lines in Scotland for Scenery.

THIS Hotel is situated on the banks of the Lochay, at the head of Loch Tay, amongst some of the finest scenery in Scotland, including Finlarig Castle, the burial-place of the Breadalbane family, Inch Buie, the burial-place of the old Clan M'Nab, and the Falls of Lochay, Auchmore House, Kinnell House, the romantic Glen Lyon, Glenlochay, Glen Dochart, Ben Lawers, and Ben More. Parties Boarded during May and June. Salmon fishing begins 5th February and ends 31st May. Trout fishing Free. Coach runs between Killin, Kenmore, and Aberfeldy, to meet trains north and south from each end.

Posting Establishment complete.

Parties staying at this Hotel can make the tour through the Trossachs and back by Loch Lomond and Glenfalloch in one day.

BUS FROM HOTEL MEETS NORTH AND SOUTH TRAINS.

ALEXANDER STUART, *Proprietor.*

KINGSTOWN.

ROYAL MARINE HOTEL,

KINGSTOWN.

FIRST CLASS FAMILY HOTEL.

Faces Dublin Bay and Kingstown Harbour.

Two minutes from Royal Mail Packet Pier.

FOURTEEN MINUTES FROM DUBLIN BY RAIL.

LUGGAGE PER MAIL SHOULD BE LABELLED "KINGSTOWN."

CONISHEAD PRIORY

HYDROPATHIC MANSION, NEAR ULVERSTON:

Resident Physician.—Dr. THOMAS MARSHALL (Edin. Univ.)

HOT, COLD AND TURKISH, SEA AND LAKE WATER BATHS.

Summer Terms, Board and Baths, commencing 1st April, £3 : 3s. per Week.

"THE SCOTSMAN" writes—"Conishead Priory, known far and wide as one of the finest of old English mansions, is now opened to the public as a Hydropathic Establishment. Visitors to the English Lake District will not fail to recall the architectural beauty and enviable situation of the building. The Establishment will be specially welcome to persons who may be in search of healthful relaxation, or of the beautiful in nature. The grounds are, on one side, washed by the waters of the sea, and the house is yet by its happy situation sheltered from the violence of the storm coming either from landwards or seawards. The attraction of the place is enhanced further by the fact, that the Priory is set down at a spot specially convenient for making the tour of the Lakes. The grounds in connection with the Priory extend to 150 acres, about sixteen of which are beautifully laid out in garden and shrubbery, and include excellent croquet and tennis lawns and a bowling-green."

The Guide-Books for the district refer to the Priory as "The Paradise of Furness."

Excursions can be made from the Priory, either by coach or rail, to any part of the English Lake District, returning in the course of the day ; and Excursion Parties are arranged on extremely moderate terms.

Lawn Tennis, Croquet, Bowling, and the Scotch Game of Golf, &c.

PROSPECTUS ON APPLICATION TO "THE MANAGER," CONISHEAD PRIORY, NEAR ULVERSTON,

N.B.—The Priory is recommended by high Medical Authority as a most desirable WINTER Residence. The Directors have completed a new and admirable system of Heating, which is guaranteed to maintain a Summer temperature in the House throughout the coldest months of Winter.

WINDERMERE.
CLOUDSDALE'S CROWN HOTEL.

(Patronised by Royalty, and American Presidents.)

THE pre-eminence of the CROWN is indicated by the fact that the Hotel has been made a Postal Telegraph Station by Government Authority.

As Head-quarters for Families and Tourists desirous of visiting the other Lakes and Mountain Scenery of this Picturesque District, the CROWN, both by reason of its central situation and convenient access, is acknowledged to be unequalled.

It faces the Lake and Steam Yacht Piers.

The District Coaches run from the CROWN for Ambleside, Grasmere, Keswick ; also for Ullswater and Coniston during the Season.

NINETY BEDS.
Table d'Hote Daily at 6.30 P.M.

OMNIBUSES attend the arrival of Trains at Windermere Station, and Steamers at the Pier.

WINDERMERE.
FERRY HOTEL.

"The most beautiful spot on Windermere is the Ferry."—*Christopher North.*

THIS New and Large Hotel is situated on the Western shore of Windermere, and has most pleasing views of Lake and Mountain. It contains Drawing, Dining, Billiard and Smoking Rooms, etc. The Steam Ferry plies constantly, and Steamers in connection with the Midland and Furness Railways call at the Hotel Pier.

Every description of Pleasure Boats, Carriages, &c.
'Bus from the Hotel meets the London and North-Western Trains at the Station.

TARIFF ON APPLICATION TO
BRUCE LOGAN, PROPRIETOR.

WINDERMERE HYDROPATHIC ESTABLISHMENT.

Overlooking "Queen of English Lakes," with magnificent views of mountains and lake.

CHARMING House; elegantly appointed; every comfort and convenience; well ventilated; heated by hot water and open fireplaces. Good table and accomplished *Chef;* moderate terms. The Turkish Bath is PERFECT, with a constant current of hot oxygenised air passing rapidly through it. It can be enjoyed by persons unable to bear the ordinary Turkish baths. Russian, Electro-magnetic, Vapour, and all other baths. Fine Billiard Room with two tables. Resident Physician. Omnibus meets all trains. For prospectus address Manager, Windermere.

D

LEAMINGTON.

THE REGENT HOTEL.

A FIRST-CLASS FAMILY AND HUNTING ESTABLISHMENT.

FLYS AND OMNIBUS

MEET ALL THE G. W. AND L. AND N. W. TRAINS.

POSTING, &c.

L. BISHOP, *Proprietor.*

LIMERICK.

THE GLENTWORTH HOTEL.

THIS neat Hotel has been prepared with great care and at considerable expense, for the accommodation of Ladies and Gentlemen visiting Limerick.

The Commercial Room (and Writing Room attached), the Ladies' Coffee Room, and the Gentlemen's Coffee Room, will stand comparison with any of the kind in Ireland.

The GLENTWORTH claims the support of the general Public for the superiority of its accommodation in every Department, including Sitting Rooms, Bed Rooms, Bath Rooms (Hot and Cold Water), &c. &c.

The Wines and Liquors have been selected with the greatest care.

The GLENTWORTH is the nearest Hotel in the city to the Railway Station, Banks, Steamboat Offices, Telegraph and Post Office, and to all public Places of Amusement.

Omnibus attends the arrival of all Trains and Steamers.
Night Porter attends the Night Mail.

P. KENNA, *Proprietor.*

14, 15, & 16 GLENTWORTH STREET, LIMERICK.

LIMERICK.

CRUISE'S ROYAL HOTEL,

J. J. CLEARY, PROPRIETOR.

THIS long-established and well-known FIRST-CLASS HOTEL is now conducted under the sole superintendence of the Proprietor, and possesses everything requisite to promote the comfort and convenience of the NOBILITY, GENTRY, and TOURISTS, and affords particular facilities to Commercial Gentlemen, having first-rate SHOW-ROOMS, together with MODERATE CHARGES.

Omnibuses attend all Trains, Steamers, &c. &c. &c. ; also a 'Bus attends the Night Mails for the convenience of Gentlemen coming by the late Trains.

N.B.—This is the PRINCIPAL HOTEL IN THE CITY, and is capable of accommodating over 150 persons, together with a splendid Suite of Drawing-Rooms.

HOT, COLD, AND SHOWER BATHS.

CAUTION.—This is the only Hotel in the City called THE ROYAL HOTEL.

COMPTON HOTEL

SPACIOUS COFFEE ROOM, with the LADIES' DRAWING ROOM adjoining.	**CHURCH STREET.** **LIVERPOOL.**	The Finest COMMERCIAL, BILLIARD, and SMOKING ROOMS in the Town.

THIS magnificent building is now the most central Hotel in Liverpool for Families and Visitors, containing 250 rooms, handsomely furnished, with every modern luxury and home comfort.   Private Suites of Rooms.

Adjacent to the several Railway Termini and River Landing Stage.

CHARGES STRICTLY MODERATE.

WILLIAM RUSSELL, *Proprietor.*

LIVERPOOL.

SHAFTESBURY HOTEL,

28, 30, and 32 MOUNT PLEASANT, LIVERPOOL.

THREE minutes' walk from Central and Lime Street Stations. Omnibuses from the Landing Stage, the Steamers, and the Exchange, pass every few minutes. Post-Office nearly opposite.

Terms Moderate.

Acknowledged to be one of the best Temperance Hotels in the Kingdom.

LLANDUDNO.

THE IMPERIAL FAMILY HOTEL.

(CENTRE OF BAY.)

IN consequence of the EXTENSIVE PATRONAGE which this Hotel has enjoyed since it was opened in 1872, it has been found necessary to ADD A NEW WING.   APARTMENTS *EN SUITE.*

ELEGANT BILLIARD SALOON FOR THREE TABLES.

An Omnibus attends all Trains.   EXCELLENT STABLING.   *Tariff on Application.*

JOHN CHANTREY, PROPRIETOR.

LLANGOLLEN.

EDWARDS' HAND HOTEL.

THE "HAND,"

Unequalled for the Beauty of its Situation on the Banks of the Dee.

Several Bed-Rooms and Sitting-Rooms have been added to the House to suit the requirements of Families visiting this delightful Neighbourhood.

BILLIARDS.

Omnibuses from this Hotel meet all Trains at Llangollen Station.

LOCH AWE, DALMALLY.

PORT SONACHAN HOTEL.

SITUATION unrivalled ; views magnificent. Visitors will find this Hotel replete with home comforts. Messrs. M'Brayne land passengers from the Columba Steamer and from Loch Awe Station (Callander and Oban Railway) at the Hotel Pier.

FISHING ON LOCH AWE FREE.   BOATS AND BOATMEN IN ATTENDANCE.

POSTING IN ALL ITS BRANCHES.

Charges strictly moderate.

THOMAS CAMERON, *Proprietor.*

LOCH EARN HEAD.

LOCH EARN HEAD HOTEL,

BALQUHIDDER, PERTHSHIRE

12 miles by rail from Callander.

(Under Royal Patronage. Twice visited by the Queen.)

THIS Hotel, which has been long established, has excellent accommodation for Families and Tourists, with every comfort and quiet, lies high and dry, and charmingly sheltered at the foot of the Wild Glen Ogle (the Kyber Pass). It commands fine views of the surrounding Hills and Loch, the old Castle of Glenample, the scenery of the Legend of Montrose, in the neighbourhood of Ben Voirlich, Rob Roy's Grave, Loch Voil, Loch Doine, and Loch Lubnaig, with many fine drives and walks. Posting and Carriages. Boats for Fishing and Rowing free. A 'Bus to and from the Hotel for the Trains during Summer. **Coaches to and from Crieff daily in Summer.**

R. DAYTON.

The Callander and Oban Railway is now open. Parties breaking the journey here can proceed next morning with greater comfort.

LOCHLOMOND.

INVERSNAID HOTEL

THE landing place for Loch Katrine, The Trossachs, Aberfoyle, &c. This Hotel has been considerably enlarged.—The additions comprising Large Dining Rooms, several Bed Rooms, Drawing Room, Billiard Room, &c. All newly furnished.

The scenery surrounding is unsurpassed.

Carriages can be had on hire, and there are also excellent boats and boatmen to be had for the use of Anglers or Excursionists on the Loch.

Arrangements can be made by Parties for Board by the Week or Month.

ROBERT BLAIR, *Proprietor.*

LOCHLOMOND.

TARBET HOTEL,

(OPPOSITE BEN-LOMOND)

A. H. M'PHERSON, Proprietor,

IS the finest and most commodious Hotel on the Lake, and commands the best View of Ben-Lomond. Large additions comprising Bed Rooms, Billiard Rooms, and Ladies' Drawing Room have just been added to the Hotel.

Coaches direct for the far-famed Glencroe, Inveraray, and Oban, will commence running on 1st June.

Tourists *en route* for Trossachs and Callander can leave per 10.15 A.M. Steamer, next morning, in connection with the Steamer down Loch Katrine.

Small Boats on the Lake, and Guides to Ben-Lomond, to be had at the Hotel.

May 1881.

LOCH LOMOND, LUSS HOTEL.

ROBERT M'NAB.

POSTING.   PLEASURE BOATS.   FISHING FREE.

INCHTAVANACH and the STRONE BRAE command the most extensive, magnificent, and picturesque prospects of this, the far-famed

"QUEEN OF SCOTTISH LAKES."

LOCHLOMOND.

ROWARDENNAN HOTEL,

Foot of Ben Lomond.

B. JARRATT begs to return his sincere thanks to Tourists and others who have so kindly patronised him for the last thirteen years. Visitors will find this Hotel clean and comfortable, with every attention. Rowardennan is the best and shortest road to Ben Lomond, and the only place where Guides and Ponies can be had, by which parties can ride with ease and safety to the top, the distance being only four miles to the very summit.

The Loch Lomond Steamers call at Rowardennan Wharf six times a day on their route up and down the Loch.—*May* 1881.

LOCHLOMOND.

BALLOCH HOTEL, FOOT OF LOCHLOMOND.

THE above first-class Hotel is beautifully situated at the foot of the "Queen of Scottish Lakes," and at an easy distance from the Railway Station. Visitors will have every comfort, combined with moderate charges. Parties purposing to proceed by first Steamer up Lochlomond would do well to arrive at the Hotel the previous evening.

Visitors staying at this Hotel have the privilege of going through the Grounds and Flower Gardens of Sir James Colquhoun, Bart., and Mr. Campbell of Tillychewan, and have permission to visit "Mount Misery," which commands 17 miles of the most beautiful portion of Lochlomond—23 islands being comprised in the view. Excellent Trout and Salmon Fishing. Posting in all its branches. Boats for the Lake.

MRS. GEORGE M'DOUGALL, *Proprietrix.*

LOCHLOMOND.

COLQUHOUN ARMS HOTEL, ARDLUI.

Under New Management.

THIS Hotel is situated at the Head of Lochlomond. During the season, coaches in connection with the Lochlomond Steamers, and Callander and Oban Railway, start from this Hotel, where seats may be secured. Carriages for Hire. Fishing on River Falloch and Lochlomond free. Boats for Hire. Parties boarded by week or month. Moderate Charges.

J. BRODIE, *Proprietor.*

TURKEY, INDIAN, & PERSIAN CARPETS.

MANUFACTURED FOR AND IMPORTED BY

WATSON, BONTOR, & COMPANY,

CARPET MANUFACTURERS TO

HER MAJESTY THE QUEEN

AND

H.R.H. THE PRINCE OF WALES.

Superior Brussels, Velvet, Saxony, and all other Carpets in the Newest Designs.

Nos. 35 & 36 OLD BOND STREET, LONDON, W.

LONDON.

UPPER NORWOOD.

NEAR THE CRYSTAL PALACE.

THE QUEEN'S HOTEL.

THIS unique establishment stands unrivalled for the exquisite picturesqueness and beauty of its situation ; its commanding and central position ; and the commodiousness and completeness of its general arrangements.   Delicate persons, to whom a light bracing air, charming scenery, close vicinity to the Crystal Palace and its amusements, and quiet seclusion, would be an invaluable boon, will find, in this establishment, their wishes fully realised.

"THE QUEEN'S HOTEL, at Upper Norwood, is like a Private Royal Residence, managed with marvellous quietness, and is replete with all domestic comforts and appliances ; being a veritable home for individuals as well as families.   Lately there have been added some new rooms of magnificent proportions, suitable for balls, wedding breakfasts, public dinners, &c.   Ladies and gentlemen can make use of a most delightful coffee room for meals, overlooking the beautiful grounds.   For gentlemen, there are billiard and smoking rooms, and also a private club.   It deserves the special attention of the nobility and gentry, and their families, who may be seeking the means of restoration to health, both of mind and body, without going far from London."—From the *Court Journal.*

SPECIAL NOTICE OF WINTER ARRANGEMENTS AND TERMS AT THE ABOVE HOTEL.

The Patrons of this establishment are respectfully informed that Tourists, Families, and others are received on most reasonable terms for the Winter months—which season has many enjoyments for Visitors at the QUEEN'S HOTEL, owing to its elevated, dry, and salubrious situation, and its convenient vicinity to the Crystal Palace and the Winter Garden, whilst it commands by Rail easy access to the West End, the City, &c.

GREAT MALVERN.

THE IMPERIAL.

THE attention of Foreign and Home Tourists seeking a salubrious and charming part of England is respectfully drawn to this Establishment, the largest and principal one in the district—comfortable, well appointed, specially adapted for Family Residence, and the charges strictly moderate.

TERMS—FROM £3 : 3s. PER WEEK,

Including Bedroom, Attendance, Meals, and use of Public Rooms.

Special Arrangements made with Families intending to reside for some time.

THE NEW AND ELEGANT SWIMMING BATH,

Part of a complete system of Baths in course of erection—IS NOW OPEN.

Tariffs forwarded on Application.

MALVERN.

THE FOLEY ARMS HOTEL

Is situate on the slope of the Hills in the highest part of the town, and from its bay-windows and Terrace the most beautiful views are obtained.

MISS FLIGHT, *Manager.*

EDWARD ARCHER, *Proprietor.*

GREAT MALVERN.

THE ABBEY HOTEL.

AN old established first-class Family Hotel, occupies one of the best positions in Malvern. Is thoroughly well warmed during the colder months of the year. Handsome suites of Apartments. Coffee-Room for Ladies and Gentlemen.

Letters addressed "Manager," insure a reply by first post.

WILLIAM ARCHER, *Proprietor.*

MANCHESTER.

KNOWSLEY HOTEL,
CHEETHAM HILL ROAD,

Only a few minutes' walk from Victoria Railway Station,

Will be found by Travellers who appreciate Good and Lofty Rooms, and enjoy the Quietude and Comfort which the noisy parts of the City cannot offer, a very acceptable house.

Omnibuses to all parts of the City pass the door every few minutes.

J. B. BRENMEHL, Lessee.

SWAN HOTEL,
MANSFIELD.

UNDER the management of Miss WHITE, daughter of the late Robert White, for 30 years proprietor. The best centre for visiting Sherwood Forest, The "Dukeries," Welbeck, Thoresby, Clumber, Newstead, Hardwick, Bolsover, &c.

"The best plan is to get a carriage from the 'Swan' at Mansfield."—Rambles among the Hills, by Louis J. Jennings.

An Omnibus meets all Trains.

MATLOCK BATH, DERBYSHIRE.

(On the Main Midland Line.)

TYACK'S (LATE IVATTS AND JORDAN)

NEW BATH HOTEL.

THIS first-class old-established Family House, acknowledged to be one of the most homely and comfortable Hotels in the kingdom, is beautifully situated on the highest and most open part of the valley, surrounded by its own extensive pleasure grounds, commanding the finest views of the grand and picturesque scenery for which Matlock Bath (the Switzerland of England) stands unrivalled. Matlock is the most central place for day excursions to the most interesting parts of Derbyshire. A Public Bus to Haddon and Chatsworth daily.

A public Dining Room and Drawing Room. Private Sitting Rooms. Coffee, Smoking, and Billiard Rooms. A large natural tepid Swimming Bath, 68 degrees. TABLE D'HÔTE daily at 6.30 p.m. Excellent Stabling and Coach Houses. Posting, &c.

An Omnibus to and from each Train.

BOOK FOR MATLOCK BATH, NOT TO MATLOCK BRIDGE.

LAWN TENNIS AND CROQUET. GOOD FISHING.

Places of interest in the vicinity :—Buxton, Chatsworth, Haddon Hall, Castleton, Dovedale, Wingfield Manor, Hardwick Hall, &c.

HYDROPATHY.

SMEDLEY'S HYDROPATHIC ESTABLISHMENT,

MATLOCK BRIDGE, DERBYSHIRE.

Physicians { **WILLIAM B. HUNTER, M.D., &c.**
            { **THOMAS MACCALL, M.D., &c.**

THIS Establishment is conducted with the same solicitude and care for the interests of the sick which have characterised it for a period of nearly thirty years, and procured it a high and wide-spread reputation under the late Mr. Smedley. Many additions and improvements have been made, and its usefulness and comfort enhanced. Electric Bells are in every Room— Electric Baths in operation, and there are commodious Billiard and Smoking Rooms.

As a **Winter Residence** this place is admirably adapted for Invalids, especially sufferers from Chest and Digestive disorders, Rheumatism and Gout. It affords warm and well-ventilated Public Rooms, Bedrooms and Corridors, covered Balconies, permitting open-air exercise in all weathers, a handsome and specially-ventilated *Turkish Bath*, and Bath-houses thoroughly reconstructed with all modern improvements. The numbers during the winter months average from one hundred to one hundred and fifty.

Prospectus on application to Manager.

MELROSE.
THE GEORGE AND ABBOTSFORD HOTEL.

THIS Hotel is now enlarged and improved, having Ladies' Drawing-Room, Dining-Rooms, handsomely furnished Suites, 40 Bed-Rooms, Baths (Hot, Cold, and Shower), Billiard Room, and all the necessary appointments of a first-class Hotel, while the charges are the same as those of minor Hotels. Being two minutes' walk from the Railway Station, and the same from the Abbey, the Hotel is the most convenient for Visitors to Melrose. The Proprietors, T. & W. Griffiths (the latter many years with Messrs. Spiers & Pond, and lately their manager for Scotland), have had great experience as Hotel Proprietors and Restaurateurs, and attend personally to all Patrons. Well-appointed carriages, with careful drivers, selected from the large posting establishment of the Hotel, have the sole right of standing in the Station Yard.

The Hotel Omnibus meets all Trains.

MELROSE.
THE ABBEY HOTEL, ABBEY GATE.

THIS is the only Hotel which is built on the Abbey Grounds, at the entrance to the far-famed ruins of Melrose Abbey. An extensive addition having been built to the Establishment, consisting of Private Sitting Rooms, Bedrooms, Billiard-Room, etc. etc., it is now the largest Hotel in Melrose, and only two minutes' walk from the Railway Station.

First-class Horses and Carriages to Abbotsford and Dryburgh Abbey.

An Omnibus attends all trains to convey Visitors' Luggage to and from the Hotel.
                                    GEORGE HAMILTON, Proprietor.

MELROSE, CLEAVER'S KING'S ARMS HOTEL.

Two Minutes' walk from Railway Station and Abbey.

TOURISTS and Visitors coming to this Hotel are cautioned against taking a cab at the Railway Station, and are requested either to take the King's Arms Omnibus (which attends all trains), or walk down to the Hotel, where Carriages of every description can be had for Abbotsford, Dryburgh, etc.

DUMFRIESSHIRE, N.B.

MOFFAT HYDROPATHIC ESTABLISHMENT
AND SANATORIUM,

Resident Physician—DR. R. THOMSON FORBES.

THIS Establishment, which occupies a beautiful situation on the western slope of the beautifully wooded Gallow Hill, and within a short distance of the far-famed "Moffat Well," is replete with every comfort for Visitors and Patients. The PUBLIC ROOMS, HALLS, and CORRIDORS are universally recognised as unsurpassed by any similar Establishment, and the BATHS are of the most varied and perfect construction.

MOFFAT has long been a favourite resort for those seeking health and pleasure, and in the Establishment there is the additional attraction of good society and varied amusements.

For full Particulars apply to C. NAU, *Manager.*

MOFFAT SPA.
ANNANDALE ARMS HOTEL,

ROBERT NORRIS, *Proprietor.*

TOURISTS and Visitors to this famous watering-place will find at the Annandale Arms Hotel first-class accommodation, combined with Moderate Charges. Commercial Gentlemen will find every attention to their convenience and interests. Omnibuses meet the Trains at Beattock Station. A Summer Excursion Omnibus runs along the route—passing "Craigieburn Wood," Bodesbeck, Grey Mare's Tail, to St. Mary's Loch, every Tuesday, Thursday, and Saturday, in connection with a Coach from Selkirk. Omnibuses ply to the Well every morning. Carriages of all kinds. Job and Post Horses on Hire.

MONMOUTH.

VALLEY OF THE WYE.

THE KING'S HEAD HOTEL
AND POSTING HOUSE.

THIS old-established Hotel, situate in Agincourt Square, the centre of the town, is replete with every accommodation for Families and Tourists, at Moderate Charges.

A SPACIOUS LADIES' COFFEE ROOM.
AND A SUPERIOR BILLIARD ROOM.
An Omnibus meets every Train.

JOHN THOMAS, Proprietor.

OBAN—CRAIG-ARD HOTEL—R. MACLAURIN, *Proprietor.*

TOURISTS and Strangers visiting the West Highlands will find that, whether as regards Situation, Comfort, or Accommodation, combined with Moderate Charges, this elegant Hotel, built expressly for summer Visitors, cannot be surpassed, while it commands an extensive view of the beautiful Bay of Oban and other romantic scenery in the neighbourhood. The Hotel is situated on an elevated plateau near the Steamboat Wharf, to which a new and convenient approach has been lately added: The Wines and Cuisine are of the first quality. French and German spoken. Table d'Hôte daily. Apartments may be engaged by the week at a reduced scale.

E

PENZANCE.
UNION HOTEL.

CENTRALLY SITUATED.

During the season a Four-Horse Brake leaves the Hotel *daily* for Land's End, Logan Rock, etc., at 9 A.M. (Sundays excepted).

Omnibuses to the Lizard pass the Hotel *daily* (Sundays excepted).

Board by Arrangement.

The Hotel Omnibus meets all Trains.

PENZANCE.

MOUNT'S BAY HOUSE.

(On the Esplanade.)

ERECTED AND FITTED UP EXPRESSLY AS A SEASIDE FAMILY HOTEL.
No expense or labour has been spared by the Proprietor. The house is furnished in the most modern style, is well supplied with *Hot and Cold Baths*, and replete with every accommodation suitable for Tourists to West Cornwall. All the Drawing Rooms command an *uninterrupted* and *unsurpassed* view of that "beauteous gem set in the silver sea," St. Michael's Mount, and the whole of the magnificent bay. During the winter Invalids will find in Mount's Bay House the comforts of a home, while the beauty and salubrity of the situation, and its nearness to the charming walks on the sea-shore, render it a healthy and delightful residence. Suites of Apartments for families of distinction. Choice Wines and Ales. Post Horses and Carriages. Charges moderate.

Mrs. E. LAVIN, *Proprietress.*

PENZANCE
QUEEN'S HOTEL.

(On the Esplanade.)

THIS magnificent Hotel has a frontage of over 170 feet, all the rooms of which overlook the sea. It is the only Hotel that commands a full and uninterrupted view of Mount's Bay. Penzance stands unrivalled for the variety and quiet beauty of its scenery, whilst the mildness of its climate is admirably adapted to invalids. Apartments *en suite*. Drawing, Reading, Coffee, Billiard-Rooms. Hot and Cold Baths. An Omnibus meets every train. Posting in all its branches.

ALEX. H. HORA, *Proprietor.*

PITLOCHRIE.

FISHER'S HOTEL,

FIRST-CLASS FAMILY HOTEL
AND
POSTING ESTABLISHMENT.

PARTIES wishing to see the magnificent Scenery in this part of the Scottish Highlands will find this Hotel (to which large additions have been made) most convenient, for in One Drive they can visit the

Falls of Tummel, the Queen's View of Loch Tummel;
The Far-Famed Pass of Killiecrankie;
Glen Tilt; The Falls of Bruar, &c.

Pitlochrie is on the direct route to Balmoral Castle, by Spittal of Glenshee and Braemar; and to Taymouth Castle and Kinloch-Rannoch, by Tummel-Bridge.

Salmon and Trout Fishing on the Rivers Tummel and Garry, and on the Lochs in the neighbourhood.

Job and Post Horses and Carriages of every kind,
By the Day, Week, or Month.

ORDERS BY TELEGRAPH, FOR ROOMS OR CARRIAGES, PUNCTUALLY ATTENDED TO.

PITLOCHRY, PERTHSHIRE.

THE ATHOLE HYDROPATHIC ESTABLISHMENT

NO expense has been spared to render this magnificent Establishment complete in all its arrangements. The locality is as widely known for the health-giving qualities of its climate as for the grandeur of its Strath and mountain scenery.

The House occupies a commanding position on the sunny side of Strath Tummel. The Public Rooms are large and richly furnished. The Turkish and other Baths are constructed on the most scientific principles, and for elegance and comfort are not surpassed by any in the country.

The Grounds, extending to 35 acres, abound in natural and artistic beauties, and contain Bowling, Croquet, and Lawn Tennis Greens, Curling Ponds, etc.

The Walks and Drives in the neighbourhood are numerous and inviting. The places of interest within walking or driving distance are—The Pass of Killiecrankie; Lochs Tummel, Tay, and Rannoch; The Falls of Bruar, Tummel, and Moness; Glen Tilt, Blair and Taymouth Castles; Dunkeld, Birnam Hill, Rumbling Bridge, The Birks of Aberfeldy, Black Spout, etc.

A special Telegraph wire connects with the House. Commodious Stable and Coach-house accommodation for Private Carriages.

WILLIAM S. IRVINE, M.D., Consulting Physician.

Prospectuses forwarded on application to ALEX. S. GRANT,

at the Establishment.

The Royal Hotel, Plymouth.

Two Lines of Railway from London and the North of England to Plymouth, viz.—London and South-Western and Great Western.

EXTENSIVE POSTING ESTABLISHMENT.

S. PEARSE, Proprietor.

DUKE OF CORNWALL HOTEL,

(Opposite the Railway Station).

POSTAL TELEGRAPH OFFICE,

PLYMOUTH, DEVON.

FIRST-CLASS FAMILY HOTEL

CONTAINING

A HANDSOME GENERAL COFFEE ROOM.
LADIES' DRAWING ROOM.
SMOKING AND READING ROOMS.
LARGE BILLIARD ROOM *(Two Tables)*.
SUITES OF APARTMENTS.
HOT AND COLD BATHS.

TABLE D'HOTE DAILY.

Address to the Manager.

ST. LEONARDS-ON-SEA.

ALEXANDRA HOTEL.

THIS HOTEL, situate in the finest position in St. Leonards or Hastings, in the centre of the parade, has been considerably Enlarged and Improved. Fifty more rooms have been added, including a new and spacious Coffee Room, and a large and handsome Reading and Drawing Room. There are elegant suites of apartments, consisting of Bed, Sitting, and Dressing Rooms, French Bedrooms, Excellent Single Rooms, Smoking Room, Bath Room, Gentlemen's Lavatory, and every other convenience.

The Sitting Rooms and French Bedrooms, Coffee Room, and Reading and Drawing Rooms, all face the sea, and in the rear of the premises is a large and tastefully laid out garden.

The Hotel is close to the Pier and Baths, has a complete south aspect directly facing the Sea, and commands an uninterrupted and extensive view of the Channel ; it is beautifully appointed, and fitted throughout with every modern appliance conducive to the comfort of visitors. Special arrangements, if desired, are made with families for lengthened periods. Tariff with all particulars will be forwarded on application to HENRY RADFORD, *Manager.*

SALISBURY.

THE WHITE HART HOTEL.

AN old-established and well-known first-class Family Hotel, nearly opposite Salisbury Cathedral, and within a pleasant drive of Stonehenge. This Hotel is acknowledged to be one of the most comfortable in England.

A Ladies' Coffee Room, a Coffee Room for Gentlemen, and first-class Billiard and Smoking Rooms.

Posting-Masters to Her Majesty. Carriages and Horses of every description.

Tariff on application to H. T. BOWES, *Manager.*

SOUTHSEA, HANTS.
OPPOSITE THE ISLE OF WIGHT.

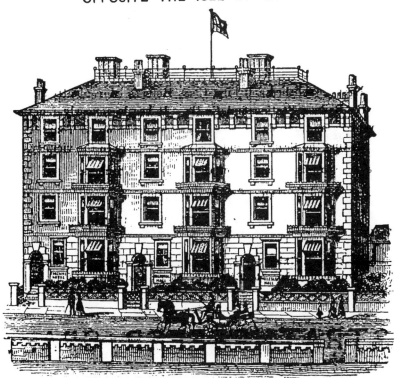

SOUTHSEA, HANTS.

FIRST-CLASS APARTMENTS, SPLENDIDLY FURNISHED, FACING THE SEA, CLARENCE PARADE.

'BALMORAL HALL.' 'WELLESLEY HALL.' 'FROGMORE HOUSE.
TRAFALGAR HOUSE. BARRINGTON HOUSE. 6 & 7 DAGMAR TERRACE.

THE healthiest spot in England ; commanding an uninterrupted view of SPITHEAD and the ISLE OF WIGHT.

There is a Splendid Esplanade, Magnificent Beach, the best Sea Bathing on the South Coast.

MILITARY BANDS ON THE PIERS DAILY.

A Spacious Common, on which Reviews are frequently held, affording to Visitors a constant source of amusement.

Steam Vessels continually leave the Pier for the Isle of Wight and other places. Assembly Rooms. Libraries. Turkish Baths, etc.

Average Mortality, 14 in 1000.

APPLY TO MANAGERS.

STIRLING.

GOLDEN LION HOTEL.

STUART, LATE CAMPBELL.

THIS Oldest Established and First-Class Hotel is conveniently situated near the Railway Station and Castle. It has been newly renovated and improved, and affords comfortable accommodation to Tourists and Families visiting the Beautiful and Historical Scenery in the vicinity.

Conveyances await the arrival of all Trains and Steamers.

Post Horses and Carriages of every description.

May 1881.   ROBERT STUART, *Proprietor.*

See Shearer's Guide to Stirling and Lakes, 1s. free by Post.
Do.   do.   to Stirling, Maps and Cuts, 6d.

ROSS-SHIRE, N.B.

STRATHPEFFER SPA.

(The Property of the Duchess of Sutherland and Countess of Cromartie.)

STRATHPEFFER (the Harrogate of Scotland) is yearly increasing in popularity, not only on account of the well-known curative powers of its mineral waters (sulphurous and chalybeate), but also because of its being one of the healthiest and most attractive places in the Highlands. Professor (now Sir) Robert Christison of Edinburgh describes the strong well as a pure sulphurous water, and the strongest known in Great Britain. Dr. Murray Thomson, Edinburgh, certified that the Strathpeffer waters deserve a much wider celebrity than they have hitherto enjoyed; that they are invaluable as a curative agent for chronic diseases of the skin, for rheumatism, and gout; and that they act fully on the liver and kidneys, and have their value in many constitutional affections. Dr. Medlock of London writes: "These waters possess several valuable properties which do not belong to any other known sulphur spring."—See Dr. Manson's Guide.

The establishment is in the hands of the Proprietrix, and is placed under the charge of a Manager. There is a resident Medical Practitioner, who has made the waters his special study for several years.

ADDRESS TO THE MANAGER.

THE BEN WYVIS HOTEL,

STRATHPEFFER SPA, ROSS-SHIRE, N.B.

THE HARROGATE OF SCOTLAND.

VISITORS to this popular Watering Place will find this Hotel replete with every comfort combined with charges *strictly moderate*. It stands within its own grounds, which comprise Bowling, Croquet, and Lawn Tennis Greens, is surrounded with grand scenery, and commands a splendid view of Ben Wyvis, the ascent of which can be accomplished from the Hotel in a few hours.

The BEN WYVIS HOTEL, which contains Public and Private Apartments *en suite*, Billiard Room, &c., is within two minutes' walk of the Mineral Wells and Baths, and of Post and Telegraph Offices.

The Hotel is within a mile of the Strathpeffer Station on the Dingwall and Skye Railway, and is a convenient point from which to visit Skye, Loch Maree, Dunrobin, &c. &c.

Orders for Apartments and Carriages punctually attended to.

APPLY TO THE MANAGER. N.B.—POSTING CONDUCTED IN ALL ITS BRANCHES

SPA HOTEL,
STRATHPEFFER.

MRS. EDWARDS begs to intimate that this Old Established Family Hotel is now open for the Season, where parties can depend on every comfort, combined with moderate charges. The Hotel is beautifully situated, and commands some of the finest views in Strathpeffer.

A conveyance leaves the Hotel three times daily to convey parties to the Pump Room free of Charge.

Posting in all its Branches.

TAYNUILT.

TAYNUILT HOTEL.

THIS Hotel is situated near Loch Etive, within two minutes' walk from the Taynuilt Station on the Callander and Oban Railway. Visitors have the privilege of Salmon and Trout Fishing on the River Awe.

JAMES MURRAY, *Proprietor.*

Post Horses, Carriages, &c.

TENBY.

ROYAL GATE HOUSE HOTEL,

COMMANDING A DELIGHTFUL VIEW OF THE BAY.

(FAMILIES AND GENTLEMEN.)

JOSEPH GREGORY, Proprietor.

THURSO.

HENDERSON'S ROYAL HOTEL.

THIS Hotel has recently been enlarged and expressly fitted up as a First-Class Hotel. The Bedroom and Parlour accommodation are ample, and well adapted to secure the comfort of Commercial Gentlemen and Tourists. Private Parlours and suites of apartments on moderate terms. Daily communication by Steamer to Stromness. Posting in all its departments. 'Bus meets all Trains and Steamers. First-class Billiard Room.

THE TROSSACHS HOTEL,
LOCH KATRINE.
A. BLAIR, PROPRIETOR.

TROSSACHS.

STRONACHLACHAR HOTEL,
HEAD OF LOCH KATRINE.

DONALD FERGUSON begs to intimate that he has lately completed extensive alterations and additions to his Hotel, and that it will be his constant endeavour, as heretofore, to secure every comfort and attention to Tourists and others favouring him with their patronage.

It is the best Fishing Station, and Boats with experienced Boatmen always in readiness.

During the season Coaches run to and from Inversnaid, in connection with Steamers on Loch Katrine and Loch Lomond.

Carriages and other Conveyances kept for Hire.

STRONACHLACHAR, 1881.

YORK.

HARKER'S YORK HOTEL,
ST. HELEN'S SQUARE.

THIS long-established First-Class Hotel occupies the best Situation in the City, being nearest to the Minster and the Ruins of St. Mary's Abbey; is free from all noise of Trains, and surrounded by the patent wooden pavement. P. MATTHEWS, *Proprietor,*

Also of the North-Eastern Family Hotel.

YORK.

THE NORTH-EASTERN FAMILY HOTEL.

(LATE ABBOTT'S.)

CONTAINS every appointment of a Modern First-Class Hotel for families and gentlemen. Situated within three minutes' walk of New Railway Station, and free from the noise of trains.

The Hotel Porters meet all trains day and night to convey visitors' luggage, and will be found under the Portico at the entrance to the station.

P. MATTHEWS, *Proprietor,*
Also of Harker's York Hotel.

WELSHPOOL.

ROYAL OAK HOTEL.

Established 200 Years.

THIS old Family Commercial and Posting House is now in complete order, redecorated for the comfort of Visitors. Powis Castle Park is close to the town, and is open to the Public.

MAGNIFICENT STABLES NEWLY ERECTED.

Post Horses, Breaks, Private Omnibuses, and Carriages.

BILLIARDS.

Omnibus meets all Trains.

WILLIAM ROWLAND, *Proprietor.*

LONDON & SOUTH-WESTERN RAILWAY,

WATERLOO STATION, LONDON.

The Shortest and Quickest Route to the South-West and West of England, EXETER, BARNSTAPLE, BIDEFORD ("Westward Ho!") ILFRACOMBE, NORTH and SOUTH DEVON, BUDE *via* HOLSWORTHY, TAVISTOCK, LAUNCESTON, PLYMOUTH, WEYMOUTH, BOURNEMOUTH, SOUTHAMPTON, PORTSMOUTH, STOKES BAY, and ISLE OF WIGHT.

Fast Expresses at Ordinary Fares, and Frequent Trains.

CHEAP TOURIST AND EXCURSION TICKETS.

Through Tickets in connection with the London and North-Western, Great Northern, and Midland Railways.

Regular Mail Steam-Ships, *via* Southampton, to and from the CHANNEL ISLANDS, JERSEY and GUERNSEY. Also Fast Steam-Ships for HAVRE, ROUEN, and PARIS, ST. MALO, CHERBOURG, GRANVILLE, and HONFLEUR.

GREAT WESTERN RAILWAY.

TOURIST ARRANGEMENTS.

FIRST, SECOND, and THIRD CLASS TOURIST TICKETS, available for two months, and renewable, with exceptions, up to Dec. 31st, are issued during the Summer months of each year, at the principal stations on this Railway, to the Watering and other places of attraction in the WEST OF ENGLAND, including:—

CLEVEDON.	EXETER.	PLYMOUTH.	SCILLY ISLANDS.
WESTON-SUPER-MARE.	DAWLISH.	TRURO.	BRIDPORT.
MINEHEAD.	TEIGNMOUTH.	FALMOUTH.	DORCHESTER.
BARNSTAPLE.	NEWTON ABBOT.	ST. IVES.	WEYMOUTH, & THE
ILFRACOMBE.	TORQUAY.	PENZANCE.	CHANNEL ISLANDS.

To North and South Wales, including—

DOLGELLY.	LLANDUDNO.	CARNARVON.	SWANSEA.
BARMOUTH.	PENMAENMAWR.	HOLYHEAD.	TENBY.
ABERYSTWITH.	BETTWS-Y-COED.	CHEPSTOW.	PEMBROKE.
RHYL.	BANGOR.	TINTERN.	NEW MILFORD.

To BUXTON.	WINDERMERE.	SCOTLAND.	MATLOCK.
ISLE OF MAN.	SCARBOROUGH.	WHITBY.	
To BRIGHTON.	ST. LEONARDS.	ISLE OF WIGHT.	MARGATE.
EASTBOURNE.	HASTINGS.	RAMSGATE.	DOVER.

And to WATERFORD. CORK. LAKES OF KILLARNEY. DUBLIN, ETC.

Passengers holding 1st or 2nd Class Tourist Tickets to the principal stations in the West of England can travel by the 11.45 a.m. Express train from Paddington, which reaches Exeter in *four hours and a quarter*, and Plymouth in *six hours and a quarter*, or by the 3.0 p.m. Express train from Paddington, which reaches Exeter in the same time, and Plymouth in *six hours*.

For particulars of the various Circular Tours, Fares, and other information, see the Company's Tourist Programmes, which can be obtained at the Stations and Booking-offices.

PICNIC AND PLEASURE PARTIES.

From May 2d, 1st, 2nd, and 3rd Class Return Tickets, available for one day only, will be issued (with certain exceptions and limitations) at reduced fares, at all the principal Stations, to parties of not less than six 1st class or ten 2nd or 3rd class passengers.

To obtain these Tickets, application must be made to one of the persons named below not less than three days before, giving full particulars of the proposed excursion.

EXCURSION TRAINS

at low fares will run at intervals during the season, to and from London, Liverpool, Manchester, Birmingham, Bristol, Worcester, Weymouth, West of England, N. and S. Wales, South of Ireland, and all parts of the Great Western system.

Full information as to Trains, Fares, Routes, etc., will be duly announced, and may be obtained on application to the Company's Superintendents:— Mr. A. Higgins and Mr. W. A. Hart, Paddington; Mr. J. Gibbs, Reading; Mr. T. W. Walton, Bristol; Mr. J. Campfield, Exeter; Mr. E. C. Compton, Plymouth; Mr. J. Peach, Penzance; Mr. G. C. Grover, Hereford; Mr. J. Kelley, Chester; Mr. H. Hughes, Birmingham; Mr. H. Y. Adye, Worcester; Mr. T. I. Allen, Cardiff; Mr. H. Besant, Swansea; and Mr. P. Donaldson, Pontypool Road (Mon.); and Mr. C. Boucher, Newport.

Paddington Terminus. J. GRIERSON, *General Manager.*

F

LONDON & NORTH-WESTERN AND CALEDONIAN RAILWAYS

WEST COAST ROYAL MAIL ROUTE

BETWEEN

ENGLAND AND SCOTLAND.

1st, 2d, and 3d CLASS TOURIST TICKETS,

Available from the date of issue, up to and including the 31st December 1881, are (during the Season commencing 2d May) issued from all Principal Stations in England to the chief places of interest in Scotland, and also from the same places in Scotland to English Stations.

Passengers by the Through Trains between **London (Euston Station)** and **Scotland** are conveyed in

THROUGH CARRIAGES

of the most improved description, and constructed specially for the accommodation of this Traffic.

Saloons, Family Carriages, Reserved Compartments, and all other conveniences necessary to ensure comfort on the journey, can be arranged upon application to Mr. G. P. NEELE, Superintendent of the L. and N.-W. Line, Euston Station, London ; the General Superintendent, Caledonian Railway, Glasgow; or to any of the Stationmasters at the Stations on the West Coast Route.

The Passenger Fares, and Horse, Carriage, and Dog Rates between London and Scotland, have been revised and reduced.

By the opening of the line of Railway from **CALLANDER** to **OBAN,** direct Railway communication is now afforded by the West Coast Route to Loch Awe, Taynuilt, and Oban.

TABLE OF EXPRESS TRAINS BETWEEN LONDON AND SCOTLAND.

DOWN JOURNEY.

STATIONS.		WEEK DAYS.						SUNDAYS.	
		morn.	morn.	morn.	morn.	night.	night.	night.	night.
London (Euston)	dep.	5.15	7.15	10.0	11.0	8.50	9.0	8.50	9.0
Edinburgh (Princes St. Stn.)	arr.	4.30	5.50	8.0	9.45	6.45	7.50	6.45	7.50
Glasgow (Central Station)	,,	4.44	6.0	8.0	10.0	6.55	8.0	6.55	8.0
Greenock .	,,	5.50	7.15	9.5	11.42	*7.50	*9·40	7.50	9.48
Stirling .	,,	5.39	..	8.24	10.27	7.21	*8.43	7.21	8.43
Oban .	,,	..	..	..	4.35	*12.40	..	12.40	..
Perth .	,,	6.50	..	9.25	11.40	8.15	*9.55	8.15	9.55
Aberdeen .	,,	10.12	..	..	3.20	12.40	*2.15	12.40	2.15
Inverness .	,,	..	..	..	8.50	2.45	*6.25	2.45	6.25

No connection from London to Places marked thus (*) on Saturday Nights.

UP JOURNEY.

STATIONS.	WEEK DAYS.						SUNDAYS.	
	aft.	morn.	morn.	morn.	morn.	aft.	morn.	night.
INVERNESS . . dep.	10.0	..	..	..	10.18	12.40	10.18	..
Aberdeen . . ,,	..	..	8.55	9.25	12.30	4.15	12.23	..
	morn.		noon.					
Perth . . . ,,	8.30	..	12.0	1.55	4.4	7.30	4.4	..
Oban . . . ,,	..	..	6.0	..	12.0	4.5	..	..
Stirling . . ,,	9.30	..	1.5	3.24	5.3	8.30	5.3	..
Greenock . . ,,	9.0	..	1.10	3.0	5.0	8.10	..	..
Glasgow (Central Stn.) . ,,	10.0	10.4	2.15	4.30	6.0	9.10	6.0	9.10
Edinburgh (Princes St. Stn.) ,,	10.0	10.35	2.25	4.45	6.10	9.15	6.10	9.15
London (Euston) arr.	8.0	10.40	4.30	5.30	4.5	*8.0	4.5	†8.15
	night.	night.	night.	morn.	morn.	morn.	morn.	morn.

From Scotland daily, except Sunday. † From Scotland on Sunday.

THE LIMITED MAIL TRAINS

Travel by this route, and are in connection with the Mail Coaches to the Outlying Districts of the Highlands. These Trains have been accelerated between London and Edinburgh, Glasgow and Perth ; and additional accommodation and increased facilities are now afforded to passengers travelling by them.

DAY SALOONS, WITH LAVATORY ACCOMMODATION ATTACHED,

Are run between London and Edinburgh and Glasgow, leaving Euston Station by 10.0 a.m. Down Express, and returning from Edinburgh and Glasgow by 10.0 a.m. Up Express on Week Days. NO EXTRA CHARGE is made for Passengers travelling in these Saloons, and Compartments are specially reserved for Ladies and Family Parties.

SLEEPING SALOONS

Between London and Perth and Glasgow, and CARRIAGES with SLEEPING COMPARTMENTS, are also run between London and Edinburgh and Greenock by the Night Trains. The extra charge for berths in the Saloons or Sleeping Carriages is 5s. in addition to the ordinary 1st class fare.

Passengers are requested to ask for Tickets by the West Coast Route.

Conductors, in charge of the Luggage, &c., travel by the Through Trains.

Dog Boxes specially provided.

Game Consignments conveyed by the Limited Mail.

FAMILY LUGGAGE.—With a view of giving greater facility for the conveyance of heavy Luggage by Passenger Trains, arrangements have been made in all the large towns for carting to the Station, at low rates, the Luggage of Families proceeding to Scotland, and also for forwarding such Luggage by Passenger Trains in advance. The charge for conveyance by Passenger Train is at the rate of 6d. per Truck per Mile, for any weight up to 50 cwts., with a minimum of 10s., and exclusive of a reasonable charge for collection and delivery.

For full particulars of Train Service, Tourist arrangements, &c., see the L. & N. W. and Caledonian Coy.'s Time Books, or West Coast Tourist Guide, which can be obtained at all principal Stations.

April 1881. *BY ORDER.*

Midland Railway.

The MIDLAND RAILWAY COMPANY provide

SINGLE-HORSE OMNIBUSES

Capable of carrying Six Persons inside and Two outside, with the usual quantity of Luggage, to meet the Express and other principal Trains at the ST. PANCRAS STATION when PREVIOUSLY ORDERED.

These Vehicles must be ENGAGED BEFOREHAND, either by written application to the Station-Master at St. Pancras Station, or by giving notice to the Station-Master at the starting point (if a Midland Station), or at *any Station en route not less than 30 miles from London*, so that a telegram may be sent to St. Pancras to have the required Vehicle in readiness.

The Omnibuses will also be sent to the Hotels or Residences of PARTIES LEAVING LONDON by MIDLAND RAILWAY, or to the Stations of the Southern Companies at which passengers may arrive from the Continent, on application being made to the Station-Master at St. Pancras, stating the Train by which it is intended to leave St. Pancras.

The charge for the use of an Omnibus will be One Shilling per mile (Driver and a reasonable quantity of Luggage included), with a minimum charge of Three Shillings.

NEW ROUTE BETWEEN ENGLAND AND SCOTLAND.

THE SETTLE AND CARLISLE RAILWAY is now open for Passenger Traffic, and an entirely New Service of Express and Fast Trains has been established between the Midland System and Scotland.

A Morning Express Train runs between London and Edinburgh and Glasgow, in each direction, with Pullman Drawing-Room Cars attached, and a Night Express Train runs in each direction between the same places, with Pullman Sleeping Cars attached. An additional Express Train will run during portions of the months of July, August, and September, in both directions. First-Class Passengers may avail themselves of the comfort and convenience of these luxurious Cars on payment of a small charge in addition to the Railway Fare, particulars of which may be ascertained at the Stations.

For the convenience of Passengers to and from the West of England and Scotland, a New Service of Express Passenger Trains has been established to and from Bristol, Bath, Gloucester, Cheltenham, Worcester, and Birmingham, in connection with the Through Service between London and Edinburgh and Glasgow.

The Up and Down Day Express Trains stop half-an-hour at Normanton, in all cases, to enable Passengers to dine. A spacious and comfortable Dining Room is provided at that Station for their accommodation.

Through Guards, in charge of the Luggage of Passengers, travel between London and Edinburgh and Glasgow by the Day and Night Express Trains in both directions.

Passengers by this Route by the Express Trains between London and Edinburgh and Glasgow are conveyed in Through Carriages of the most improved description, fitted up with the Westinghouse Continuous Break and all the most approved modern appliances.

Ordinary Return Tickets between Stations in England and Stations in Scotland are available for the Return Journey on any day within One Calendar Month of the date of issue.

BELFAST,

BY THE NEW AND SHORT SEA ROUTE *via* BARROW.

THE capacious New Docks of Barrow, situated within the ancient Harbour of Peel, under shelter of Walney Island, being now open for traffic, the Swift and Powerful First-class Paddle Steam Ships "ANTRIM," "ROE," "TALBOT," and "SHELBURNE," will sail between Barrow and Belfast (weather permitting) in connection with through Trains on the Midland and Furness Railways ; and through Tickets to Belfast, in connection with the Boat, will be issued from London, Northampton, Leicester, Nottingham, Bristol, Birmingham, Derby, Sheffield, Leeds, Bradford, and principal Stations on the Midland Railway—Return Tickets being available for One Calendar Month.

Passengers to and from London, and other Stations south of Leicester, may break the journey at Furness Abbey, Leeds, Derby, Trent, or Leicester ; and Passengers to or from Stations west of Derby, at Furness Abbey, Leeds, or Derby, taking care that from any of those places they proceed by Midland Trains.

TOURISTS' TICKETS.

SCOTLAND.

During the summer months 1st and 3rd Class Tourist Tickets will be issued from London (St. Pancras) and principal Stations on the Midland Railway to Edinburgh, Glasgow, Greenock, Oban, Melrose, Dumfries, Ayr, Stirling, Perth, Dundee, Aberdeen, Inverness, and other places of interest in Scotland.

Saloon, Family, and Invalid Carriages can be obtained for the use of parties travelling to and from Scotland by the Midland Route, by giving a few days' notice to the Stationmaster at any of the principal Stations, or to the Superintendent of the Line, Derby.

MORECAMBE AND THE ENGLISH LAKES.

DURING the Summer months 1st and 3rd Class Tourist Tickets are issued from Principal Stations on the Midland Railway to MORECAMBE, WINDERMERE, AMBLESIDE, GRANGE, FURNESS ABBEY, SEASCALE, PENRITH, KESWICK, and TROUTBECK.

Every Saturday, from May 28th to October 1st, Cheap Excursion Tickets to Morecambe will be issued from Leicester, Nottingham, Derby, Sheffield, Masboro', Barnsley, Normanton, Leeds, Bradford, Keighley, Repton, and principal intermediate points, available to return up to the Tuesday evening after date of issue.

For Fares and further particulars see Tourist Programmes and Special Hand-bills.

MATLOCK AND BUXTON.

First and Third Class Tourist Tickets are issued during the Summer Months from principal Stations on the Midland Railway, and Lines in connection, to Matlock and Buxton.

Passengers holding Tickets to Buxton are allowed to break the journey at principal places of interest on the Line between Matlock and Buxton.

RETURN TICKETS at Low Fares will be issued to MATLOCK and BUXTON, by any of the Through Trains, on Saturdays, from May 28th to October 1st, available for Return by any *Train up to the TUESDAY EVENING after date of issue.*

First and Third Class Tourist Tickets, available for Two Months or longer, are issued during the Summer Months from Principal Stations on the Midland Railway, to

Scarboro', Whitby, Filey, Bridlington, Harrogate, Ilkley, and other Stations in the Yorkshire district.

Yarmouth, Lowestoft, Cromer, Cleethorpes, and other Stations on the East Coast.

Brighton, Hastings, Portsmouth, The Isle of Wight, Bournemouth, and other Stations in the South of England.

Penzance, Plymouth, Torquay, Exeter, Weston-super-Mare, Ilfracombe, and other Stations in the West of England.

Monmouth, Swansea, Tenby, and other Stations in South Wales.

Aberystwith, Llandudno, Rhyl, Bangor, and other Stations in North Wales.

Lytham, Southport, Blackpool, and other Stations on the Lancashire Coast; and to Bath, Malvern, Leamington, Brecon, etc.

For further particulars, see Tourist Programmes and Hand-bills.

Pleasure Parties during the Season, commencing 2d May.

CHEAP RETURN TICKETS

Will be issued to parties of not less than SIX First Class, or TEN Third Class Passengers, desirous of taking Pleasure Excursions to places on or adjacent to this Railway.

For particulars, apply to the Stationmasters on the Line, or to the Superintendent of the Line at Derby.

DERBY, 1881.   JOHN NOBLE, *General Manager.*

CALEDONIAN RAILWAY.

TOURS IN SCOTLAND.

THE CALEDONIAN RAILWAY COMPANY have arranged a system of TOURS—about 70 in number—by Rail, Steamer, and Coach, comprehending almost every place of interest either for scenery or historical associations throughout Scotland, including—

**EDINBURGH, GLASGOW, ABERDEEN, DUNDEE, INVERNESS,
GREENOCK, PAISLEY, DUMFRIES, PEEBLES, STIRLING,
PERTH, CRIEFF, DUNKELD, OBAN, INVERARAY,**

*The Trosachs, Loch Katrine, Loch Lomond, Loch Earn, Loch Tay,
Loch Awe, Caledonian Canal, Glencoe, Iona, Staffa, Skye, Balmoral, Braemar,
Arran, Bute, The Firth of Clyde, The Falls of Clyde, &c. &c.*

☞ TOURISTS are recommended to procure a copy of the Caledonian Railway Company's "Tourist Guide," which can be had at any of the Company's Stations, and also at the chief Stations on the London and North-Western Railway, and which contains descriptive notices of the Districts embraced in the Tours, Maps, Plans, Bird's-Eye View, &c.

Tickets for these Tours are issued at the Company's Booking Offices at all the large Stations.

The Tourist Season generally extends from JUNE to SEPTEMBER, inclusive.

*The Caledonian Co. also issue Tourist Tickets to the Lake District of England,
The Isle of Man, Connemara, The Lakes of Killarney, &c.*

The Caledonian Railway, in conjunction with the London and North-Western Railway, forms what is known as the

WEST COAST ROUTE

BETWEEN

SCOTLAND AND ENGLAND.

DIRECT TRAINS RUN FROM AND TO

GLASGOW, EDINBURGH, GREENOCK, PAISLEY, STIRLING, OBAN, PERTH, DUNDEE, ABERDEEN, INVERNESS, and other Places in Scotland,

TO AND FROM

LONDON (Euston), BIRMINGHAM, LIVERPOOL, MANCHESTER, LEEDS, BRADFORD, and other Places in England.

Sleeping and Day Saloon Carriages.   Through Guards and Conductors.

The Caledonian Company's Trains from and to Edinburgh, Glasgow, Carlisle, &c., connect at Greenock and Wemyss Bay with the "Columba," "Iona," "Lord of the Isles," "Ivanhoe," "Gael," and other steamers to and from Dunoon, Innellan, Rothesay, Largs, Millport, the Kyles of Bute, Arran, Campbeltown, Ardrishaig, Inveraray, Loch Goil, Loch Long, &c. &c.

A full service of Trains is also run from and to Glasgow, to and from Edinburgh, Stirling, Oban, Perth, Dundee, Aberdeen, and the North; and from and to Edinburgh, to and from these places.

For particulars of Trains, Fares, &c., see the Caledonian Railway Co.'s Time Tables.

GENERAL MANAGER'S OFFICE,   JAMES SMITHELLS,
GLASGOW, 1881.   *General Manager.*

GLASGOW & SOUTH-WESTERN RAILWAY.

DIRECT ROUTE BETWEEN

SCOTLAND & ENGLAND.

THROUGH TRAINS ARE RUN BETWEEN

GLASGOW (St. Enoch) and LONDON (St. Pancras).

Via the GLASGOW & SOUTH-WESTERN and MIDLAND RAILWAYS,

Giving a Direct and Expeditious Service between

GLASGOW, GREENOCK, PAISLEY, AYR, ARDROSSAN, KILMARNOCK, DUMFRIES, &c., AND LIVERPOOL, MANCHESTER, BRADFORD, LEEDS, SHEFFIELD, BRISTOL, BATH, BIRMINGHAM, LONDON, &c.

PULLMAN DRAWING-ROOM AND SLEEPING CARS

Are run by the Morning and Evening Trains between GLASGOW and LONDON.

FIRTH OF CLYDE AND WEST HIGHLANDS, VIA GREENOCK.

EXPRESS and FAST TRAINS are run at convenient hours between

GLASGOW AND GREENOCK

(St. Enoch Station)   (Lynedoch St. and Princes Pier Stations)

IN DIRECT CONNECTION WITH THE

"COLUMBA," "IONA," "LORD OF THE ISLES,"

And other Steamers sailing to and from

Kirn, Dunoon, Innellan, Rothesay, Kyles of Bute, Ardrishaig, Oban, Inveraray, Largs, Millport, Kilcreggan, Kilmun, Lochgoilhead, Garelochhead, &c.

Through Carriages are run by certain Trains between GREENOCK (Princes Pier) and EDINBURGH (Waverley), and by the Morning and Evening Express Trains between GREENOCK (Princes Pier) and LONDON (St. Pancras).

RETURN TICKETS issued to COAST TOWNS are available for RETURN AT ANY TIME.

Passengers are landed at Princes Pier Station, from whence there is a Covered Way to the Pier, where the Steamers call; and Passengers' Luggage is conveyed FREE OF CHARGE between the Station and the Steamers.

ARRAN AND AYRSHIRE COAST.

An Express and Fast Train Service is given between GLASGOW (St. Enoch), PAISLEY, and TROON, PRESTWICK, AYR, ARDROSSAN, &c.

From ARDROSSAN the Splendid Saloon Steamer, "BRODICK CASTLE," sails daily to and from the ISLAND OF ARRAN, in connection with the Express Train Service.

Fast Trains provided with Through Carriages are run between STRANRAER, GIRVAN, AYR, &c., and GLASGOW (St. Enoch) and EDINBURGH (Waverley).

IRELAND.

A DAYLIGHT SERVICE is given by the Short Sea Route *via* STRANRAER and LARNE, and a NIGHTLY SERVICE is given by the Royal Mail Steamers *via* GREENOCK, and also by the ARDROSSAN SHIPPING COMPANY'S Full-Powered Steamers *via* ARDROSSAN.

For particulars as to Trains and Steamers see the Company's Time Tables.

APRIL 1881.   W. J. WAINWRIGHT, *General Manager.*

GLASGOW, BELFAST, BRISTOL, CARDIFF, AND SWANSEA.

Carrying Goods for Newport, Exeter, Gloucester, Cheltenham, etc.

The Screw Steamships
AVON, SOLWAY, SEVERN, PRINCESS ALEXANDRA,
or other Vessels,
Are intended to Sail as under:—

GLASGOW to BRISTOL and SWANSEA—Every Monday, at 2 P.M.
GLASGOW to BRISTOL and CARDIFF—Every Friday, at 2 P.M.
BELFAST to BRISTOL and SWANSEA—Every Tuesday.
BELFAST to BRISTOL and CARDIFF—Every Saturday.
BRISTOL to BELFAST and GLASGOW—Every Wednesday and Friday,
SWANSEA to BELFAST and GLASGOW—Every Saturday.
CARDIFF to BELFAST and GLASGOW *via* BRISTOL—Every Monday.
FARES from GLASGOW—Cabin, 20s.; Steerage 12s. 6d.; Soldiers and Sailors, 10s.
   ,,   from BELFAST—Cabin, 17s. 6d.; Steerage, 10s.
RETURNS for Cabin and Steerage at Fare and a half, available for TWO MONTHS.
These Steamers have splendid Cabin accommodation for passengers.

For Rates of Freight and further particulars, apply to

WILLIAM SLOAN & CO., 140 Hope Street, Glasgow.

ABERDEEN

AND

LONDON

Average Passage
36 *Hours*.

THE ABERDEEN STEAM NAVIGATION COMPANY'S STEAMSHIPS

BAN-RIGH, CITY OF LONDON, or CITY OF ABERDEEN,
will be despatched (weather, etc., permitting) from ABERDEEN, and from The Aberdeen Steam Navigation Co.'s Wharf, Limehouse, LONDON, every Wednesday and Saturday.
FARES—including Stewards' Fees—*Private Cabins* accommodating four passengers, £6. *Private Cabins*, if occupied by fewer than four passengers, £5.
Single Tickets—First Cabin, 30s.; Second Cabin, 15s.; Children under fourteen years, 15s. and 10s. *Return Tickets*—available for three months—45s. and 25s.; Children, 25s. and 15s.
Passengers will please observe that during the season the Co.'s steamer 'Ich Dien' will start from the Temple Pier, Thames Embankment, one hour before the advertised times of sailing, conveying passengers and their luggage alongside the Aberdeen Steamers free of charge. Porters in the Company's service will assist with the luggage.
For further particulars apply to JOHN A. CLINKSKILL, Agent, The Aberdeen Steam Navigation Co.'s Wharf, Limehouse; and 102 Queen Victoria Street, E.C., London; or to CHARLES SHEPHERD, Manager, Waterloo Quay, Aberdeen.

LEITH AND LONDON

THE LONDON & EDINBURGH SHIPPING COMPANY'S

SPLENDID FAST-SAILING SCREW-STEAMSHIPS

MALVINA (New Steamer),

MARMION, IONA, MORNA, OR OTHER OF THE COMPANY'S STEAMERS,

Sail from VICTORIA DOCK, LEITH, every *Wednesday* and *Saturday* afternoon ; and from HERMITAGE STEAM WHARF, LONDON, every *Wednesday* and *Saturday* morning.

For Rates of Freight and Fares, apply to THOMAS AITKEN, 8 Commercial Street, Leith.

Dr. J. COLLIS BROWNE'S
CHLORODYNE.
THE ORIGINAL AND ONLY GENUINE.

CHLORODYNE is the best remedy known for Coughs, Consumption, Bronchitis, Asthma.

CHLORODYNE effectually checks and arrests those too often fatal diseases known as Diphtheria, Fever, Croup, Ague.

CHLORODYNE acts like a charm in Diarrhœa, and is the only specific in Cholera and Dysentery.

CHLORODYNE effectually cuts short all attacks of Epilepsy, Hysteria, Palpitation, and Spasms.

CHLORODYNE is the only palliative in Neuralgia, Rheumatism, Gout, Cancer, Toothache, Meningitis, &c.

The Right Hon. EARL RUSSELL has graciously favoured J. T. DAVENPORT with the following:—
"Earl Russell communicated to the College of Physicians that he received a despatch from Her Majesty's Consul at Manilla, to the effect that Cholera has been raging fearfully, and that the only remedy of any service was CHLORODYNE."—See *Lancet*, December 1st, 1864.

From W. Vesalius Pettigrew, M.D.
I have no hesitation in stating that I never met with any medicine so efficacious as an Anti-spasmodic and Sedative. I have used it in Consumption, Asthma, Diarrhœa, and other diseases, and am perfectly satisfied with the results.

From Dr. B. J. Boulton & Co., Horncastle.
We have made pretty extensive use of Chlorodyne in our practice lately, and look upon it as an excellent Sedative and Anti-spasmodic. It seems to allay pain and irritation in whatever organ and from whatever cause. It induces a feeling of comfort and quietude not obtainable by any other remedy, and it seems to possess this great advantage over all other Sedatives, that it leaves no unpleasant after-effects.

CAUTION.—The extraordinary medical reports on the efficacy of Chlorodyne render it of vital importance that the public should obtain the genuine, which bears the words "Dr. J. Collis Browne's Chlorodyne."
Vice-Chancellor Wood stated that Dr. J. COLLIS BROWNE was undoubtedly the Inventor of CHLORODYNE; that the whole story of the defendant Freeman was deliberately untrue.
Lord Chancellor Selborne and Lord Justice James stated that the defendant had made a deliberate misrepresentation of the decision of Vice-Chancellor Wood.
Chemists throughout the land confirm this decision that Dr. J. C. BROWNE was the Inventor of CHLORODYNE.

Sold in Bottles at 1s. 1½d., 2s. 9d., and 4s. 6d., by all Chemists.
SOLE MANUFACTURER:
J. T. DAVENPORT, 33 GREAT RUSSELL STREET, BLOOMSBURY, LONDON.